Debs at War
1939–1945

How Wartime Changed Their Lives

ANNE DE COURCY

PHOENIX

A PHOENIX PAPERBACK

First published in Great Britain in 2005
by Weidenfeld & Nicolson
This paperback edition published in 2006
by Phoenix,
an imprint of Orion Books Ltd,
Orion House, 5 Upper St Martin's Lane,
London WC2H 9EA

5 7 9 10 8 6 4

A CIP catalogue record for this book
is available from the British Library.

ISBN-13 978-0-7538-2078-0
ISBN-10 0-7538-2078-1

Typeset by Butler and Tanner Ltd, Frome and London

Printed and bound in Great Britain at
CPI Group (UK) Ltd, Croydon, CRO 4YY

The Orion Publishing Group's policy is to use papers
that are natural, renewable and recyclable products and
made from wood grown in sustainable forests. The logging
and manufacturing processes are expected to conform to
the environmental regulations of the country of origin.

www.orionbooks.co.uk

Contents

Illustrations

Illustrations

The author and publishers thank the following for their kind permission to reproduce photographs: Camera Press, 35; Country Life, 33, 34; Hulton Getty, 1, 2, 38, 39, 40, 44, 54, 65, 66; Illustrated London News, 6, 7, 37, 45; Imperial War Museum, 43, 51, 52, 53, 55, 56, 57, 58, 59, 60, 61, 62, 63, 64; Lavinia Orde, 21, 28, 42, 46, 49, 50. The remaining photographs are from private collections.

Preface

History is made all the time, not just by the noisy clash of politics, economic currents or overpowering personalities but by the everyday texture and attitudes of contemporary life – things impossible to judge accurately from the standpoint of hindsight. It is generally accepted that the words and writings of those who actually lived through a period are an invaluable historical contribution and help to bring it truly to life.

Within a decade or two, the era before the Second World War, and a little later the war itself, will become what is known as 'history' – that is, there will be no one alive who can actually remember these years, and how radically different they were from life as it is now lived. Stoicism is only one of the national qualities that seems to have disappeared.

The women I spoke to for this book described a society quite unlike the Britain of today. For them, the contrast between their peacetime lives and the war was sharper than for any other section of British society. They had been brought up largely in isolation from anyone not of their particular background, in conditions of material privilege yet often at a physical and emotional distance from their parents unknown in any other stratum of society and with a code that regarded 'making a fuss' (which included making oneself conspicuous as well as complaints) as something not to be tolerated.

All of them had been debutantes in the years before the war; they had made their curtsey before the King and Queen and become fully-fledged members of the social class in which they had been brought up. Until they emerged into this adult world, they had been protected, cocooned and kept in chaste ignorance under their parents' sway, conditions that often lasted until their expected destiny, marriage.

When war broke out, with or without parental approval they rushed to join up rather than wait for call-up papers. Indeed, many had begun what became their wartime work or service as soon as their age permitted, well before hostilities began. The realities of war and the accompanying culture shock liberated many from the straitjacket of their upbringing, giving the confidence that comes from successfully coping with challenges and responsibility on one's own. Their voices are the experiences of a minority which, though small, was a not insignificant element of the complex social history that has produced the country we are today. As such they deserve to be heard.

Anne de Courcy
London and Gloucestershire
January 2005

Acknowledgements

First and foremost I owe an enormous debt of gratitude to all those women set out on pages xiii and xiv, who allowed me to talk to them and who answered my questions so freely and fully. One of the nicest aspects of this was the feeling that I had made many new friends. I would also like to thank them for the photographs they so kindly lent me.

I am also most grateful to Lady Brinckman, Sir Edward Ford, Genevieve Edis, Carol Goddard, Alan Hodson, Vickie Macnair, Miranda Villiers and Jane Wykeham-Musgrave for their help in tracking down potential interviewees; and to Christian Grant, Lady Moyra Ponsonby, Lavinia Holland-Hibbert and Denise Woosnam for permission to quote from their diaries, and to Vickie Macnair for permission to quote from her husband Peter's letters. I would also like to thank Sarah Baring and Esme, Countess of Cromer, for making available to me their fascinating memoirs, *The Road to Station X* and *Born with Silver Spoons*. And, as always, it is impossible to overstate what I owe to my editor, Benjamin Buchan.

Former Debutantes Interviewed
(married surname in brackets)

Mary Armitage (Lady Freeland)
Ursie Barclay (Lloyd-Owen)
Diana Barnato (Barnato Walker)
Daphne Brock (Davie)
Jean Campbell-Harris (Baroness Trumpington)
The Hon. Val Canning (Hon. Mrs Sutcliffe)
Fiona Colquhoun (Lady Arran)
Ann Darlington (Cameron)
The Hon. Anne Douglas-Scott-Montagu (Hon. Lady Chichester)
Cynthia Denison-Pender (Mortimer)
Lady Margaret Egerton (Lady Margaret Colville)
Jean Falkner (Meade-Fetherstonhaugh)
Virginia Forbes Adam (Charteris)
Fanny Gore Browne (Hugill)
Christian Grant (Lady Bowman)
Frances Grenfell (Campbell-Preston)
The Hon. Esme Harmsworth (Countess of Cromer)
The Hon. Lorna Harmsworth (Hon. Mrs Cooper-Key)
Rosemary Hodson (Trollope)
Lavinia Holland-Hibbert (Orde)
Judy Impey (Macfarlane)
Suzanne Irwin (Lady Terrington)
Pamela Joyce (Mackrill)
Lady Cynthia Keppel (Lady Cynthia Poston)
Lady Barbara Legge (Lady Barbara Kwiatkowska)
Elizabeth Lowry-Corry
Diana Lyttelton (Viscountess Hood)
Renée Merandon du Plessis (Lady Iliffe)
Susan Meyrick (Green)

Cynthia Miller (Pitman)
Lady Elizabeth Montagu Douglas Scott (Duchess of Northumberland)
The Hon. Sarah Norton (Hon. Mrs Baring)
Sheila Parish
Mary Pollock (Coad)
Lady Moyra Ponsonby (Lady Moyra Browne)
Diana Quilter (Tennant)
Anne Reid (Paget)
Betty Shaughnessy (Lady Grenfell, later Mrs Lawson)
Fortune Smith (Duchess of Grafton)
Lady Anne Spencer (Lady Anne Wake-Walker)
Cecilia Sprot (Lady Whitelaw)
Lady Barbara Stuart-Wortley (Lady Barbara Ricardo)
Joan Stafford King-Harman (Lady Dunn)
Mary Toulmin (Morrison)
Denise Woosnam (Patterson)
Penny Woosnam (Kavanagh)
Rosemary Wynn (Record)

Chapter 1

Childhoods

'... taken down to say
good morning to our mothers'

All over England, the daughters of the upper classes were growing up in similar fashion. Although it was received wisdom in the Twenties and Thirties that the 1914–18 war – the Great War, as it was known – had changed everything, shattering the rigid social hierarchy and formal etiquette of pre-war Edwardian days, in practice very little had altered.

There were superficial changes: the parents of these girls now drank cocktails, danced in smart restaurants, wore shorter, less constricting clothes, went to the cinema, and visited the French Riviera in the summer, all unheard of in that distant, golden, pre-war era. But underlying these activities, the customs and practices of their world remained very much the same. The demands of the social calendar, with its emphasis on sporting activities, dominated many of their lives. As one contemporary source points out: 'When people in high society in those days spoke of "economising" it usually meant making do with one footman instead of two or giving up the under-gardener.' And most still lived in anything from stately homes or 'places' (the next down) to halls, manors or pleasant country houses.

Some lived permanently in the country, renting a London house (or availing themselves of the hospitality of a London-based relation) only for the Season when a daughter was being 'brought out' – that is, making the transition from schoolroom to grown-up world via presentation at Court and attendance at as many balls, dances and social events as possible.

Grander families had their own town houses, opened only for a few months each summer, some palatial, all big enough to hold a dance. For many years, as a child, Lady Margaret ('Meg') Egerton did not dare explore the whole of Bridgewater House (in St James's), the immense London mansion of her parents, Lord and Lady Ellesmere. 'I was far too frightened of getting lost to go into the back premises or the remoter rooms.'

Such houses were of course staffed by servants who carried out all the work of the household, a fact that was still taken for granted (in 1939, the number of domestic servants stood at around 1.25 million) both by the very rich and by those who described themselves as 'not having much money'. Mary Pollock's doctor father, a distinguished paediatrician, kept a butler, cook, housemaid, nanny and nurserymaid at the family house in Evelyn Gardens, although Mary described her family as being not particularly well off. In Scotland, the Ellesmeres had around thirty servants, including a house carpenter and grooms, taking some of them to Bridgewater House from May to the end of July when they came to London for the Season. At one stage, when the six Egerton girls were growing up, the Bridgewater staff included three ladies' maids.

'I was four when I first went to Bridgewater House,' recalled Meg Egerton. 'A whole carriage in the train was hired and we came down with Nanny. The butler, the cook and the footmen came but the housemaids stayed at Mertoun. There was already a housekeeper and resident staff at Bridgewater House, with a hall porter who would double as a footman. We brought our chauffeur down as well but we also had another one in London because there was so much going on.'

At Warwick House, in St James's, the London home of the

Honourable Esmond Harmsworth,* there was a butler, three footmen, an under-butler, a housekeeper and a number of maids. 'One didn't know them except for their surnames,' said his daughter, Lorna. 'The kitchen had a cook and kitchen maids and my father had three chauffeurs – one who worked for the family, my father's personal one and one of the staff, who took things down to our house in the country or brought things back from the greenhouses.'

Other houses were like little villages. At Wentworth in south Yorkshire, the largest house in England, surrounded by lawns black with coal dust from the adjacent mines, the corridors were so long and the turnings so complicated that the footman who showed guests to their rooms would unwind a ball of string to enable them to find their way back to the drawing room. Sheila Parish's mother was the favourite granddaughter of the great Prime Minister, William Ewart Gladstone; and her rich Gladstone uncle and his wife, who had no children, lived at the old family home, Hawarden Castle in Flintshire. 'We were treated as their children and went there for all our holidays. We had ponies and a swimming pool in the garden and when we grew out of that he made a lake for us.

'In London we had a reasonable-sized staff – cook, kitchen maid, parlour maid, housemaid, batman (my father had been in the Army), nanny, nursery maid and daily. But at Hawarden the staff was enormous – two butlers, four in the kitchen, four housemaids, twenty in the garden and lots out in the park and farms.

'At Christmas all the staff families came in and there was an enormous tea, after which we and the village children acted in a nativity play. Then we stood round a vast Christmas tree, with gardeners holding sponges on sticks to douse the candles when they got too low, while we gave out presents to the children – there must have been 150 of them. Then we all sang carols.'

---

* He became the 3rd Viscount Rothermere in November 1940.

'We had nine servants inside, two pantry, three kitchen, two upstairs,' said Cynthia Denison-Pender. 'But I never had any feeling of belonging to a privileged class – our staff were my friends. They didn't tell my parents if I'd done something wrong and for my twenty-first they all gave me something special.'

Aristocratic households, especially those of the older generation, often maintained the formality of an earlier era. When Lady Barbara Legge and her sisters and brother stayed with their grandparents, the Earl and Countess of Dartmouth, they went out for picnics in a brougham* driven by a coachman, with a small boy, wearing a top hat, standing at the back ready to spring down and open gates.

Most housework in the 1930s was done by hand, chiefly by housemaids in their cotton print uniforms; vacuum cleaners had been invented but many employers thought them new-fangled. Servants could be dismissed without notice for such crimes as immorality – maids were quite often found in bed with footmen, unsurprisingly, as the latter were frequently chosen for their looks – dishonesty, or drunkenness. This last was a particular hazard for butlers, who had charge of the wine cellar. 'Our first butler was dismissed after shutting himself in the cellar when my parents were away and systematically drinking one bottle of wine after another while filling the empties with his urine,' recalled Esme Harmsworth, sister of Lorna.

Cold was a routine fact of life. No cars (let alone aeroplanes) were heated; few houses had central heating; draught exclusion was a phrase as yet unknown, and year-round open windows were considered healthy. 'Nobody would come and stay with us in winter,' said Barbara Legge, 'as our house, Godmersham Park [between Canterbury and Ashford], was the coldest house imaginable.'

* The first four-wheeled carriage drawn by only one horse and invented by the 1st Lord Brougham.

Society, in the sense of 'Society', was much smaller and almost entirely class-based: that is, the people written about by the gossip columnists of the day were a smallish network of the rich, titled and influential, sometimes infiltrated by the famous or the very determined.

Column inches filled today by 'celebrities' then featured elegant or titled members of the upper classes as icons of success or glamour. Young and beautiful peeresses were used to advertise the virtues of cold cream or, if socially prominent – that is, figuring in magazines like the *Tatler*, *Sketch* or *Bystander* that chronicled the doings of this small group in gushing prose – were lent clothes by the grandest couturiers to wear in the London Season or at country house parties, in the same way that Hollywood designers today dress actresses for the Oscar awards ceremony.

Pictures of the aristocracy at play – Lord's, a polo match, Ascot – were a spectacle for the public. Debutantes learned this early when crowds lined the Mall on Presentation Court days, peering in at car windows as the procession of chauffeur-driven cars inched its way towards the gates of Buckingham Palace, and gave their verdict on the occupants.

For this small, exclusive and self-recognising set, social ostracism was a form of death. Divorce, for example, carried such a stigma that no divorced person was allowed into that holy of holies, the Royal Enclosure at Ascot, where all their friends were meeting and greeting. When Betty Shaughnessy, then Lady Grenfell, was divorced from her first husband shortly before the Second World War, her stepfather, the courtier Joey Legh, asked her to go and tell the King and Queen herself at Windsor.

'I remember this awful thing, going up by myself to their part of the Castle. Luckily the King, who was terribly sweet, was at a meeting. I went in to the Queen in her boudoir. "This is all very sad," she said. "Sit down, Betty. I just hope that you will be happy and the dear children won't be too upset. These awful rules ... you won't be able to come to official parties now, you know, but of course privately you still will."

'Then she sighed and continued: "I know you love racing ..." I said: "Yes, Ma'am, I know I won't be allowed in the Royal Enclosure."'

Within the home, children led a life almost completely separate from their parents. For younger children, this took place mainly in their day and night nurseries (or, in larger houses, the nursery wing), with formal visits to their mother and father after tea. Primped, starched, brushed and combed by Nanny, they would enter the drawing room to greet the two adults who had given birth to them.

'You didn't really want to go downstairs to see them after tea,' said Meg Egerton. 'They didn't play with us children. We sat in the drawing room, seven of us on the sofa, then shot out of the room like scalded cats, back to the red landing. Once through the glass door at our end you were in heaven, you were in the nursery wing.'

Even as they grew older many children led such separate lives from adults that for hours no one might know where they were. Lady Margaret, who spent nine months of the year in Mertoun, the Adam house on the banks of the Tweed bought by her father in 1913, ran wild most of the time. 'Nobody bothered where you went. We climbed enormous pine trees and couldn't get down and made omelettes out of birds' eggs. The river was actually quite dangerous. If one had slipped down that bank ...'

Yet even in the remoter parts of Scotland or rural England, there was one great link with other children: the weekly, or monthly, dancing class in the local county or market town. 'We lived in tweed kilts, jerseys and Burberries,' said Jean Falkner of her Galloway childhood. 'We had nothing much else except the velvet party dresses and bronze shoes which we wore to dancing class every month.'

In London the favoured dancing teacher was Miss Vacani. 'She was very small and wore enormous high heels,' said Barbara Legge, taken to classes with her younger sister by their nanny. The fascinated children also noted the teacher's unusual underwear. 'When she demonstrated to us how to twirl when waltzing, her skirt used to fly out and we could see that she was wearing silver knickers decorated with red roses!'

Children's clothes, though, were utilitarian rather than decorative, conforming to a social ideal rather than to personal taste. Little dresses were smocked by Nanny or a mother's lady's maid, sailor suits were popular for little boys; in winter, jerseys and skirts hid Chilprufe vests and pants. 'We weren't allowed to wear shoes until we were about ten,' Barbara recalled. 'Out of doors in the winter we wore gaiters with buttons, and boots – wearing boots was supposed to make your ankles strong.'

Betty Shaughnessy was another who saw little of her parents as a child. 'We went down to the drawing room, changed, after tea for about half an hour – about half past five to six. Sometimes Mummy had people to tea. Then we were fetched up to the nursery again. Also they were away nearly every weekend in the summer and in the winter too, shooting.'

Many children learned everything, from the daily routine to behaviour, from what would nowadays be called the hired help. 'As a child one was of course brought up by the servants, not our parents,' said Esme Harmsworth. 'We knew the domestic staff better than anyone else. We had Nanny, an under-nurse and nursemaid looking after us three children. The nurseries themselves were on the wrong side of the green baize door – the twilight zone between the staff and the parents. We didn't have thick carpet like our mother and father; we had linoleum and the bits of carpet we did have were pretty threadbare but we were waited on hand and foot – there was a nursery footman.

'In the morning, when our parents were at home – which

wasn't that often – we were taken down to say good morning to our mother for ten minutes and then in the evening – if they were in – there was the children's hour. We went down, all dressed up – oh! those nasty prickly organdie sleeves – and hair brushed and Nanny had to shove us through the drawing-room door as we didn't really want to go in at all. Once there, we had to be seen but not heard. They were usually either playing bridge or mah-jong. When they had visitors I was terrified.'

The gulf between even loving parents and their children was enormous. 'My childhood was very happy and I was close to my parents, particularly my mother,' said Barbara Legge. 'Did my parents ever cuddle me? Certainly not my father. Twice a year, at Christmas and on birthdays, he used to play with us and that was wonderful. My mother always came and said good night to us and heard our prayers.'

Fortune Smith, 'very close' to her parents, was one of many who only began to have lunch 'downstairs' (in the dining room with her parents as opposed to the nursery or schoolroom) at the age of ten. 'I'd just gone to my first day school and I was so proud of my uniform I kept my blazer on all day.

'We had supper in the nursery and then the schoolroom until quite an old age – I didn't really have dinner downstairs until I was about fifteen. We had a bed time all through our lives at home and I went to bed at ten really almost until I came out.'

Fortune and her brothers saw more of their parents than many. They were taken to France by their mother and father every Easter holidays to look at the chateaux on the Loire and in the summer, with another family, to a deer forest in Inverness-shire.

The concept of 'teenager', with its specific needs, desires, vocabulary and cultish, independent life had not been invented. Children did what their parents told them and never, ever answered back. 'I wasn't really close to my parents,' said Jean Falkner, who on their Galloway sheep farm saw more of hers than most children. 'I was terrified of my father. He hardly ever spoke and when he did he was very noncommittal and brusque – although he could suddenly make the funniest remark. My mother was a matriarch and very bossy. I was in awe of her. What she said went. Her rules were rules. I wouldn't have dared answer her back.'

Other children found contact with their parents anything from difficult to unhappy. 'When we became old enough to have dining-room lunch we used to rehearse in the hall what we would say to our father, as otherwise he wouldn't understand,' said the Hon. Val Canning, the daughter of Lord Garvagh and granddaughter of the seventh Earl Fitzwilliam. 'We were also allowed downstairs at tea-time and we used to have to play those awful board games which I've always hated since. The thing is my mother doted on my father and hadn't really got a lot of time for us.'

Parents could be distant to a degree that seems almost sadistic now. 'My mother never once came to say good night to us,' said Meg Egerton. 'And I only remember two occasions when my father came upstairs to our rooms – once when I had appendicitis at fifteen and again when I was ill in London. I don't resent the strictness of our upbringing but I do resent the lack of affection.'

Anne Reid was another who suffered, both from fear of her parents and from their remoteness. 'Until I came out, I only ever had meals in the dining room with my mother and father on Christmas Day and Easter Day.

'These dining-room meals were torture. My father never used physical violence but mentally he could be very cruel – tremendously sarcastic. My mother was frightened of him and so were the servants.

'He was a great stickler for punctuality. If he said: "Be ready in the hall at eleven o'clock" I jolly well had to be there at five to, as eleven was considered late. If we left a light on at bedtime, outside my bedroom, there was a frightful scene and I had to pay a shilling.

'The one good thing is that after him nothing was terrifying, so I've never been frightened of anybody since.'

Christian Grant, the daughter of Sir Arthur Grant of Monymusk, was equally terrified. Growing up in a huge, icy, Scottish castle, often hungry, she was beaten by her father with a cane for real or imagined misdemeanours from time to time – once, for hovering outside the dining-room door to eat the scraps that came out from a grown-up dinner party.

Such parents occupied their time in ways that have since changed out of all recognition. For many men, sport of some kind served as a work-substitute, at least as far as absorbing the drive, energy, intelligence and time that would today have been poured into a career: building up a shoot, a pack of foxhounds or a racing stables was a lifetime's occupation. In any case, much social life was based around horses, with hunting prints adorning the walls of country houses and the bookshelves packed with hunting memoirs and the complete works of Surtees and Nimrod. (Shooting replaced hunting in counties like Norfolk.)

The fathers of others were heavily involved in local government or looked after family estates. Rosemary Wynn's father, Arthur Wynn, ran the Rhug estate in Denbighshire that belonged to his father, Lord Newborough (though as a second son he would inherit neither it nor the family money needed to maintain it).

Some soldiered, in peacetime an altogether more leisurely affair, with plenty of leave for hunting or polo. 'During the winter there was no question of doing any soldiering,' wrote General Sir Cecil ('Monkey') Blacker, then a subaltern in the 5th Iniskilling Dragoon Guards, in his memoir *Monkey Business*. 'It was understood that every officer would depart for two months to hunt, taking with him his two chargers plus one or two troop horses and as many soldier grooms as were needed to look after them.' For those who worked in the City the rewards were good, thanks to the 'old boy' network, while today's frenetic pace and exhausting hours were unknown.

The mothers of these children also had to fill their days. A number worked hard at different charities and, in the country, ran anything from the village Girl Guide troop – often handed on to a daughter – to the Mothers' Union and Moral Welfare Association. Elizabeth Lowry-Corry's mother did exquisite embroidery.

For the smart set in London, life could be relentlessly frivolous – appointments at hairdressers', fittings at dressmakers' (most had their clothes made, though ready-made was gradually creeping in), perhaps cocktails at the Ritz followed by a luncheon there, a visit to an exhibition or to a jeweller's to buy a wedding present, tennis, golf, bridge and a charity tea or committee. Then it was home, often complaining of exhaustion, to change for dinner – always a long dress and black tie even when *à deux* – followed by the theatre, with supper and dancing afterwards. Betty Shaughnessy's mother, Sarah Legh, who all her life employed a lady's maid, rested on or in her bed every day for at least an hour before facing the rigours of the evening.

For the children of these elegant couples, tucked away on the nursery floor, Nanny was, unsurprisingly, the focus of their lives. Most grew up with Nanny wisdom and Nanny dicta – 'There's no such word as can't,' 'Two wrongs don't make a right,' 'No cake till you've had your bread and butter' – entering the subconscious of future generations. 'We adored our Nanny and she was very insistent on good manners,' said Sarah Norton, the daughter of Lord Grantley. 'If there was naughty behaviour at the tea table it was: "We did not ask Mr Rude to tea." Questions like "Nanny, where are we going?" drew the reply, "There and back to see how far it is and don't scuff your new shoes." If we asked, "Nanny, how old are you?" she would smile and say: "As old as my tongue and a little older than my teeth."'

The pre-war Nanny was a quite different figure from the child carer of today. The massive slaughter of fighting men in the 1914–18 war had resulted in a whole generation of single women – the maiden aunts trumpeting through the pages of P. G. Wodehouse were as much a reflection of real life as an inspired creation – and the profession of nanny attracted many who would otherwise have been mothers themselves. With, of course, a few exceptions, this pre-war nanny was a loved, unchanging figure who regarded her employer's children as her own and often remained with the same family all her life, perhaps moving on to look after the children of one of the daughters when the last of her charges went to boarding school. Betty Shaughnessy was not the only one to claim: 'Our nanny was like a mother to us. We confided in her but not in our parents. They were strangers. We were also very fond of our nursery maid. We would go to Hyde Park with two prams, Nanny always pushing the one with the baby in it.'

Girl children were often lonely. Unlike their brothers, sent away to school, they were frequently governess-educated, the lucky ones in a schoolroom with the daughters of their parents' friends of the same age. 'I longed to go to school,' said Meg Egerton. 'I loved games and I wanted to meet other people.'

Those living in the country tended to have few friends, owing to the distances between similar families, although some had parents with time to spare for them. Others were left to their own devices until, with luck, they were sent to school at the age of between twelve and fourteen. Suzanne Irwin was one of these. 'As a child, I saw a lot of my parents. I saw nobody else really. I had my governess, Ruthie, our nanny, my pony and the dogs and that was my life. There were no children of my sort of age near by. I did very much miss young people.'

Some children were sent off for months, even years, at a stretch. Diana Quilter was despatched to Paris at the age of twelve, with her older sister and a governess. 'We stayed off the

Avenue Victor Hugo and I went to a lycée. They worked very hard, those French children, and I didn't know much French. For a whole term I wasn't able to do any work and sat reading Dumas on a bench outside. When I came home I did lessons with the daughter of a friend and her governess for a year and then I was sent off to Florence. And at seventeen to Bavaria, to one of the old Gräfins who were desperate for some hard currency. I was there three terms then I was dragged back, protesting violently, to do the Season.'

Parents who sent their offspring abroad were not always aware if a child was frightened or mistreated. Val Canning had a governess whom she and all her siblings loathed. 'She particularly hated me and used to report me to my mother for all sorts of things I hadn't done. So I was always being punished, which wasn't pleasant. When I got to school I was amazed how nice everybody else's parents were.'

It was a life when *not* being looked after by others would have seemed unimaginable. Anne Reid described her life, as 'living in the lap of luxury. There were twelve living-in staff and my mother (who was French) had a personal maid brought over from France.

'While I was growing up, Nanny looked after all my clothes. She took them away, washed and pressed them or took them to the cleaners – I left everything on the floor. I didn't know how to make a bed, sweep a floor or boil an egg. Other people did everything for me.'

Parental wealth, however, was no guarantee of a cosseted life. For Meg Egerton, life was spartan rather than luxurious. 'We had the same iron bedsteads the housemaids had, with the same distemper instead of paint on the walls. Our upbringing was very strict – we weren't allowed cake and jam on the same day and if you forgot something you were banished to the attics. You were told what to do and told to get on with things. If you were ill there was no sympathy but "What a tiresome child you are" and you were sent up to the attics.'

It was made perfectly clear from an early age that boys were the superior sex. They, rather than girls, were the recipients of tips – gold sovereigns if they were lucky. 'One only rode in term-time as in the holidays the ponies were kept for my brother, who was made a god,' said Meg Egerton. 'In the same way, one could only fish on the Tweed, which ran below our house, when nobody else wanted to.'

Riding was very much a part of life for those living in the country. At the family house in Sussex, with its staff of ten, Fortune Smith and her three younger brothers all rode. 'We didn't absolutely have to but it was expected that we would. We had a groom who brought the ponies to the door and when we rode, as we did most days, we just chatted to him – he'd been a prisoner of war in the First War and he taught us elementary German as we trotted along. I was rather a nervous rider – I didn't grow up to be a horsy person.'

Female education focused on those accomplishments thought to be fitting to a gentlewoman: notably, a fluency in foreign languages and a knowledge of the arts, rather than the acquisition of learning. There was an emphasis on letter-writing. Telephones, for which calls had to go through an operator, were not the casual means of communication, open to the entire family, that they are today. 'My parents never talked on the telephone – that is to say, they never chatted,' said Elizabeth Lowry-Corry. 'It was used for emergencies. Before I came out, I never once received a telephone call at home.' If situated in the hall, the telephone was usually answered by the butler, while grander houses sometimes had a 'telephone room' which afforded some privacy.

Tuition was frequently given by governesses rather than in a school, and often these governesses were from abroad. Daphne Brock was one child who was educated entirely by governesses. 'I learned French before English and spoke to my parents entirely in French, although my father [an Admiral of the Fleet and an academic] read to me in English. I saw my mother largely in her bedroom when she was getting ready to go out and being helped by her French maid, Jeanne, so again we always talked French. Then, from the age of five to eleven, I had a French nursery governess.

'When I was eleven my parents decided I should learn another language, so along came a penniless Austrian countess whom my parents had met in Austria as my next governess. The result was that as well as learning German I learned more about the Hapsburgs than about the House of Windsor.'

At Althorp, Lady Anne Spencer (the aunt of Princess Diana) lived a nursery and schoolroom life, although seeing plenty of her parents. 'I had a wonderful nanny until I was eleven and then two French governesses – I never went to boarding school, which is why later life was so difficult.

'Lessons were with girl friends, who came to us as weekly boarders. My second French governess was wonderful – I learned a lot about life from her, including how to wear clothes. We learned history, geography, grammar but not maths which proved to be a bore later when measuring up carpets. I did German with another governess. My parents wanted me to become a well-rounded woman, fluent in languages and cultured.'

Sarah Norton was another who learned from French and Spanish governesses. 'My mother thought it useless for me to be taught maths – there would always be somebody to do that for me – so she had me taught Latin and Greek by a tutor, which she thought much more important.'

Sarah was the exception: most upper-class girls learned nothing of the classical languages, a mainstay of their brothers' education. When Cynthia Denison-Pender went to the well-known boarding school, Downham, near Bishop's Stortford, at the age of thirteen, she found there was little emphasis on education. 'It was a very social school – our parents sent us there because we met the right girls. We weren't highly educated and we didn't extend our intelligence – it wasn't asked of us.'

Fortune Smith went to a similar school, Southover, in Lewes, when the eldest of her three younger brothers was sent to prep school. 'My father used to say that it was so rare for anyone to pass the School Certificate that if they did we were given a day's holiday.'

Most went to finishing schools or their equivalent: visits of several months to the house of some impoverished French, German or Italian noblewoman who would take in up to half a dozen girls, teaching them the language of the country and as much as possible of its art, music and culture. They were taken to museums, cathedrals and concerts, always as heavily chaperoned as if they were the inmates of a harem belonging to a hyper-proprietorial sultan. Nothing considered the least bit 'racy' was allowed to assault eyes, ears or, heaven forfend, the person.

'The cinema was out of bounds because of the white slave trade – someone might inject you with a needle and you'd wake up in South America and if you went to the hairdresser, someone sat there to make sure you weren't assaulted,' said one girl. 'We had to leave the opera before the last act of *Faust* because the ending was not considered "suitable".'

Chapter 2

A Question of Upbringing

'You won't need exams'

Upper-class women grew up expected to 'do' – in the sense of gainful employment or physical tasks involved in looking after themselves or others – very little. The process began in the nursery, when Nanny or a nursery maid picked up fallen clothes, washed and ironed them and tidied up generally. When the young woman was old enough to have a lady's maid this invaluable creature would put out her mistress's clothes, run her bath, mend – often for the household – wash, iron, pack her suitcase, accompany her on weekend visits and even put her jewels away in the safe when she arrived home late from a party. In many households with a number of servants, the bell was rung for even the smallest task – putting logs on a fire, for instance.

For the mothers of these debutantes, life had a pattern equally serviced by others. After talking to Cook in the morning and writing letters, thank-you notes for the night before and invitations for the future, there were visits to the hairdresser, lunches with friends, wedding presents to choose for others, and endless fittings at the dressmaker's. All these occupations were fitted round the implacable demands of the social or, in the country, sporting calendar.

Honesty was still the norm among all social classes. 'My father was Chairman of Rolls-Royce and used to work in

London every day,' said Fortune Smith. 'He used to leave the car, unlocked, at Haywards Heath Station – one thought nothing of it. And we never locked the front door – that was unheard of.'

England seemed a much safer place then. From the age of twelve Fortune was allowed to bicycle, alone or with a friend, wherever she wanted in the countryside around her Sussex home. 'We used to go for miles. There was very little traffic and no one thought of risks of any other kind.'

Punctuality was another virtue instilled from birth. Lateness, as children were taught, meant that you disrupted other people's lives, in particular those of the servants whose tasks were made much more difficult if the family did not keep to a regular routine. 'Being late for meals simply wasn't countenanced,' said Jean Falkner. 'My father had an absolute rule that everybody had to be down for breakfast at eight o'clock and all my life I've been simply terrible in the morning. He used to get very angry if one was late – even in the war when I'd come home on leave exhausted.'

Meals were regular, and much more formal, with – during the day – everyone going for a wash-and-brush-up five minutes beforehand, while parents invariably changed for dinner in the evening.

It is difficult for anyone living today to realise how much the idea of class, in the sense of unchanging social order, underlay everyday life. Of course there were exceptions to the 'us and them' rule, in the sense that all barriers fell before the exceptionally successful, talented – Noël Coward and Cecil Beaton spring to mind – or the very wealthy, such as the society hostess Mrs Ronald Greville.* But for all practical purposes, the boundaries of class defined ordinary life for much of the country.

---

* Mrs Ronald Greville was the daughter of the Scottish beer baron John McEwan by his cook. An immensely rich, caustic and noted Edwardian hostess, she owned a splendid Regency house, Polesden Lacey, near the North Downs in Surrey, which she lent to the Duke and Duchess of York (later King George VI and Queen Elizabeth) for their honeymoon.

'There was a total demarcation between the servants and us,' said Jean Falkner. 'It makes me go hot and cold now.

'I was completely conscious of it while growing up. Where we were living in Scotland we were totally isolated and the only people we had to play with – unless relations came to stay – were the children of the shepherds.

'I had a great friend of my age, a shepherd's son called Jim, whom I adored. He taught me how to tickle trout, corner a sheep and catch it with the handle of a crook, skin rabbits and salt and cure moleskins. Suddenly one day when I was about eleven my mother called me into the drawing room and said I couldn't have Jim to play with me in the house any more.

'Actually it was more brutal than that. She made me realise that there was a reason Jim could no longer play with me in the house and come to meals and do everything with me, though I could still go out and play with him. I didn't question this – one didn't question decisions then – but I was very puzzled and terribly upset and miserable. My mother just had these rules that she seemed able to impress on me without my actually knowing what they were. Soon afterwards Jim was given jobs and began to work.

'If I'd got seriously involved with anyone like that later I can't think what they'd have done. I can't imagine. They'd have been *horrified*. When I was fifteen, I fell in love with the bootboy, who was later sacked by my father.

'When we were sent down to stay with my grandmother it was rather the same but in reverse. She told the butler's wife to bring up their baby for me and my younger sisters to play with – I mean, play with like a doll. We also had children from the village summoned up for us. We used to dress them and undress them and wash them, like living dolls.'

Class differences appeared in the most unlikely of situations.

Nudism had been imported from the Weimar Republic in the early thirties (entry to nudist camps was strictly controlled to avoid charges of immorality; prospective members had to obtain the written consent of husband, wife or fiancé(e)). At the superior nudist camps the butlers and maids who brought along refreshments had to wear loincloths and aprons respectively to denote their lower social status.

A prejudice that seldom percolated down to nursery or schoolroom was a certain low-level anti-Semitism. Parents who would never have dreamed of any physical manifestation of this still tended to believe that there was, if not an international conspiracy of Jewish bankers, at least a very powerful network. Even Sir John Simon, Foreign Secretary in the National Government of the 1930s, found it necessary to explain that he was really a Welshman who happened to have a Jewish-sounding surname.

Implicit in the upbringing of the upper classes was the belief that emotion, if allowed at all, should be severely restrained – particularly if it involved misery or complaint of any kind. Feelings, unless agreeable, were expected to be kept under wraps.

Pamela Joyce, taken to the funeral of a family friend when she was quite young, was given a warning about self-control by her father. '"Now, darling," he said to me, "we don't want any tears. You just keep yourself in hand – control yourself." There was no question of showing any sort of emotion. It was very British – self-discipline, I suppose.'

In Fortune Smith's family, emotions were never discussed. 'We were expected not to cry if we hurt ourselves, and to be good losers – the stiff upper lip and being a good loser was very much the thing. The boys went to school when they were eight and a half and that was it – nobody showed emotion about it. In fact I don't ever remember seeing my mother cry.'

For both sexes, this early training in stoicism would be tested to the full in the difficult and often dangerous situations of the war, while the unacknowledged miseries of homesickness at boarding school and the strategies evolved for coping with life among a crowd of unrelated boys or girls of the same age was a useful preparation for existence in a barrack room of strangers.

Fear could certainly never be acknowledged. Lady Margaret Egerton, brought up to ride, was terrified most of the time. 'We all rode. I was scared stiff but you didn't ever say so – one could never tell anyone what had happened or how frightened you were. We had no ponies suitable for children – one kicked you off and the other ran away but that didn't stop my parents putting us on them. When I was a bit older my horse would run away out hunting and crash into furious old colonels.

'And if we got cut when we were climbing trees we were expected not to cry when iodine was poured into our wounds.'

In part this was due to the fact that obedience to parental dictates was a given. Fortune Smith was one of many who said: 'You very much did what your parents told you then. I would never seriously have considered flouting their wishes.'

Along with this tamping down of emotional expression was a concomitant hatred of disclosure that went far beyond a simple distaste for self-revelation. Affairs might rage but outside the charmed circle no one knew about them; the idea that a 'leak' might trickle from Government circles to the general public would have been unimaginable; and publicity was anathema. Except for the columns of the *Times*'s Court and Social page – the bulletin board of the upper classes – and the glossy magazines (well, one could not very well stop a photographer snapping one in a particularly fetching outfit, could one?), which were considered harmless and indeed amusing, publicity was to be avoided at all costs as the acme of vulgarity. After the 1939 Pytchley Hunt Ball, Jean Falkner received a letter from the makers of Ponds. 'It offered what seemed like a goldmine to me if I would let myself be photographed for an advertisement for their cold cream. When I told my father he blew his top. "People like us don't do such things!" he said furiously. I was bitterly disappointed.'

Almost the greatest difference between then and now was in the position of women. It was only a decade since the mothers of the girls growing up before the war had received the franchise on equal terms with men (in 1928) but this advance did nothing to dispel the received wisdom of generations that boys were the superior sex. Boys had much better educations, went to universities, chose professions, earned money or inherited it – in short, had command over their lives, while their sisters passed smoothly from the care of a father to that of a husband.

For the young women of the thirties, marriage was both goal and destiny. 'One just assumed one would marry,' said Ursie Barclay, daughter of a substantial Norfolk family. 'Looking back, I suppose that in those days before the war my parents would have wanted one to marry well – I mean, if I'd come home with one of the farm labourers and said: "He's coming to dinner" that would not have gone down. If I'd fallen in love with a sergeant during the war neither of my parents would have liked it although Mummy, I think, would have tolerated it.'

'Of course we all hoped to get married,' said Frances Grenfell. 'There was no question of us getting a job. I remember my mother saying: "There are a million unemployed, and most of them are starving. You cannot take their jobs." So one wasn't trained and had no prospects. It was marriage or nothing.'

'I never expected to earn money,' said Lady Barbara Legge. 'It would have shocked my parents very much if I'd said I wanted a job. I didn't need one and there was a lot of unemployment so they would have been horrified at the thought of me working.'

～

Education, therefore (apart from languages), for these daughters of the upper classes who had no need to 'better' themselves, was considered at best a waste of time, at worst something likely to put off a potential suitor, whose masculine dignity might be offended by a wife cleverer and more knowledgeable than himself. 'I was quite ambitious,' said Fanny Gore Browne, whose father was Chairman of Southern Railways. 'But I wasn't allowed to go to university. My brothers – who both went to Cambridge – said to my mother: "Don't let her go to Oxford, she'll turn into a bluestocking."'

As Mary Pakenham wrote of her Season a few years earlier:* 'I acquired the unsavoury reputation of being "intelligent". No harder word was used. No harder word was needed.'

Some, like Lady Barbara Stuart-Wortley (the daughter of the third Earl of Wharncliffe), met active opposition on the question of education. 'Men don't like educated women,' said her mother firmly. 'But it's very important to know how to ride.' So the children were given a pony each and went hunting once a week during the winter.

'My sister Josceline and I lived for riding,' said Barbara Legge. 'We were desperate to ride – it was the one thing we really loved doing. Otherwise we were totally uneducated.' Other parents, like those of Diana Quilter, might not have forbidden a daughter to go to university but the idea – as in her case – simply would not have crossed their minds.

A few girls wanted their futures to include more than marriage. 'I did have ideas about doing something,' said Lavinia Holland-Hibbert. 'I planned to be a political secretary before I married. I belonged to something called the House of Citizenship and went visiting Borstals. I spent much of my leisure writing notes about foreign affairs in my room.

'If Mummy came in I hid them because I was shy about it. She wouldn't have disapproved but she would have thought I should have been out playing tennis – being indoors was not exactly a sin, but rather an indulgence. It didn't matter what the

---

* Mary Clive, *Brought Up and Brought Out* (1938).

weather was like – you went out and did something.'

Cynthia Keppel, granddaughter of the Earl of Albemarle, also had what she called 'aspirations' but the culture in which she grew up was too powerful. 'I enjoyed school, the lessons, actually learning. But when I grew up there was no idea of girls having a career or going to university. I had a wonderful aunt and if I *had* wanted to go to university, she certainly would have helped me. But somehow I felt, because of my upbringing, that marriage was the ultimate aim of any girl and this was a kind of invisible obstacle to my even considering a university.'

Suspicion of the well-educated woman was widespread. Mathematics, science and the classics were considered among the subjects too 'hard' for the female mind.

Sometimes active impediments were placed in the way of those attempting to help themselves. When Barbara Stuart-Wortley, deeply worried about her lack of education at the hands of an incompetent French governess, went to her father's library to look up the meaning of a list of words she did not understand in one of his dictionaries, she was found there by her father who assumed, even in the face of her denials, that she was looking up profanities and 'improper' words. From then on, the library was banned to her.

Val Canning was not allowed to take exams, so unnecessary for girls did her parents think any form of education. 'When I wanted to take exams my mother said: "You won't need to, you'll get married straight away." I longed for education but I got very little. The result was that I wasn't capable of doing a job – I was offered one or two but my parents didn't think it suitable for me to take one.'

For those who did go to school, the reality was sometimes unpleasant. Parental visits were few and far between – many parents saw boarding school as a handy way of ridding themselves of their children for three months at a stretch – and, in any case, visits were generally rationed to two or three a term.

The atmosphere at school was often cheerless. At one of the

smartest girls' schools, Heathfield (in Berkshire), though the food was good and the pupils were waited on by uniformed maids, silence at meals was absolute, with talking penalised in much of the building. Nobody was allowed a soft toy or favourite book, photographs were limited to two from home, and the universal rule of strict propriety required that curtains had to be drawn round each cubicle when its occupant dressed or undressed.

'Our whole education was about getting to know people,' said Lavinia Holland-Hibbert. 'At school you went to stay with girl friends who had house parties.'

A few had other ideas. 'I wanted to do a job – I wanted to learn about pictures and how to clean them,' said Cynthia Denison-Pender. 'My particular friends were quite ambitious. We'd met enough people with titles not to be impressed by that or to feel it was the be-all and end-all of life to marry one. And I certainly didn't want to marry early on.'

All through childhood and adolescence, discipline was inculcated in girls no less than in boys, with both drilled in the way they were expected to behave. Choice was a luxury, unknown to many until they were officially adult. There was an insistence on good manners, especially to older people, for whom respect was fundamental.

Children – and girls were considered to be children until the moment they 'came out' – were supposed to keep their elbows off the table, eat what they were given (to the last crumb; sometimes to be sent upstairs to finish off the gradually cooling mutton chop or rice pudding they had been served with), never answer back and sit up straight. 'For goodness' sake, hold up!' Lady Elizabeth Montagu Douglas Scott's mother would say to her.

Despite the 'seen but not heard' rule, the art of conversation was equally important. 'One day when I was about fifteen there were thirteen to lunch – considered an unlucky number – and I was made to be the fourteenth,' said Lady Elizabeth Scott, daughter of the Duke of Buccleuch. 'I sat there getting on with my lunch and I felt my mother's eyes on me. She mouthed "Talk!" and I went scarlet.'

Elizabeth's mother also chose her clothes, taking her daughter to the dressmaker ('Even with my trousseau she took me to the dressmaker and the hatmaker – one had to have a brown overcoat, a blue overcoat and a black overcoat and everything else went with that').

Even when girls were technically grown-up, the parental sway was not over. 'I was invited to go to the cinema by a very attractive man, ten years older than me,' recalled Suzanne Irwin. 'When we got back and I came upstairs my mother called me into her bedroom where she was sitting up in bed. "I heard Russell's car pulling up outside," she said, adding reprovingly: "You were a very long time coming in." I told her that of course we were just talking.'

Lady Elizabeth remembers going to a party with her mother and being given a glass of sherry. 'My mother came across and said: "What are you drinking?" I said: "A glass of sherry." To which she said: "At your age! Why?" And by then I was twenty-three.'

Alcohol was so seldom drunk by young upper-class girls that it was often a source of suspicion to them. 'When my sister and I went to FANY [First Aid Nursing Yeomanry] camp in Strelsall we were asked out to a bath and meal by some friends who lived the other side of York,' said Barbara Legge. 'They gave us each a drink, the first time we'd ever drunk alcohol. Driving back through York I suddenly saw a goat on the road. I was so convinced it was a drink-induced hallucination that I looked at Josceline and said: "Did you see that?" Only when she said "Yes" did we realise it was a real goat and not the drink.'

Outward expressions of love, as a public manifestation of the dreaded emotionalism, were kept severely at bay; so much so that in most of these upper-class families such feelings were never expressed. 'My mother played the piano beautifully and my father would sing,' said one girl. 'I think that was their only outlet for deep feelings, which were never displayed, or discussed.'

Sometimes this meant that physical contact between parents and children was virtually non-existent. One pair of sisters, sent to a convent at the ages of ten and eleven because their mother believed a Catholic education was not only the cheapest but also the best, reeled with surprise when greeted on arrival with a kiss from the nuns ('We were never kissed by either of our parents').

Nowhere was this lack of intimacy more unequivocally demonstrated than in the matter of imparting sexual knowledge. Despite the upheavals of the 1914–18 war, the freedoms of the dance-mad twenties and the advent of the cinema with its constant emphasis on love and romance, sex was still the Great Unmentionable.

'My mother avoided the subject like mad,' said Jean Falkner. 'Once when we were driving past our hens and one was being ridden by a cock, I said: "Oh, look! What are they doing?" and I was brushed off. When we got home I went back to the question again and still my mother didn't tell me.'

Yet parents who brought up their daughters in a state of profound sexual ignorance were often themselves indulging in more or less flagrant love affairs. Sarah Norton's mother, the beautiful Jean, was the long-term mistress of Lord Beaverbrook, a fact well known to everyone in her circle – except for her son and daughter. 'We were completely unaware of her affair with Lord Beaverbrook,' said Sarah. 'I hated him although I didn't know why.'

Many girls went into puberty ignorant of bodily changes. 'I was scared stiff when I found I was growing pubic hair,' said one. 'I thought something monstrous had happened to me.' 'No one told me about getting the curse,' said another. 'I suppose I was a bit early – eleven or twelve. I thought I was bleeding from some wound and for three days I didn't tell anyone. I wore bits of cotton wool until one day Nanny discovered what had happened. I wouldn't even have discussed it with my sister – we'd been brought up not to talk about our bodies.'

'When my period arrived I was a bit puzzled,' said another. 'We had a marvellous old nanny and all she said was "Oh, stay in your bed, I'll get your mother." She wasn't going to take any responsibility. So my mother came and explained it to me in such convoluted terms that I simply didn't understand at all. I just about got that for some reason this was going to happen every month. I remember saying to my mother: "Oh dear, it sounds much easier to be a bird".'

Another girl, who was equally ignorant, first menstruated at a smart Newmarket race meeting where she had been taken with her mother and the Aly Khan to see one of his horses run. On first discovery she thought it was a disease, probably fatal, until her mother said solemnly: 'You have become a woman!'

The silence about menstruation, as about anything else to do with sex, pervaded even girls' schools. 'I was told not to let out the fact that I'd started in case some of the others hadn't,' said one girl. 'So when I got the curse I had to hide an ST [sanitary towel] up my knicker leg and disappear to the loo.'

One mother brought the subject up while hacking home from hunting with her daughter, who remembered: 'I was frightfully embarrassed – I remember running my hunting crop down my horse's neck so that I didn't have to look at her. It was the only time she ever spoke about anything to do with the human reproductive system.'

This obfuscation was nothing, however, to the impenetrable fog that shrouded anything to do with copulation.

'My mother never told us the facts of life,' said Lady Barbara Legge. 'I think she tried once or twice but, really, we didn't want to hear. There was a tremendous embarrassment in talking about sex – it was simply never mentioned. We did know a bit because Godmersham was a farm and we used to see the sheep having lambs. But you don't always connect animal behaviour with human.'

The mother of Virginia Forbes Adam was one of the few – the very few – who spoke openly to her daughter. 'She was extremely extrovert and told me everything about life. She told me all about my periods and drew pictures of my youngest brother inside the womb so that when I began to go to dances I didn't feel a complete innocent – though later on, when I became engaged, an erection was quite a shock.

'I also heard about lesbianism when I stayed for one term in 1939 with a Swiss governess who took English girls in Paris. When I got back I talked to my parents about it and they said: "And who told you that?" I'd bought a paperback book in France on the subject.'

Much more the norm was the experience of another woman who, totally ignorant of sexual matters when she became a nurse at the beginning of the war, remained so until her marriage two years later. 'My mother never spoke to me about sex. Even on my wedding night I didn't know what was going to happen.' When asked by the present writer if she was horrified when she found out, she reflected for a moment before saying: 'No – but I *was* surprised.'

She was not the only one who found the truth difficult to grasp. The actress Joyce Grenfell, who married Frances' half-brother Reggie, was another never given the slightest information during adolescence. 'The morning she was being married her mother thought she had better tell her,' recounted one of her cousins. 'Joyce said: "Oh Ma, do shut up. I simply don't believe you – that means being upside down."'

Country girls, in theory, had a better chance of learning about the mechanics of sex through watching animals but few connected the activities of bulls or boars with human reproduction. When Lady Barbara Stuart-Wortley and her sister

Anne asked their mother about the facts of life she refused to tell them. 'She'd start talking vaguely about the birds and the bees, which meant nothing to us. I think my sister must have learned somehow, because one day when we were out riding with the groom and going through a farm we saw a sow being mounted by a boar and Anne said to me: "One day a man will do that to you." I just looked at her and said: "Don't be so disgusting."'

The fear of pregnancy outside marriage was, as one girl put it, 'held like a flaming sword over our heads'. Although the ideal for most parents was their daughter's marriage to a 'suitable' young man whom she loved, preferably at an early age, sometimes their dire warnings were couched in terms so mysterious that they were counter-productive.

'My older sister was very pretty and attractive. My mother put the fear of death into her over misbehaviour leading to pregnancy before marriage but never explained what this was, so my sister thought that if you were kissed you had a baby,' said one. 'The result was that she was terrified of young men, put them all off in case they tried to kiss her and didn't marry until she was nearly thirty.'

Kissing as the highroad to pregnancy was a common misconception. Coming back alone in a taxi with a young man who had taken her to a nightclub (both of which were strictly forbidden), the eighteen-year-old Lady Elizabeth Montagu Douglas Scott sat on the edge of the taxi seat with her arms folded repressively across her chest. 'I *knew* that if he kissed me I might have a baby.'

Few of these cocooned young girls had any idea how babies arrived. 'I certainly hadn't a clue,' said Jean Falkner. 'While I was still at boarding school, at the age everyone began to look at boys – about sixteen and a half, I suppose – the son of some friends of my parents kissed me under an apple tree. I was absolutely terrified – I thought it meant I'd have a baby.'

Most parents would do anything rather than speak to their

children about sex. 'It was a subject you simply didn't discuss, even with your daughter,' said Ursie Barclay. 'I learned a bit at school but I certainly didn't know about erections. The one thing everyone was scared stiff of was getting pregnant – then, it really was something to be ashamed of. So even when you were frightfully in love you didn't dare go too far'.

'I think the reason my parents didn't talk to me about the facts of life was that they didn't even talk to each other about it,' said Esme Harmsworth. 'It's always puzzled me how they managed to have us at all.

'I grew up in total innocence. I was enlightened at my day school by a friend when I was about fourteen. I couldn't believe it – I thought it was frightfully funny and thought immediately of King George V and Queen Mary and went off into howls of laughter, saying: "I don't believe a word of it – *they* couldn't possibly have done that sort of thing!"'

Nor were books or other publications any help as the most that the enquiring mind of puberty could expect was a row of asterisks when love reached its right climax – although it was known that more 'explanatory' books could be purchased abroad.

'My parents never discussed emotions or the facts of life with me,' said Jean Campbell-Harris. 'Never, ever. I grew up in complete ignorance. We talked about sex at boarding school but we had a very strange idea of it. Everything was drawn from *Lady Chatterley's Lover* – I bought a copy in France and put it inside a Jane Austen dust cover.

'There was an immense amount of protectiveness. The result was that you could get into dreadful trouble and not know why. Jean Borotra, the tennis star, knew my family and so when I was in Paris just before the war he asked me out. I wasn't allowed to go and I couldn't think why – to me he was a hundred years old.

'So when sex did hit you it was awful bad luck. The first time I was kissed with an open mouth I was appalled. I thought it revolting. I was seventeen and I said to my mother: "This is just revolting – is it a usual thing?" She simply said: "Oh, you'll learn about these things."'

'Even when I was going to get married I didn't know much,' said Barbara Stuart-Wortley. 'I begged Mummy to tell me more details. But she wouldn't. After the ceremony she said: "Oh, darling, I've put a few things in your case that might be useful to you." She'd put a tin of Vaseline in but she didn't tell me how to use it – I simply didn't know. And I think David [Ricardo] was as ignorant as me – his parents wouldn't tell him. Instead, they asked one of the masters at the school to talk to him.'

Fiona Colquhoun was yet another who was never told the facts of life. 'My mother never discussed it with me, although we were very close. I think she was frightened of telling us – or perhaps nervous is a better word. I don't know why, but she definitely was. I only finally learned just before I was married – but from a cousin, not my mother. Nor did she like me going out. If a young man called to take me out, she disliked it.'

The agonies of embarrassment suffered by the mother who did attempt to broach this then-taboo subject often caused misunderstandings.

'Before I went to boarding school my mother thought she ought to talk to me about the facts of life,' said Ursie Barclay. 'We were going downstairs and she said: "You do know how babies come, don't you?"

'As I didn't I answered: "Not really." She said: "Well, you know what your rabbits are always doing?"

'I thought of how they were constantly nibbling their patch of lawn, so I said "Sort of." And she changed the subject straight away, saying, "What are you going to wear tomorrow?" So for a long time I thought conception had something to do with eating grass.'

Chapter 3

Coming Out

'The whole point was to find a husband'

For girls in the upper echelon of society, the ritual of 'coming out' at the age of seventeen or, more usually, eighteen was set in stone. It followed a regular pattern: first, a base would be set up in London for the coming campaign (for such it often was). This could be a rented house in London, preferably with a first-floor drawing room big enough for a dance, the opening up of a town house by those lucky enough to own one, or an arrangement to stay with a conveniently placed aunt, cousin or grandparent. The new debutante's mother would give, and attend, numerous luncheons at which introductions were made and lists of eligible young men and other debutante daughters were exchanged; the girls themselves would give and go to endless girls' tea parties. The soda fountain at Selfridges was a favourite mid-morning rendezvous for groups of girls to meet and discuss the previous night's ball as the Season got under way.

With a state visit of the King and Queen to the US and Canada planned for May, the Season of 1939 started early. During March several Presentation Courts were held at Buckingham Palace, at which these debutantes (an average year saw around 1,200) would be presented to the King and Queen, generally by their mothers. Only a married woman of ostensibly unblemished reputation, who had been through the same procedure herself, could present a debutante, which ruled out both maiden aunts, however virtuous, and divorcees. Sometimes impecunious women of good social standing, such as Lady Clancarty (known as Lady Blank Cartridge) and Lady St John of Bletsoe, would present – for a sizeable sum – the daughters of rich and socially aspiring parents who would not otherwise have infiltrated this annual ritual.

The Season proper began on the first Monday in May with the opening of the Royal Academy Summer Exhibition in the morning and Covent Garden grand opera that night. There followed a frenetic round of cocktail parties, dances and balls. By the end of the thirties, many of these parties were held in hotels rather than private houses so that more people could be asked. Favourites were Claridge's and the Hyde Park Hotel because of its position overlooking the park. There would be dinner parties beforehand, organised among her friends by the hostess giving the dance, and supper at the dance itself, followed by breakfast at or soon after 2.00 a.m. It was said that a young man who owned a tail coat and white tie could eat free for the whole of the summer.

When the Season ended, in the first few days of August, the exhausted participants would either retire to the country, or to Cowes to sail, or to Scotland to shoot (the grouse-shooting season began on 12 August).

So important was the curtsey to the Sovereign considered to be, together with the whole breathtaking round of the Season, that strenuous efforts were made to partake of it even when the necessary cash was in short supply. Some girls from poorer families, though necessarily from the 'right' social background, managed to circumvent this.

'My mother said I couldn't come out because she couldn't afford it,' said Christian Grant. 'But I had been left £200 by an old governess so I paid for it myself. My dance cost £100 – I shared it with another girl.' Christian's dance was on 11 May 1939 at 6 Stanhope Gate (a favourite party venue), ostensibly given by the Dowager Lady Grant and Lady Schuster.

'My grandmother was very keen that I should be presented,' said Rosemary Hodson, mother of the writer Joanna Trollope. 'My mother had been brought up in luxury but my father as Rector of Minchinhampton had very little money so presentation wasn't on the cards. Then my mother thought about it and realised that it needn't cost us much more than our train fare to London.

'Our dresses were made by the village dressmaker and – as you had to have either a bouquet or an ostrich-feather fan – my grandmother, who had masses of these fans, lent us hers, as well as giving me the feathers for my hair. She also lent us jewellery and long white gloves. We went to stay with a kind aunt in Hampstead who lent us her Rolls and chauffeur, with a friend of the chauffeur's as the extra man you had to have in the front.'

Before this momentous summer, most of the young women involved had been 'finished' in small schools or smart but impoverished families in France, Germany or Italy, from which they were supposed to come home both culturally enriched and linguistically fluent. It also gave many their first taste of freedom, albeit carefully rationed.

'My Season was led up to by being abroad for two years,' said Lady Elizabeth Montagu Douglas Scott. 'I spent three months in Munich to learn German, then went to Italy for two terms, then home for the Christmas holidays. At the beginning of 1939 I was taken to the local hunt ball, for which we had lots of young people to stay who I didn't know and was terrified of. Then I was sent back to France for the third of my languages – such a short time that I learned nothing – and told to get ball dresses in Paris with the help of the lady I lived with. I came back in May and was plunged straight away into a ball.

'It was a total disaster. I didn't know a soul. First I went to a dinner party – I didn't know anyone there for a start – then going up the stairs of this huge house in the Finchley Road there was such a crush you were squeezed to bits and couldn't see anyone. I had a dance with my father and then lost him, after which I didn't know what to do. Eventually I found my mother and cried, "Oh please take me home! I hate this" and she very kindly did. I thought, Oh dear, this is going to be a nightmare life. But gradually one got to know people, and young men who danced with one, and I really enjoyed it.'

Food played a prominent part, with formal dinner parties of several courses beforehand, so that guests arrived at the dance around 10 p.m. Some time after midnight there was supper, with dishes such as quails, lobster, cold chicken in aspic, asparagus, and strawberries and cream, with breakfast – bacon and eggs, kidneys, salmon kedgeree and coffee – to follow. There was plenty of champagne but most of the girls drank little or nothing. For some of those accustomed to school or nursery food, these delicacies were a delightful novelty. 'Quail was often on the menu – I'd never eaten it before, nor asparagus,' said Val Canning.

Few families owned a London house large enough in which to give a ball. Some of those who did, whose own daughters were perhaps too young or already grown up, would let them out for the Season; other dances were given at well-known venues rented for the night. The dance given for Joan Stafford King-Harman on 5 May 1937 was at a house rented by her parents in Cadogan Square, decorated throughout with tulips by Constance Spry – then the last word in floral chic. 'It would be put in the paper that one was in London for the summer and then piles of advertisements would come through the door,' said Joan. These would be for anything from clothes, invitations from the famous caterer and tea shop, Gunter's, to offers of free sittings from photographers.

'Most of the young men couldn't dance for toffee, they went round with their arms pump-handling. It was always white tie and most of them wore gloves. It was all frightfully proper – if anyone danced cheek to cheek, they pretty well had to announce their engagement.'

Some girls came off better than others in the matter of partners. Even among debutantes, protocol was observed, so that girls with titles were always placed next to the host – the father of the girl in whose house the dinner was taking place. 'I didn't know any men but usually you could be sure of at least two dances, as the rule was that the two men on either side of you at dinner always asked you to dance,' said Lady Margaret Egerton. 'But because of my title I was always seated beside the father, so was done out of one of these dances.'

Many debutantes hated their own dances. Sheila Parish shared hers with a girl whose mother was a lady-in-waiting to Princess Alice, who insisted on coming to the dinner party beforehand and then to the dance. There followed an episode that showed both the formality of all such occasions and the extraordinary reverence in which royalty was held. 'Because Princess Alice was coming it meant that I, as daughter of the joint hostess, had to go and have dinner with my friend's mother and twenty old fogies, instead of dinner with other young people, including young men who would have danced with me.

'By the time we arrived everybody had filled up their cards. As I knew no boys and very few girls I spent most of the time up in the cloakroom. So my dance was hell.'

Girls like Sheila who had grown up without brothers, or knowing many boys, often had a sticky start to their Season. 'The awful thing was waiting with one's little dance card, hoping it was going to be filled up,' said Susan Meyrick. 'If it wasn't, you had to pretend you were talking to someone or dart to the ladies' loo. The debs were pretty catty, noticing who was a wallflower.'

Other girls were luckier. 'All my mother's friends had boy children, so I grew up with these galumphing boys who wouldn't let me play football with them,' explained Sarah Norton. 'But it meant I did have friends when the terrible moment of the first debutante dance arrived. And as the only girl they knew was me, I had lots of partners. So although I hadn't wanted to be a debutante I just loved it. I had lots of boyfriends but no proposals – you weren't allowed to go out with them.'

Frances Grenfell also had insurance, in the shape of twin boy cousins with whom she was great friends. 'I said to them: "Look here, you jolly well dance with me when I'm not dancing." And they said: "All right, that's perfectly fair – as long as there's not a duke's daughter ahead of you", although girls with ducal mothers were guarded like the crown jewels – young men had quite a job getting through to them.

'In any case, the mothers sitting on the bench watched to see that their little darlings didn't dance too much with the same person – if they did, they would break it up a bit.'

For some, looks and personality countered the repressive influence of an upbringing where personal vanity was severely discouraged and, as in Christian Grant's case, confidence eroded. 'I'd been brought up to believe that it was wrong to think one was pretty or attractive or that anyone would take any notice of one. And then this door opened and there were young men falling in love with me. It was wonderful, like the doors of paradise opening, to realise that one wasn't, as one had always thought, stupid and boring and "who wants to hear what *you've* got to say".'

'I was terrified of young men when I first met them,' recalled Lady Elizabeth Scott. 'My brother was young and my childhood was very quiet. Two or three families who lived near, whom one knew very well, were the limit of our social life. So I was flung into the Season, no conversation at all, no education really. I must have been very dull but I loved dancing and music and got excited by it. Luckily the other girls were a terribly nice lot and we became great buddies.'

Strict sexual segregation sometimes meant that potential partners were unavailable. Diana Lyttelton was the daughter of the well-known Eton housemaster George Lyttelton (and sister of the great jazz trumpeter Humphrey Lyttelton), with a whole generation of potential partners growing up around the parental house. 'But Pa thought blooming girls in the middle of a boys' school was not a good idea so we were all sent to boarding school at eleven.

'Thus my debbing was not a glittering career. I wasn't shy but I knew nobody. Nobody ever asked me to a nightclub and I certainly didn't find a husband. Nor did I want to – I didn't have a boyfriend during the Season. We rather slogged through it. Mummy came up rather gloomily and sat on benches round the various ballrooms and we lodged with an aunt and uncle who made no concession to the fact that we'd been out late – breakfast was at nine and removed at ten past if we weren't there.'

Debutantes were chaperoned to an extent that any eighteen-year-old girl today would find unbelievable. They were taken to and from dances, watched while there (under lights bright enough to dispel any chance of a stolen kiss). Some were forbidden to walk down St James's Street even in daylight (it was lined with London's most famous and exclusive men's clubs), presumably in case they were approached by clubmen bent on luring them into unknown depravities. One girl who was, highly unusually for those days, allowed to attend the London School of Economics, had to be chaperoned there and back by her lady's maid since travelling alone was out of the question.

Since going anywhere alone with a young man was also strictly forbidden, the smart thing for a popular debutante was to sneak off to a nightclub in mid-dance with a favourite boyfriend, returning to the party in time to go home, so that she was not missed by her chaperoning mother. 'We thought it was terribly dashing but it was really very innocent,' said Susan Meyrick.

Sometimes the mothers themselves complicated things. Lady Elizabeth Scott's mother always took her to dances 'but then she'd disappear to a nightclub and come back and collect me. One evening I discovered I could slip away too but wherever I went I'd have to ask at the door: "Is my mother here?" If the answer was no I could go in with my friend. Mr Rossi at the 400 was a great pal and he'd say: "Careful, careful, she's here!" So we'd go to the Florida or the Café de Paris instead, with one's eye on the watch, to be back by three.'

Some girls were sent to dinner parties with the family chauffeur and then put in the charge of the dinner-party hostess. Others were brought home by their mothers, who had been sitting all night on the small gilt chairs ranged round the ball-room. Christian Grant was one seen home in this way, either by her mother or by one of her mother's women friends. 'If the latter, I had to put my dancing shoes in my mother's bedroom, so that if she woke up she would see them.'

The popular Christian, who had no intention of ending her evening so early, easily circumvented this ploy. 'I would simply put on another pair of shoes and go out with a young man to a nightclub. I never lied about it – but then, if she saw the shoes, she never asked me.'

Some girls were chaperoned – or were expected to be chaperoned – the whole time. Anne Douglas-Scott-Montagu, the daughter of Lord Montagu of Beaulieu, asked to join a cousin's party to watch the 1939 Derby, reached the house in South Audley Street from which the group was to set out, having caught a bus from her grandmother's house in Thurloe Square. When she arrived, the first question was: 'Who's brought you?' 'Nobody's brought me,' said Anne, 'I came on a bus.' Her cousin's mother replied incredulously: 'Did your mother let you come alone? Didn't she send her maid or anybody with you?'

Chaperonage had some advantages. 'My mother or my father or both took me to every dance and sat there until it was time to go home,' said Lady Anne Spencer. 'The nice thing about having a chaperone was that it meant you could have somewhere to sit and someone to talk to if you hadn't been asked for that dance.'

While some girls took easily to meeting a mass of strangers or semi-strangers in their own age-group, others found it a horrific ordeal – one girl so hated the idea of coming out that her mother sent her to a psychiatrist to overcome her reluctance. 'I was quite scared of being presented as I was frightened of doing the wrong thing,' said Fiona Colquhoun. 'In any case, I thought my coming out was a waste of time – I'd rather have had the money as I always wanted to fly.' (Later, as Lady Arran, she would break the offshore world speed record.)

Still others were simply bored. Lady Moyra Ponsonby, one of those who had her own lady's maid (the daughter of her father's head chauffeur), found going out night after night exhausting. 'I would rest after tea and fall fast asleep. My maid would come in and wake me and I would have given anything not to go out again that evening and do it all over again, though it did get a bit better later when one had one's favourite boyfriend.'

Virginia Forbes Adam counted herself fortunate to miss that strenuous summer. 'My grandmother was a painter and had married very young to get away from Harewood, where she said the whole duty of man was hunting, shooting and fishing. I was the same – I set my teeth and ears against the Season. I missed it because I was just too young but I was sent to Queen Charlotte's Ball in 1940. My mother lived for my coming out and was terribly disappointed when the war put a stop to it for me. She was an immensely social person who loved the dressing-up, the going to balls, but I couldn't bear the thought. She was so determined that I should have a dance that she gave a ball for me when the war ended.'

Queen Charlotte's Ball, in aid of the famous maternity hospital, was one of the highlights of the debutante calendar. It was run by the ubiquitous Lady St John of Bletsoe; the debutantes of that year, wearing mandatory white, would process down the grand staircase into the ballroom of Grosvenor House, where they would curtsey to a giant cake. (Later, when the Court Presentations stopped in wartime, Queen Charlotte's Ball took over as the unofficial marker of a girl's coming out – even in

1944, when people had to bring their own food and drink, 1,300 tickets were sold at £3 each.)

'We were all given a free make-up that afternoon,' remembers Frances Grenfell, 'and came out looking rather like Coco the clown. After our curtsey we were given a badge to wear, with a stork on one side carrying a baby and on the other the words "For Services Rendered". I had to get rid of it, my brothers ribbed me so much.' The badge was pinned to a crimson satin heart, which the girls wore slung around their necks on a crimson cord.

~~

Contact between the sexes was as strictly controlled as possible. 'We may have been great innocents but we certainly knew what not to do,' said Joan Stafford King-Harman. 'The year I was coming out my mother said: "Don't let a man kiss you unless you're going to marry him."'

Virginity, the great unmentionable – most girls would have blushed at hearing the word – was as prized as in an entrant to a Turkish harem. In part this was owing to the fear of pregnancy – no unmarried girl could hope for assistance with birth control nor would she have known where to go for it – springing from the atavistic belief that only by marrying a virgin bride could a man be absolutely sure that the child of the union was his own. In part, too, purity was valued for its own sake. 'I and all my close friends would have considered ourselves defiled if we hadn't come to marriage as virgins,' said Sarah Norton. 'Even when you became engaged it made no difference. Virginity lasted right up until the wedding night.'

'The boys didn't expect to go to bed with you,' said Lorna Harmsworth. 'They went to the Bag of Nails.* We understood

* A Soho nightclub with a somewhat louche reputation, famous for its black jazz band.

that they went there – it was taken for granted. I don't think we worried about not knowing about sex. You see, we had romances.'

For the vast majority, there was a kiss in the taxi and no more than that – if that.

'I don't think I was properly kissed until I was in the Army,' said Lavinia Holland-Hibbert. 'Hand-holding going home in the car was the thing. You had these huge fur rugs at the back of the car because there was no heating and the great thing was to get with your chap under the fur rug while you were being driven by somebody.

'The two great slogans we used about dangerous boys were MTF and NST – Must Touch Flesh and Not Safe in Taxis'.

Naturally, there were occasional exceptions to the rule of chastity. 'We all knew who they were as the men talked,' said Christian Grant. 'I learned everything about who went to bed with whom from men blathering, which was very silly of them because it must have stopped a lot of other girls doing it. They talked about them in a joky way. "Oh, lucky old Pongo, he's going out with X – we all know where that'll end up." There were two girls in my year who were known to go to bed with people. They both married rich peers and we all thought: How unfair.'

Other aspects of sexuality were not so much a mystery as unheard of. 'I had no idea what a homosexual man was and when some of the better-looking men didn't pounce, one could not make out what was wrong,' said Christian. 'Pouncing was the understood thing – I think one would have been slightly insulted if they'd taken you out to dinner and not put an amorous arm around you in the taxi.'

Girls wore bright red lipstick and curled their eyelashes with tiny tongs. Yet although allowed make-up, they often had their clothes chosen for them by their mothers. 'The frock that my mother bought for me when I was presented was narrow with puffed sleeves,' said Sarah Norton. 'I thought it was perfectly hideous and told her so but she paid no attention. "You're going to wear it and that's that", she said – she chose all my clothes for me.

'But things got better as luckily I had an eighteen-and-a-half-inch waist and the designer Victor Stiebel began to dress me for nothing. He used to make my waist even smaller by putting a guêpière round it and would pull this so tight that I couldn't eat whatever dinner I was given that night. I had to give back these ball dresses at the end of the Season but was allowed to buy them cheaply, for twenty pounds, if I wanted.'

Most clothes were made by dressmakers, required several fittings and cost anything from £2 10s for a pleated chiffon dance dress to £10 for a Court dress. Silk stockings were treasured and carefully mended, hats and gloves worn on all outings. 'Today I bought a hat,' wrote Christian Grant on 16 January 1939. 'I walked half round London looking in shop windows and finally bought a very plain little black felt with a sailor brim and a filmy veil tied in a bow behind. I planted two ostrich feathers on the crown – and there was the hat which, with several changes of trimming, would last me till the summer.'

Val Canning, who in 1938 had suffered such a horrendous car accident on her way home from the Italian finishing school to which her parents had sent her that her coming out was postponed for a year, was then sent to the Monkey Club in Pont Street ('I don't think my parents really wanted me at home') for yet more 'finishing'.

There she learned dressmaking from Queen Mary's dressmaker, Reville, alongside Cecil Beaton, and was chosen to paint the furs for the Reville catalogue as she had learned miniature embossed painting in Italy. Kept short of money by her parents, she had to manage as best she could.

'I found out where there was a charity shop, in a scruffy part of Pimlico. When the rich girls around me wanted to sell their dresses second-hand, I took them there for them and bought the ones I liked for myself – paying the shop's price, of course. That was all right but shoes were a different matter. My feet were bad because my mother would never buy new shoes for me at school so they were always too small and distorted my feet.'

'The peak of the dress mountain was a very pretty girl who lived in Millionaires' Row [Kensington Palace Gardens] who was never seen in the same dress twice,' said Christian Grant, who had four evening dresses and two short ones. 'I had an allowance of ten pounds a month on which I was supposed to dress myself and get my hair done. The only thing my mother gave me was my Presentation dress and if I were asked to stay anywhere she would buy my railway ticket there – if she approved of where I was going.'

Debutantes who came out in 1936 – the year King George V died – could wear only the Court mourning colours of white or black until June. Most chose black, thrilled at the idea of wearing a colour usually reserved for older and more sophisticated women.

An extract from Christian Grant's diary of 1939 shows both the entertainments then available and the prevailing attitudes towards them. 'I was rather flattered when Christopher Scott asked me to go to the Scottish Art exhibition with him. It was the first time anyone had taken me to anything intellectual. We went on to a sherry party. Afterwards we had dinner at La Coquille and I went home to change before going to the Florida. There was a marvellous all-black cabaret with tap dancers, crooners, hula-hula girls and two witch-doctors who danced to the beat of tom-toms. I cannot decide if I admire Christopher for his frankness or dislike him for his obviousness but I know when he tried to hold my hand I wouldn't have any. We trekked off home about three o'clock.'

Girls were usually given two Seasons, the second an altogether more relaxed affair, after which parents felt they had done their duty in providing their daughters with as wide a pool of 'eligibles' as possible from which to choose friends – and husbands. For, as Barbara Legge commented: 'Really, the whole point of the Season was to find a husband – if not then, well, certainly later.'

In a girl's second Season, chaperoning rules were generally relaxed – though sometimes only slightly. 'The first time I went out alone with a man I was allowed to go to the Berkeley with my American cousin whom I didn't like,' said Diana Barnato, the daughter of Woolf 'Babe' Barnato, the famous thirties racing driver. 'My mother went to the head waiter and said: "You will see that my daughter leaves at eleven, won't you?"'

At the same time, it was thought that a girl in her second Season would know so many men that she could produce her own partners. 'In your second season you were often asked to bring a partner to dances,' said Lavinia Holland-Hibbert. 'And if you hadn't been asked to a dinner party beforehand you had to find somewhere to dine with him first. It was always the Ladies' Carlton – Mummy had an account there. You sat in a discreet corner and whispered.'

Fiona Colquhoun put the alternatives starkly. 'I remember sitting in the train coming up to Glasgow and wondering which was the best – whether to have another Season, or get married. I hadn't met Boofy [her future husband] then, so it was just in theory. Then I met him that weekend, and that decided me.'

~

The real *raison d'être* of the entire Season was, of course, presentation at one of the Courts that took place in March that year. Rules as to what a debutante should wear were strict. Trains, for instance, hung a regulation two-and-a-half yards from the shoulder; the three white ostrich feathers (black in the case of a widow) had to be attached to the head in the 'Ich Dien' motto manner, slightly to the side of the head. 'You were sent a long form detailing how low the neckline and the back should be, how wide your train and how much of it must rest on the floor,' said Anne Reid. 'Huge crinolines or excesses of any kind were banned but the dress didn't have to be white – although most were.

'Mine was pale aquamarine and Mummy's was coral. People peered into the cars on the Mall but in a very friendly way, gazing at my mother in her tiara and jewels and me in my Prince of Wales feathers. My father and mother took me, driven by the chauffeur and with a "man on the box" – a chap in front sitting next to the driver, which was a requirement of the Palace. Ours was our odd-job man, William.'

Rosemary Hodson was presented on 11 May, the first Court in 1938. 'We began by leaving Hampstead, where we were staying, at 2.30, for a date at the Palace at 7.00 p.m. We'd taken books, because we knew there'd be the long wait in the Mall. God only knows what would have happened if we'd wanted to go to the loo but luckily no one did.

'The crowds in the Mall peered in at the cars, like in a zoo, with their noses actually pressed to the glass. 'Come and look at this one!' they'd shout. We were photographed by Movietone News – a picture that still sometimes comes up.

'I remember the Throne Room was filthy – the white walls were so grimy they had turned a dull khaki. And all round us were tiaras that had obviously been kept in the bank and no one had bothered to clean them. I've always loved clothes and fashion and have made my own clothes since I was sixteen, so I was quite aware of how diamonds should look. My grand-mother's sparkled but all those marvellous tiaras just looked as if they'd been painted in charcoal.

'After our curtseys we all lined up in the gallery beside the Throne Room and the King and Queen came down, his hand held high and hers resting on it as in a fairy-tale. We were then taken down to the basement and given champagne in what looked like tooth mugs and Windsor pies – little small round shiny mutton pies – which was a traditional thing.* About midnight we finally got out, then it was off to the photographer, Lenare, to be captured in all our finery. There was such a queue we didn't get in until 4.00 a.m. By the time we finally got home it wasn't worth going to bed.'

Most thought of curtseying to the King and Queen as an ordeal. Would they be sufficiently graceful, maintain their balance, or even trip over their train on the way out?

'I was terrified of the curtseying,' said Susan Meyrick, who was eighteen when presented in 1938, with a dance a year later. 'I'd practised for hours beforehand but I was still very scared. Luckily I only had one curtsey, to the King, as the Queen was away because her father had died. I remember noticing the Duke of Kent because he was so good-looking. The King looked as though he'd been made up, he was so tanned.'

Sarah Norton recounted her curtsey training at the hands of the legendary Miss Vacani, whose dancing classes had been attended by most of the offspring of the upper crust. '"Now my darlings, stand up straight, poise is most important. Sarah Norton, don't look at your feet – they are meant to move, not to be gazed at, darling."'

This supposedly easy obeisance to the King and Queen was actually quite tricky. The curtseyer had to bring her left leg behind her right leg and bend the knee almost down to the floor, keeping her head high and eyes straight forward. Going down was not too bad but coming up was almost impossible without wobbling.

Christian Grant wrote an account of the day she was presented: 16 March 1939 (the day of the invasion of Czechoslovakia). 'After lunch I refused all invitations and went to bed. It sounds odd but I was going to be presented that evening and wanted to look my best.

---

* The catering was done by Lyons, a teashop chain famous for its 'Corner House' shops.

'Punctually at 4.30 I got up, had a bath and started to dress. I put on a pair of elastic pants, a pair of gossamer stockings and a pair of silver shoes. Then over my head went my pink-and-silver brocade dress, cut on Empire lines, with a train in the same material and with a bouquet of pink carnations. My feathers were fixed, my long white gloves pulled on and I was ready.

'After my photograph had been taken, we got into the car and drove round and round, up the Mall, down Birdcage Walk, up the Mall again. Luckily we were halfway up the Mall when the Palace gates opened, so we knew, when we parked in the forecourt, that we would get into the Throne Room. I ate some sandwiches and powdered my nose. The lights of the Palace shone around us and I could see some of the other debutantes in the cars near us busily titivating.

'After a bit the beefeaters arrived in covered wagons and soon afterwards we were driven up to the door. We got out and walked upstairs and down a passage to the Throne Room. I felt marvellous, not a bit frightened, just wonderfully elated and a bit regal. It was the only time in my life I have envied the Princesses – for I would have given almost anything to go on living in the fairy-tale world in which I found myself. Everything in the Palace was so unexpectedly big – the passages were high and spacious, the Throne Room ceiling seemed somewhere in the clouds.

'We sat down on gilt chairs and looked around. Facing us were tiers of seats, to our left were more seats under the musicians' gallery, while on our right were seats for the Court – and the thrones!

'Quite soon the Court arrived, followed by Their Majesties' procession. Solemnly they paced into the Throne Room, the musicians struck up the national anthem, the people rose and three men in uniform appeared, walking backwards and bowing as they walked. It was all so impressive I shouldn't really have been surprised if the Almighty Himself had appeared.

'Their Majesties entered slowly, with great dignity, and sat down in front of the canopy. The Queen was wearing a very full white dress, scattered with gold sequins, and two pages so arranged her long train that it looked like a waterfall flowing down the steps of the throne.

'As we were sitting in the first section we were among the first to be presented. We went out of the Throne Room, down a passage, and into the Throne Room again, near the King and Queen. In the doorway I handed my presentation card to an official and two lackeys spread my train behind me. My card was passed from hand to hand nine times and my name was announced by the Lord Chamberlain as I arrived in front of the King.

'Curtseying was awfully easy and the Queen gave me a sweet smile though the King only bowed rather stiffly. Afterwards we were shown into seats just by the door where everyone came in.'

Some girls were presented in Scotland. 'I was sent up in the train with my feathers in a box to stay with my aunt at Stobo Castle [now a health resort],' remembers Penny Woosnam, the younger daughter of the great athlete, Max Woosnam.* 'I was presented at a Holyrood Court. We knew a lot of the Archers – the Household Cavalry of the North – who lined the route for the debs. The King came down and spoke to me for ages – I was amazed.'

Her older sister Denise had had the opposite experience. Her presentation took place at the 1936 garden party given by Edward VIII. Halfway through the presentations, just after Denise had made her curtsey, the King got his aide to announce that the rest 'could consider themselves presented' and left to play golf with Wallis Simpson.

---

* He was Manchester City's only amateur football team captain (in 1922), took a tennis Gold Medal in the 1920 Olympics, was in the winning doubles team in the 1920 Davis Cup and the Wimbledon doubles in 1921.

While the Season was not so much a marriage market as a way of introducing the daughters of the upper classes to possible future mates, a few parents put pressure on their daughters to marry well.

'We were brought up to marry a wealthy man and be the hostesses of our houses. That was my expectation of my future,' said Val Canning. 'It was made very clear to me by my parents that I was expected to marry well.'

'I looked on the Season as being launched into my grown-up life but Daddy was definitely interested in us making good marriages. They both hoped I would marry the Duke of Northumberland – then they fixed on another immensely rich man in Lincolnshire they thought I should marry. But I wasn't in love with him.

'I'd already met my future husband. When I told my mother one morning when she came in to draw my curtains after a dance that I was engaged she said: "What rubbish!"

'And when I married him at twenty-one my parents were quite disgusted – they thought I should have married someone wealthy or with a title, like my sister Diana who married the Duke of Newcastle.'

Most parents, like those of Lady Anne Spencer, were far more relaxed ('though I do know that for some it had to be the son of a duke or marquis'). For Anne Reid, too, there was no pressure to marry well, 'although I wouldn't have been allowed to marry a Jew – my father was very anti-Semitic – nor would my mother have liked me to marry someone penniless.'

~~~

After the hectic pleasures of the summer months the social round shifted into a lower gear. Some families retired thankfully to peaceful houses in the country, others held house parties that often hinged on some sporting activity – grouse shooting and stalking in Yorkshire and Scotland or, later in the year, hunting – where the meeting and mingling of the young continued.

As winter approached, hunt balls took the place of summer dances. In the winter of 1938 the beautiful Woosnam sisters went to thirty, all round England, staying in different houses, clothes packed in large trunks, wrapped in tissue paper to avoid creases.

A feature of these gatherings was the cold. Very few houses had central heating, thermal underwear had not been invented, and the hot-water supply to the few bathrooms was usually temperamental – *Punch* magazine regularly ran cartoons featuring The Man Who Took all the Hot Water before Dinner. Even visiting the bathroom down the icy corridors of a cavernous Scottish castle was an ordeal and, unless the hostess had thoughtfully provided a hot-water bottle, the clammy embrace of her trousseau linen sheets meant that sleep sometimes took a long time coming. The wiser debs would race along the passages to dress by the nursery fire (nannies always seemed to have a good fire going, if only to air the clothes of their charges). Fortunately, wearing a fur cape at dinner was an acceptable way of keeping warm.

Chapter 4

The Approach of War

'I stood in the room that had been my nursery,
listening to Chamberlain declaring war'

Seventeen-year-old Elizabeth Lowry-Corry was being 'finished' in Dresden in 1938, studying music and German. Before she went her parents, worried about the international situation, had consulted their cousin Lord Halifax, the Foreign Secretary, who said: 'I should let her go but tell her she must come back straight away if you send her a telegram.'

The menace of Nazi Germany had increased steadily as the thirties wore on. The Munich crisis in September 1938 provided a temporary respite, grasped at with despairing hope by those who thought that no one who had experienced the slaughter of the 1914–18 war – as Hitler had – could willingly plunge his country into such conflict again.

Few of the upper classes believed, as did some of the country's leading left-wing intellectuals, that communism offered the only bulwark against the increasing menace of fascism. Equally, many had ties of blood or friendship with the grand German families. There were, too, the historical links with Germany that ran from the Hanoverian kings to Queen Victoria, a living memory to most parents of that pre-war generation. So they continued to send their daughters to be 'finished' not only amid the art and operatic treasures of Paris, Rome and Florence but to Munich and Dresden for their music, architecture and museums.

Here these sixteen-year-olds, fresh from their cloistered schoolrooms, often saw for themselves the terrors of Hitler's Germany – more evident in some towns than others.

Staying with a musician's family in Munich, Elizabeth Lowry-Corry witnessed the country's anti-Semitism at first hand.

'My host played the viola in the orchestra of the Dresden Opera House, the Staatskapelle, or State Opera, which was the most prestigious. As it was the State Opera it meant that he was a civil servant, which in turn meant that he could neither be a Jew nor be married to a Jew.

'Neither he nor his wife were Jewish but they had great friends who were – I remember meeting some who were able to escape. One of their greatest friends was the first cellist, and in order to keep his job he had had to divorce his Jewish wife – I have to say he'd stopped liking her by then. But his lady-love was also a Jewess and that wasn't so jolly and he had a big sorrow. It seemed very romantic to me.

'Also there were notices on the shops saying *Arisch*, which means Aryan, or *Keine Juden* – No Jews. I thought it was simply dreadful, quite wrong. One realised that Hitler was very wicked.'

Elizabeth was determined not to pay even the usual lip-service to the regime. 'Only once was I a bit nervous about this. All the Germans one met were very nice to one and very keen on the English and hoping there would be peace with them. Then there was a huge concert in which the Vienna State Choir were singing, during which of course they sang "Deutschland, Deutschland, über Alles", and the whole audience stood up and raised their arms in the Nazi salute. I kept my arms clamped firmly to my sides – although I must say I did have a shiver. But no one took any notice and at that point I think we all hoped there wouldn't be a war. I got home at the end of June and then there was Munich.'

Lady Anne Spencer was one of those for whom being

'finished' meant that she was in Vienna during the Anschluss (Hitler's invasion of Austria in 1938). 'We had been taken to the opera one evening and when we emerged the family we were staying with met us outside in floods of tears, saying: "There is no more Austria. Hitler is arriving." They were distraught.

'We kept in touch with the British Embassy but we couldn't get away for a fortnight. There was shooting in the streets outside our flat so we had to keep a low profile. As we wore Union Jacks on our jackets and talked English we were all right but all the Jewish shops were desecrated. We were apprehensive rather than frightened. Once we went out into the Ringstrasse and saw Hitler and Goebbels and Goering and Himmler all driving about in huge cars and being acclaimed by the Austrians. Some of our teachers became Nazis though some didn't. Eventually we three girls came by train from Vienna to Ostend and from the window we saw all the German troops pouring over the hills from Bavaria into Austria. Our parents met us at Victoria, very glad to see us back.'

In the House of Commons on 14 March, Winston Churchill declaimed: 'The gravity of the events of 12 March cannot be exaggerated. Europe is confronted with a programme of aggression, nicely calculated and timed, unfolding stage by stage, and there is only one choice open, not only to us but to other countries, either to submit like Austria, or else to take effective measures while time remains to ward off the danger, and if it cannot be warded off, to cope with it.' Even then, not everyone listened to him.

A few months later, at the time of the Munich crisis, the Spencer family was preparing for a flood of evacuees at Althorp, moving every spare mattress into the stables.

Also in Austria at the time of the Anschluss was Anne Douglas-Scott-Montagu. 'The year before I'd been in France and I was in Paris when Hitler paid a grand visit. We stood in the streets to see him. So during the Anschluss I was very aware of this dreadful man in the background. And being involved with the Red Cross at Beaulieu, with my mother, of course alerted me that we were preparing for a possible war.'

Anne Reid, too, was aware of the political situation because in Austria she had seen that all Jews had to wear yellow arm-bands. 'My father was a cousin of Neville Chamberlain, so we sometimes went to parties at Downing Street. He joined the Anglo-German Friendship League, just to annoy Mama, to tease and be irritating – and it did annoy her.'

Not everyone viewed Germany as a threat. 'My father was devoted to Hitler before the war started,' said Val Canning. 'He had pictures galore of him in Ashby, which my mother hastily put away when war was declared.'

Diana Quilter, who had spent a year travelling with a friend, staying at embassy after embassy, returned from Peking via Germany in the spring of 1938. 'I was with my eldest sister in Bucharest and on the way back I wanted to stay with Anna Montgelas, the German friend I'd stayed with before in Bavaria, where I'd met the sort of Germans I would have met over here in England – minor and major aristocracy.

'But it was the time of the winter sports there and when I arrived in Munich Anna hadn't got room for me, so she asked if I could stay with Unity Mitford. I stayed with Unity for a fortnight only as my father was in a great state, saying I should come back quickly, there were great preparations for war.

'Unity was enormous fun, very generous and extremely nice to me. On one occasion I had lent her a book and she was returning it to me on the way to where the winter games were being held. Anna and I were at breakfast and she dashed in.

'"Do hurry!" she said. "I've got the whole German Government with me." Outside were streams of black Mercedes – she was in the front one, sitting with the Goebbelses. She talked a lot about these members of the German Government.

'I saw Hitler often. Music was what I was chiefly studying and I went to the opera a great deal. We'd find ourselves in seats with Hitler sitting just behind us.

'Life was very exciting. It was heady wine. The Jewish question didn't come up as far as I was concerned – until I learned afterwards that Unity had been given her Munich flat by Hitler, who had turned out the Jewish couple who occupied it.'

⌒

Daphne Brock, whose father, an Admiral of the Fleet, was known as the cleverest man in the Navy, was used to hearing the coming war discussed endlessly. Her parents were unusual in sympathising with her intellectual ambitions, suggesting that she went to stay with her last, Austrian, governess in her flat in Vienna in order to attend the university. 'So it was quite social. I collected a German young man, an upper-class Prussian, who took me to the Nuremberg Rally of 1937, when I was just seventeen. I'll never forget the sound of the troops, who wore metal soles, goose-stepping down roads that had been specially metalled, and the ranting, the "Sieg Heils" – I can hear them still.

'After the Rally my young man took me for a walk. We could never talk about anything inside the flat unless the wireless was on very loud as so many flats were bugged, and I knew never to say anything inside a car. He said: "I took you to Nuremberg so that you can go home and tell all your friends about it." He didn't need to say anything more. He came to stay with us in England. He was killed at Stalingrad.'

Despite these horrors, the proprieties still held. Daphne Brock was made to return to England in March 1938. 'I was caught in a nightclub by Sir Nevile Henderson [the British Ambassador to Germany] and it got back home so I was hauled back.'

Some of the more spirited sixteen- and seventeen-year-olds made their dislike of the regime plain. Lavinia Holland-Hibbert, sent to Munich in 1937 after the obligatory spell in Paris, used to bicycle down the Judengasse, ostentatiously refusing to salute the monument to the Nazis who had fallen in the Beerhall Putsch of 1923.

Sarah Norton prosecuted her campaign of dislike more actively. She had been sent to Germany in 1937, aged sixteen and, thanks to politically minded parents who encouraged her to listen to meal-time talk, she was, although so young, aware that something was 'very wrong'. She had wanted to go to Italy 'because I thought the young men there would be more attractive but – perhaps because of that – I was sent instead to Munich, much against my will. I loved the people I lived with but I hated being in Munich, I thought German was a perfectly hideous language and I got into trouble with the Nazis.

'In Munich they were everywhere and there was a very nasty atmosphere. We knew something bad was going on because there was rationing and things like butter and marmalade were difficult and above all because fear was written on people's faces as they saw the Nazis strutting about like cocks in a barnyard. You could sense the fear so much you could almost smell it.

'At first we satisfied ourselves with the sport of circling the Odeonsplatz in the city centre without raising our right arms in the statutory salute to Hitler. This maddened the Gestapo but they didn't dare arrest us because we were foreigners.

'Then we began to visit the Carlton tea rooms, regularly frequented by Hitler and his cronies. We would choose a table as close to them as we could get and stare at them with all the distaste we could express. Sometimes we would pull faces at them. It was pretty childish but it gave us pleasure. We used to see Unity having tea and gaping at Hitler. We just thought she was a bit barmy. Hitler was usually dressed entirely in grey, which gave the effect of a haunting spectre with black piercing eyes that drilled into you. Goering on the other hand favoured an all-white uniform, with medals and decorations hung on every spare inch of his tunic, and he was so fat that his bloated stomach bulged over the tablecloth. Goebbels and Streicher looked so subhuman that they defied description.

'We eventually decided these visits were a waste of time and money and we had to do something more serious to show our hatred of the regime. There was a horrible anti-Jewish newspaper called *Die Juden*. It was so awful that nobody bought it but the Nazis were so determined people should read it that they put it up in glass-covered frames on street corners.

'We – my friend and I – would sneak out at night and break the glass of these frames and tear the newspapers down. The noise would bring the Nazis running but they could never catch us – we were young and fleet and wearing gym shoes, they were in jackboots and carrying heavy batons. The son of the people we lived with was, like all the young Germans, in the Hitler Jugend and we were terrified he would testify against his parents or say what we were doing was somehow their fault – he wouldn't have hesitated. So we used to put four aspirins in his after-dinner coffee before creeping out.

'Then we found that the Nazis had put wire round the frames to stop us breaking them, so we just bought wire-cutters. Eventually, running round a corner, I was caught and they wrote to the Foreign Office and said I had to be sent home. I was terrified at what my mother would say – I thought she would be furious. But all she said was: "At least you've learned the language."'

Some heard of the threatening international situation through influential or politically minded parents. 'We talked politics all the time at home,' said Frances Grenfell. 'My mother never learned to drive a car so when I passed my test she used me as a chauffeur and I would take her to the House of Commons to try and see MPs. When I had my Season she was very much into what Hitler was doing because of her work for the International Committee of the YWCA,* and so very, very aware long before others. I think my parents knew very well what was happening but simply couldn't face the idea. They were madly pro-Chamberlain. Really, they just hoped like hell.'

* Young Women's Christian Association.

As daughters of a newspaper family the two Harmsworth girls heard constant talk about the growing menace of Hitler. 'My grandfather Harold Rothermere had tried very hard to get Britain armed at the time of disarmament,' said Esme Harmsworth. 'Finally he was so disgusted he went off and bought a bomber and gave it to the Government. He had a house in the South of France where we all used to congregate, where he would discuss the coming war with Winston Churchill, who was a regular visitor, both of them saying: "What can we do?" So we all expected it.'

For those with a father in one or other of the armed services there was usually little illusion. 'I was sure from the age of fifteen that there would be a war and I was desperately worried,' said Mary Armitage, the daughter of a general who had served in the 1914–18 war.

'We had always heard about the Great War and its awful slaughter, and there was the terrifying thought of all my three brothers being killed. Then there was that film by H. G. Wells, *The Shape of Things to Come*, which showed the aftermath of a terrible war and people living in caves. Every time you went to the cinema you saw awful things about the Spanish Civil War, with the bombing. We had a pacifist headmistress, who used to say we should let the Germans overrun us. I argued with her so she hated me and did her best to put me down.'

Mary's friend Ursie Barclay had come back from finishing school in Paris for Christmas 1938. 'By this time my mother had been asked to start the first company of ATS [Auxiliary Territorial Service] in Norwich – that's how they formed the ATS, by asking people like my mother to form companies. She was about fifty then, a JP and in the Red Cross. I was very conscious that a war was coming. I read the papers, everyone belonged to the TA and then there was my mother running this company of ATS. And the boyfriend of my older sister brought the Life Guards to camp near by.'

'For us the next war was a foregone conclusion,' recalled

Cynthia Keppel. 'Coming down to lunch in the dining room I'd hear my parents talking – of course, one always listened to grown-up talk – and my father would always say "when the next war comes". He had been a regular soldier, through the first war and for a while afterwards.'

Pam Joyce, an only child whose father had also served as a regular soldier in the Great War and, at forty-five, had married her nineteen-year-old mother, would listen to her parents talking about the likelihood of war without, she said, really taking it in. 'My father had inherited a share in the Carrera mines in Italy, so he left the Army and took my mother out there, where I was born. We lived there until 1935 when my father began to worry about the political situation in Europe and thought he would bring us home.

'He was even more aware of it because he had had to go on business trips to Germany – there's some wonderful marble in Germany – where he knew a lot of the old German aristocrats. They were worried sick and were trying to get themselves out of Germany as quickly as possible. So it was a regular subject of discussion.'

Fortune Smith was aware of the danger in a general sense. 'My father had been a very young officer in the first war and when the Rhineland was occupied we suddenly saw him in tears, saying: "This is a sign there'll be another war." It was an incredible shock to us because this behaviour was totally unlike him. As time passed I realised my parents were apprehensive, but they didn't talk about it to me.'

For Fanny Gore Browne it was the same. 'My father was in World War One. Later he became a Territorial and ended up commanding the Leicestershire Yeomanry – we had our holidays in Leicestershire because both my parents hunted. In August 1939 he and my two elder brothers were back in uniform.

'My family is enormous – twenty-four first cousins on one side, most of them older than me – so the talk was very general about war. To us there was no question but that it was coming.

And at school they talked about the war, though my head-mistress was an ardent pacifist, which I found very distasteful.

'Also, my father was a banker, with a lot of Jewish friends, so I remember very clearly when he came back from Berlin and said to us: "Make no mistake about it, there will be a war." He had been horrified at what he had seen in Germany and by what his Jewish friends had told him.'

Some girls found out what was happening for themselves. 'I took the *New Statesman* and the *Spectator* from time to time as a deb, and I went to Ashridge Conservative [Management Training] College,' said Lavinia Holland-Hibbert. 'I was certainly aware there was a war coming – I knew a lot about the first war, especially the role of horses.

'During my first Season, in 1938, I joined the FANYs [First Aid Nursing Yeomanry], run by all these lesbian ladies with trilby hats standing in front of the fire with their skirts hiked over their bums, and the rank and file very aristocratic young women. I went to camp, drilled by Guards sergeants, and had a passing-out parade in front of Princess Alice.

'In my second Season I gave up the ball at Blenheim – the ball of the Season – to go to FANY camp, where I read the whole of *War and Peace*. I quoted Day Lewis to myself: "Who live under the shadow of war, what can we do that matters?"'

Denise Woosnam learned much of what was going on from her half-French mother, who had not only lived through the 1914–18 war but whose own parents had been through the Franco-Prussian War of 1870. 'The moment the Munich crisis happened she was off to Manchester – we lived in Cheshire – organising bandage-making and knitting. My sister had already said she would be a VAD [member of the Voluntary Aid Detachment] but I knew I couldn't be a nurse – I would have fainted at the sight of blood.'

The Munich crisis of September 1938 brought Mary Pollock home after one term in a Paris finishing school to her family in London. 'We thought war was coming so I did an ARP [Air

Raid Precautions] course in Chelsea Square, first aid at a church near Sloane Avenue, a cooking course in Buckingham Palace Road and I learned to drive.'

Rosemary Hodson was more alert to the crisis than her parents. 'My brothers and I were absolutely aware of the coming war but our parents were in denial. Having been through one war they couldn't bring themselves to believe another was coming. But we children knew all the time. We talked about it a lot, to our friends, among ourselves.'

A few found that the subject of a possible war was simply not one for discussion at the lunch table. 'At sixteen I'd been sent to stay with a French family in Paris to learn French,' said Jean Falkner. 'I adored it all. I did classes at a French school in the morning, was taken sightseeing in the afternoon and spent Sundays with some French Huguenot relations – their sons, my cousins, were at the French cavalry school, Saint-Cyr – and through all these French people I was well aware there was a war coming.

'I went home twice during this period and I kept saying: "I know there's going to be a war." But it was all brushed aside and hushed up. My parents wouldn't listen – in their eyes I was a child and children weren't listened to. They never talked about it. Either they didn't want me to know or they themselves were unaware.'

For others, the hectic whirl of the Season was all-consuming – even though, for the first time, the list of those presented at Court was knocked out of the following day's *Times* by the news of the German invasion of Czechoslovakia in March 1939. 'I wasn't at all conscious of the international situation,' said Christian Grant. 'Whether I just shut my eyes I don't know but it certainly didn't impinge on me. I doubt if I even read the paper – probably only the engagement column of *The Times*. Papers tended to belong to parents.'

Her diary bears this out. The entry for 9 April 1939, Easter Sunday, reads: 'Came down yesterday to Nigel Parker's for the weekend. It was a lovely sunny morning and everything was so beautiful that by common consent we banned any mention of the crisis that was raging.'

On the 27th Christian (who was to fling herself whole-heartedly into war work later) wrote: 'Tea with Joan Heywood, who tried to persuade me to join the ATS or something. I always feel that I should join something but the women in them are all so tough and it would mean giving up deb dances. They can wait a bit longer for me because, after all, one only comes out once in one's life.'

After the Season, Susan Meyrick and her family went to their house in Anglesey. 'I'd had no idea of the world situation. None. I had no idea the war was so close, although my brother took a great interest in Hitler and what was going on. We were in Anglesey when war was declared, my brother with a broken leg, and the joke was that we had a footman there who was called up before him.'

Without television, and the kind of instant communication of today, most news was gleaned from newspapers. Like radios (or wirelesses, as they were then called) these went first, unques-tioningly, to the head of the household – the father – who would quite often remove the newspaper to his study after perusing it at breakfast. Few daughters, in consequence, especially those exhausted from dancing night after night, got much of a chance to read them.

Barbara Stuart-Wortley, like many other girls, got much of her information from the young men she danced with. 'I didn't read the papers much but during the Season I met various young men – one in particular that I was fond of – who said: "Without a doubt there's going to be a war and we'll all be called up." So I became conscious of the situation not through my parents but through the young men I met. It must have been ghastly for them, realising they would be called up and anticipating the same sort of slaughter as before.'

Lady Elizabeth Montagu Douglas Scott learned in much the

same way. 'I'm afraid I didn't give a thought to what was going on outside. Whatever was going on in Germany completely passed me by. I don't think I read a newspaper much, either. I was sleeping, eating, chatting, dining, dancing – that was all.

'Then, at the end of July, that came to an end and we went back to my home in Scotland, where in August lots of friends came to shoot and they all had their uniforms in their bags.' (Many of those ready to fight immediately, incidentally, were the same ones who had voted in 1933 for the Oxford Union Debating Society motion that 'this House would in no circumstances fight for King and Country'.)

One or two, like Lorna Harmsworth, were caught abroad. 'In the summer of 1939 we were in Monte Carlo – their Season started at the beginning of August. Suddenly we had to leave in a great hurry at the end of the month.' Her father, Esmond Harmsworth, aware of what was coming after the Molotov–Ribbentrop pact of 23 August 1939, rushed the whole household to Paris and there spent all his remaining francs on buying jewellery. 'I got a pair of Van Cleef and Arpels earrings. He bought three pairs in different colours and gave two to the other two women in the party.'

In her diary for 23 August Lady Moyra Ponsonby recorded the agreement that finally blew the last faint hope of peace away. 'Germany has made a non-aggression pact with Russia – which we have been trying to negotiate for several months.

'*August 24*. All sorts of evacuation and blackout plans are being broadcast over the wireless. We are told to prepare for the official evacuation order. We are making all sorts of preparations here.'

Her father, the ninth Earl of Bessborough, had constructed a small theatre from a squash court at their family home, Stansted Park, in which plays were performed twice a year to a capacity audience of two hundred. (Later this theatre was used for Home Guard lectures.)

'*August 25*. Papa decides this morning to cancel the theatricals because of the threat of war. The trouble is we must prepare the theatre and green room and the steward's room in case of 50 evacuees – an orphanage from Portsmouth.'

Even under the shadow of war the old taboos held sway. In 1938 Esme Harmsworth and the other girls at Mrs Lestrange's finishing school in Florence were allowed to spend an evening in a neighbouring villa, owned by the grandmother of one of them, Rosalind Cubitt. This was Mrs George Keppel, almost three decades earlier the last and favourite mistress of Edward VII (and great-grandmother, through Rosalind, of the Duchess of Cornwall), who had discreetly retired to Florence some years after the death of her royal lover.*

'Mrs Keppel was a large and friendly lady,' wrote Esme, 'and her terrace gave us a fine view of the roofs of Florence and the fireworks display. We were given a plentiful supper and our hostess spoke to most of us, was jolly and kindly in a down-to-earth way and gave us all a good time.' Some parents were a little surprised when their daughters wrote home to tell them where they had been, since Mrs Keppel's name still had a notorious ring even after so long a time, and they did not regard her as a suitable person for their daughters to meet.

Other Keppels were also on the Continent as war drew nearer. 'My father, stepmother, youngest brother and I had driven down through France to a small hotel on the Atlantic coast, near the Spanish frontier, which we were sharing with some cousins who lived in Gloucestershire and their two little boys,' recalled Cynthia Keppel. 'We'd had a wonderful drive down – for me, the first time I'd had those delicious French restaurant meals.

'So there we were in this little hotel on the edge of the sea

---

* In June 1940, after escaping from Italy, Mrs Keppel took up residence at the Ritz Hotel in London for the rest of the war.

when my father came into the bedroom in his dressing gown and said, "The Russians and Hitler have made friends – we must all go back to England straight away."

'My stepmother [Lady Bury] had recently been made head of the WVS [Women's Voluntary Service] in Norfolk, where we lived, so she had to fly back to be ready to receive evacuees.'

The Keppel family drove Lady Bury to Bordeaux airport, managed to get her on a plane and then set about making their own way home, spending the night at Rouen before driving to Le Havre. Here they found a queue of cars snaking for miles as all the English holiday-makers tried to get home in a hurry.

'We had to leave the cars and just get on what ships we could,' said Cynthia Keppel. 'We had an overnight crossing, sleeping on deck, and arrived at 6.00 a.m. at Newhaven. Then we went to a hotel in Brighton and slept, and then home. The cars all arrived safely later.'

The reality of war struck home to Mary Pollock at her parents' weekend cottage near Ewhurst in Surrey. 'A few days earlier, the evacuees began arriving. I went to the Village Hall to help with them, tying labels on their arms saying where they were to go to, trying to see that brothers and sisters were kept together and that no one lost their belongings. On Sunday 3 September, I was in the middle of doing that when someone outside in a car with a radio switched it on and we all gathered round and heard Chamberlain's voice saying that we were at war.'

Pamela Joyce was with her parents that morning. 'We heard the declaration of war on a crackly old wireless, at home. Daddy was horrified but said he had rather been expecting it, and my mother broke down completely. She sobbed: "But, darling, it's only twenty years since the last one." She'd had nearly all her lovely boyfriends killed in it. Which is why I suppose so many girls like her married older men.'

Christian Grant's memory of that historic moment is equally vivid. 'I stood in the room that had been my nursery, listening to Chamberlain declaring war. There was no one else there. I was utterly stunned.

'Then we became very busy because the house where I grew up was being turned into a convalescent home. But because of the Phoney War there were no wounded soldiers, so I had no work to do. Looking back on it, I wish I had gone into nursing, got myself properly qualified and become a nurse. But nobody thought it was going to go on for all those years.'

At the air-raid warning that soon followed the announcement of war Val Canning's father herded his family into a passage where they all sat holding their gas masks. These had been issued to civilians at the end of September 1938: the fear of a gas attack was very real – thousands of crippled ex-servicemen were living reminders of the horrors of gas attacks on the Western Front during the First World War and the Italians had used gas in their invasion of Abyssinia in 1935. Older children and adults had plain masks; younger children were given 'Mickey Mouse' masks with goggle eyes and a snout-like filter; small babies had whole-body masks into which filtered air had to be pumped with a hand bellows. Hand rattles would alert the public to a poison-gas raid; the ringing of hand bells would indicate that the attack was over.

War would, of course, mean privations. 'Father said, almost gleefully: "Now you'll have to go without jam and marmalade, you won't be able to do this, that and the other, and you'll probably have to do war work,"' Val remembered. 'We were straight away put to knitting woollen squares for blankets as we walked round our huge grounds.'

Girls who had been dancing all summer found it difficult to imagine that in a few days their lives could change totally and forever.

'Until eleven that morning I could not believe that there could possibly be a war,' said Moyra Ponsonby. 'Then on the day itself I began to think I'd been wrong. Going into one of the rooms at Stansted, I heard the radio on and it was

Chamberlain's voice giving the ultimatum. The third footman, who was standing there, burst into tears.'

For many, like Fortune Smith, the announcement of war was given an unreal, not to say bizarre, twist by hearing it while sitting in church. 'The vicar gave us the news that we were at war from the pulpit of Slapham church.'

Jean Campbell-Harris, just back from finishing school in Paris, was with her family in Canterbury Cathedral. 'We'd heard the news on my mother's car radio. The Red Dean* was in the middle of preaching his sermon when the air-raid warning sounded, and he hurried from the pulpit to the crypt, to which we all went down until the All Clear.'†

Elizabeth Lowry-Corry, at home with her family on their estate at Edmonstone in Suffolk, was another who heard the news in church. 'It was a lovely hot day. The service was being taken by a marvellous old temporary priest. We were having our usual staid Matins, then at eleven o'clock he said: "War has been declared" and we had the most tremendously moving Holy Communion service – we were all in floods of tears going up to the altar rail.'

Even for those who had scarcely been aware of the crisis that had escalated at such terrifying speed, the immediate sense of doom when war was declared was overwhelming. 'I remember so vividly thinking: "This is the end. The end of our lives," said Lady Elizabeth Montagu Douglas Scott. "The end of the world."

'Then I suppose, after we'd thought about it for a bit, we got the feeling: "Well, we're still here – what do we do first?" Certainly any men at home were joining up and most of one's friends had already joined up.

---

* Hewlett Johnson, Dean of Canterbury, was known as the Red Dean for his outspoken support of communist and socialist regimes.
† A first (mistaken) air-raid warning followed within minutes of the Prime Minister's announcement.

'We settled down to working things out in a different way – probably very good for us. We'd never thought about anything seriously until then.'

Lavinia Holland-Hibbert, far more aware than most of what had been going on in Europe and more prepared than many, felt a kind of guilty excitement. 'Although I knew that really, underneath, I absolutely loathed the war, I wanted to experience it. The strange feeling was knowing one ought to be dreading it but at the same time being really excited and wanting to experience something which would give one's life significance.'

'On September the third I was in the dining room having a late breakfast and we had the wireless on and heard Chamberlain,' said Lady Barbara Stuart-Wortley. 'It just made me feel cold – cold right through – with horror.

'Cold, and fear, and the realisation that everything was going to be different and that the way we had been living was going to be completely changed, for ever.'

Chapter 5

Joining Up

'I wasn't going to get on with anything else
until we'd finished with Hitler'

The advent of war triggered a mass flocking to the colours
for men of military age and fitness and, for women, to war
work or the women's services.

All of these women were volunteers. It was not until December 1941 that the National Service (No. 2) Act required all (medically fit) single women and childless widows between twenty and thirty to make themselves available for war work.* If they registered before they were due for call-up, they could choose what they wanted to do, from joining one of the women's services to working on the land; if they did not register, they would have to go wherever they were directed.

There were a number of options. These ranged from working in factories or hospitals to the various women's services: the ATS (the Auxiliary Territorial Service), the FANYs (First Aid Nursing Yeomanry, later to be subsumed into the ATS), the WRNS (Women's Royal Naval Service or, more commonly, Wrens), the WRAF (Women's Royal Air Force) and the Women's Land Army.

The ATS, based on the earlier WAAC (Women's Auxiliary Army Corps), was founded in September 1938, while the Wrens,

---

* In 1943 the age was lowered to nineteen.

WAAF (Women's Auxiliary Air Force) and Land Army – though disbanded in 1919 – could trace their ancestry back to the last years of the 1914–18 war. The FANYs had an even earlier history, as mounted nurses in the Boer War; unlike the other women's services, this remained operational throughout the interwar years.

A girl who wanted to nurse could either take a professional nurse's training or, with a first-aid course under her belt, become a VAD – a member of the Voluntary Aid Detachment affiliated to the British Red Cross or St John Ambulance.

Factory work gobbled up many eligible women, since every possible factory was turned over to the making of aeroplanes, tanks, ships, shell casings, bombs and other weapons or defences. At the beginning of 1941 the Government opened training centres for women who wanted to become skilled workers in the engineering trades (within two years, two out of five workers in the aircraft industry were women).

For most of them, the work was hard, the hours long (often up to sixty hours a week) and the pay low. However, many welcomed this chance to earn a little money of their own and the independence it gave them – and the feeling of patriotism was intense.

Girls from the upper classes often had a head start in certain kinds of war work. Many of their mothers were local heads of the Red Cross or St John's, or had been co-opted to form ATS detachments, so these girls could find themselves taking first-aid courses or joining the maternal detachment.

Other mothers belonged to, or ran, sections of the WVS (Women's Voluntary Service), inaugurated by Stella, Marchioness of Reading, at the behest of the Government and which, when war was declared, had 165,000 members drawn from groups who were unable to join up or do essential war work, such as the elderly, those with dependants or the housebound. The first major task of the WVS was to handle the evacuation of $1\frac{1}{2}$ million children from large cities to the country – taking them by car or train to one of three WVS receiving nurseries where their hair was washed and they were provided with a complete wardrobe. WVS members, dressed in their uniforms of green tweed suits with red piping and matching hats, also provided transport for hospital patients and did welfare work for the troops. Many girls too young to join up helped their mothers with these tasks. By the end of the war, 241 WVS members had been killed in action on the Home Front.

Among those who rushed to join up was Cynthia Denison-Pender. At her small finishing school in France in 1938 she had absorbed its proprietor's belief that war was inevitable. 'When I came back from Mademoiselle Fauchet, believing that there would be a war, I made my older sister join the FANYs.

'I went to all these lectures with my sister, took the exams with her, and by the time war broke out we were both fully qualified and I'd passed my driving test – I was just eighteen. We had our uniforms – which we had to pay for ourselves.

'We were called up on September 6. We were supposed to get a telegram to alert us, saying "Auntie entered speed test". We never got it. Instead we got, "Auntie crash, come quickly". My father had the most wonderful purses made for us that you wore round your waist, with a small flask of brandy and a five-pound note in them for emergencies.

'We got everything ready, and went in my sister's car to the camp at Bovington. We stopped in Sherborne to buy something at Woolworths and when we came out we met the Dorsets marching up the street. They'd never seen women in uniform before and a cheer went up.'

Lavinia Holland-Hibbert, so convinced war was coming that she had already joined the FANYs, was another who received the FANY 'radiator' code. 'On Friday 1 September I got up early and went cubbing [fox-cub hunting] with my father. Then we went round to every house in the village [Beckley] pleading with them to house evacuees. We found places for thirty-two.

'Next day I got my secret, sealed mobilisation orders. On receipt of a telegram saying "Radiator burst" I was to open them. It arrived at 7.20 p.m. on the day war was declared, and I immediately sent one back saying "Radiator mended" which meant I would report in six hours. After dinner my father took me to Oxford where I joined the Twelfth Oxford Motor Company. I remember we had to have bicycles. I painted mine in the FANY colours, pale pink and baby blue.'

Suzanne Irwin had also become a FANY that summer. 'When war was declared I'd already got part of my uniform and I was on my way to the Portree balls on the Isle of Skye with a young man I was mad about.* I'd been chasing him and had at last captured him. He had a marvellous Lagonda and as we went through Glencoe he asked me to drive it past him at 100 m.p.h. as he wanted to see what it looked like, but I wouldn't.

'We'd got as far as Mallaig, where the boat for Skye leaves from, when my father rang up and said: "You've been called up. A telegram has come from the FANYs and you've got to report for duty." I went home, collected my uniform and reported for duty in a ghastly place in North Wales, where we were given a furniture van as an ambulance.† Then things began to get serious and I went to Edinburgh and we drove ambulances and staff cars and had a lot of fun – the third Cavalry Training Regiment was in barracks there, so there were parties with young men. As some of the people who'd known my father were still serving I was allowed to ride their horses on my day off in the hills behind Edinburgh, which was lovely.'

Hunting, said Lady Barbara Legge, was really the cause of her joining the FANYs. 'My younger sister Josceline and I joined in early 1938. The reason was that we'd had a simply

---

* After the Season proper, balls and Games began in Scotland in early autumn.
† In many country districts, buses were commandeered to serve as ambulances, resulting in a skeleton service.

wonderful day's hunting – the horses had gone very well, we felt we'd been very brave and everything had gone right. We were riding home, twenty miles away, still in a euphoric state, with a neighbour and she said to us: "Oh, will you join the FANYs?" Yes, we said – we'd have said yes to anything at that moment, we were so pleased with life.

'As FANYs, we were supposed to learn about the insides of cars and at one meeting I was asked what I knew about the carburettor. "It's filled with oil and hair," I said confidently. My father's old chauffeur used to teach us and I hadn't realised he'd put an h on "air".'

Ursie Barclay had joined the ATS in early 1939 instead of doing a Season with her older sister Iona. A year earlier, her mother had been asked to form the first company of ATS in Norwich and the two girls, along with half a dozen of their friends, joined.

'I suppose I went into the ATS because my mother told us to. And it was such an easy option, living at home. We drove up to the barracks every day with Mummy, who was the company commander – we were storewomen and clerks in the company offices. We left home about 8.15 and got back about five.'

When Lady Margaret Egerton went home to Scotland briefly during June 1939 – roughly halfway through her Season – she decided to join the Army. Without telling her parents, who she knew would disapprove, she enlisted in the Roxburghshire ATS where her friend Cecilia Sprot (later to marry the politician Willie Whitelaw) was already a sergeant major.

'Then came September 3 and I was called up. My parents were livid because I'd never told them I'd joined up. So I didn't dare moan about the conditions.

'I used to go off on a bicycle the fifteen miles to HQ each day. The boss lady was a lesbian, with an Eton crop and a deep voice. We sort of knew it – we were suspicious but we wouldn't have voiced such a thing. "Egerton," she said to me, "you will learn to type." So there I was typing with two fingers and nearly dying of fright when the War Office telephoned as I didn't understand all the abbreviations they used.

'After a month our boss lady was made Queen AT of Scotland and she took us with her to the HQ, the North British Hotel [in Edinburgh's Princes Street], run by a company of ATS who were all peacetime clerical. I ran messages with files and was general dogsbody.

'We lived in a flat with the boss – she behaved absolutely properly – and we ate at the canteen. We used to get exhausted – we would sit up in bed cleaning our buttons. Once I was so tired I went to sleep on an island in Princes Street waiting for my tram.

'Everything was a rush. It took a quarter of an hour to get into Edinburgh and a quarter of an hour back. We thought if we took five minutes too long it would affect the war effort – we were terribly patriotic.'

Cecilia Sprot had become a Territorial sometime earlier. 'I was at home when war was declared. Next moment I was into my uniform, gas mask in my bicycle basket, and straight down to the office on my bicycle.

'I was used to mixing with different sorts of people as I ran the Guides and Brownies in our village but of course country people were more innocent. I hadn't met anyone from a large town – these were much more worldly.'

With the idealism and energy of youth, girls who only a short time before had been dancing all night planned what they could best do to aid the war effort. Sarah Norton, who had been sharing a flat with a pretty Canadian girl called Osla Benning (later a girlfriend of the Duke of Edinburgh), was one of them.

'Osla and I decided we were not going to wait to be called up. We thought: what is the most important war work we can do? We didn't fancy the women's services' uniforms – except for the Wrens – so in April 1940, we went and offered our services to the Hawker Hurricane fighter aircraft factory in Slough. We had a six-month training course, then I was put on to wiring the cannon gun on the Typhoon. The test pilots used to come and pick up the planes.'

Some girls joined up almost on a whim. Fanny Gore Browne, in Oxford doing a secretarial course ('after I'd left school my parents didn't really know what to do with me'), was out walking with a friend during their lunch hour when she spotted a poster saying that the WRNS recruiting officer was at the Church Hall.

'We walked in, joined a short queue, and were interviewed in turn. The Wrens, being a much smaller service than the other two, were able to be far more selective. They demanded three character references – I think the other services only wanted two – so I got one from the father of a school friend who was the bursar of Queen's College, another from an old family friend in Leicestershire who was chairman of Leicestershire County Council and a third, academic, one.

'The way they weeded their applicants was by saying that while, yes, they were recruiting, it was only for cooks and stewards, which made a lot of girls turn tail and walk out. They wanted to be certain that people really wanted to join.

'I'd read an article in *The Times* the previous week saying that they'd got this wonderful new invention called radar. It sounded fascinating so I said to the Wren recruiting officer that what I'd like to do was specialise in radar. She looked totally blank and said it was cooks and stewards only, so I agreed. Before we left we'd both signed on the dotted line.

'A month later we both received an official letter calling us for an examination. I was very nervous because I thought I was almost bound to fail – I'd had a very sickly childhood, with rheumatic fever – but it was fairly perfunctory. I wasn't asked if I'd had any serious illness so I didn't tell them.

'It didn't go down terribly well when I told my parents, partly because of the health thing. I think they expected me to nurse but at the back of my mind I knew I didn't want to do that. By this time, 1941, we already had friends who'd been wounded. I had a car by then and I'd been taught to drive by our chauffeur, and with a friend I used to go to the Churchill Hospital in Oxford and take out a wounded friend for picnics. I'd seen enough to know that nursing was not for me.

'Really, we'd only joined the Wrens on a whim. I think we both fancied the navy-blue uniforms – we Wrens did look marvellous whereas the other services, through no fault of their own, didn't.'

One who came to the WRNS by a circuitous route was Elizabeth Montagu Douglas Scott. 'I knew that saving petrol was very important so the first war job I did was really to save petrol. I got up every morning at five thirty to drive the pony and cart to the farm three miles away to pick up our milk. At the same time, I looked around, took a first-aid course and offered my services to anyone who wanted them, such as canteen work. There was always plenty to do on the farm – there was no machinery or anything like that – and all the farm boys were getting called up at once. So if they wanted an extra hand in the woods I'd go along and if I had friends to stay I made them do it too.

'The following year I joined the Civil Nursing Reserve so that I could go and nurse anywhere. This meant training in Dumfries to get the necessary hours to be a trained nurse. Because I wasn't yet called up I spent most of that year learning nursing, doing canteen work or seeing friends.

'I was called up at the end of 1940 and then worked in a military hospital near Dumfries for a year. There wasn't enough to do and we had a bossy matron who was always getting at me. When I'd finished my work I would read the paper or chat with patients. She came into the ward one day and accused me of being idle. I said: "But I've finished everything – I've made all the beds, cleaned the floors, emptied everything that needed emptying." She said: "Well, do it again." That was too much for me and I told her I was wasting my time, and went off to join the Wrens.

'I had an interview with Lady Cholmondeley, who was Queen Bee of the Wrens. She did her best to put me off by saying one shared a room with dozens of other girls. Then I went along, supported by a friend, to actually sign on in the Wren headquarters up the Finchley Road and be taken to my little cabin, for two, and left there. There you learned your duties and your marching and the general routine.'

In the same way that she had slipped off to a nightclub from a ball during her debutante season, Elizabeth Scott managed to escape the strict confines of the WRNS hostel.

'I had lots of friends in London and I very soon discovered the fire escape key with which I could undo the door to a little staircase from the first floor where my bedroom was out into the street. I would manage to telephone my friends, say I'd meet them at the 400,* and catch the tube at the Finchley Road station straight to Leicester Square. It was more difficult getting back as the tube stopped at midnight, so whoever I was with had to bribe a taxi to take me back. I was in uniform as I didn't have any other clothes there. I did that once or twice and was never found out. I told one or two of the other girls I'd made friends with but nobody else dared do it.'

～

Nursing, more than any other occupation, seemed to polarise opinion. Some girls could imagine doing nothing else; others loathed it.

While waiting to be called up, Daphne Brock was persuaded by a friend who wanted to get married to stand in for her in her work with Sir Harold Gillies, the great pioneer plastic surgeon. The job was teaching French and German to the airmen for whom he was building new faces.

'It was the most harrowing thing I have ever had to do. The

* The most popular nightclub of the 'smart set'. It was in Leicester Square.

first week I couldn't eat or think. To appear completely natural when in front of you was somebody without a face was incredibly difficult. The worst thing of all was after a raid on London when a small girl of about five who had received terrible burns was brought down. She was put in a side ward, in a saline bath. I shall never, never forget the sound of her screaming. Of course it upset everyone terribly. She was in such agony that we were almost thankful when the poor little thing died.'

For Lady Moyra Ponsonby, nursing was enthralling. She had hated her Season, which she found exhausting, and taken a job at the English Speaking Union. When her mother, the Countess of Bessborough, began to run a first-aid course from their London house in Eaton Square, Lady Moyra joined it. 'Almost at once I was hooked. Then I got more and more involved, and began to train.

'My first job as a real nurse was in 1938, in the Royal Free Hospital in Hampstead. On my first day in the ward one of my fellow nurses asked me if I would help her by changing a dressing. The patient, who had a groin injury, had spotted I was new and did his best to embarrass me by talking about what was immediately beneath, but I'm glad to say he failed.'

Lady Moyra began her wartime nursing career at the Royal West Sussex Hospital in Chichester, nine miles from the family seat at Stansted Park. 'The West Sussex was a casualty clearing station for the bombed people of Portsmouth. I was a St John nursing auxiliary wearing St John uniform, part time and unpaid. I was living at Stansted and I would go on my pushbike four miles to a bus stop, leave my bike in a farm shed by the side of the road and go on by bus to Chichester. I did the same journey in reverse when I finished in the early evening. I wasn't being paid then but I began to do longer and longer hours. There came a point when I thought, This is silly – I'd better train properly, and I came up to London to begin training.'

Socially, nursing received the parental stamp of approval – especially if a daughter worked at a hospital like St Thomas's –

as did the FANYs and, to a large extent, the Wrens. 'My mother didn't mind me becoming a nurse,' said Virginia Forbes Adam, who began the war by rolling bandages in Belgrave Square with her friend Rosemary Lyttelton. 'But she'd have died of horror if I'd joined the ATS. Personally, I longed to be handing out tea to the troops instead of rolling bandages.'

Training could be very perfunctory. When Sheila Parish, just nineteen, who had joined the FANYs just before the war when she turned nineteen, received her call-up papers, she set off in her little Austin car, with her own clothes and food for a fortnight, for Bovington in Dorset, where she was to learn to drive ambulances. 'I was put into an ambulance and told to drive once up and down the hospital drive and that was it. They said: "You've passed – off you go, now, with another driver, to pick up a patient and take him to Southampton Hospital."

'It was pitch black, with a storm raging, and we had to drive round quite a lot to find him. Each place we stopped at, someone said: "We're coming with you." So by the time we got to the man we'd been told to collect there were eight men in the back. This turned out to be lucky, for as we set off again in this awful storm the man suddenly went berserk. The eight men pounced on him and the ambulance rocked as we drove along.

'At Southampton the patient claimed he wanted a cup of tea. He'd calmed down so we all went into a café and took him with us. He escaped and ran back to the ambulance and knelt on the steps, clutching them tightly and screaming, "I'm a poached egg! I'm a poached egg!" as crowds gathered. It took all eight chaps to prise him away from the ambulance steps.'

Judy Impey went into the ATS because she came from an army family. 'All my friends went into the Wrens because the uniform was so glamorous but my father and both my grandfathers were in the Army so there was no question of going anywhere but the ATS. I'd been given the chance of going to Canada but I refused. I said: "I want to go into the Army because I want to defend my country." I was one of three girls,

TOP: Anne Reid, here wearing a full-skirted white dress and that favourite parental present, a string of pearls. ABOVE LEFT: Mary Pollock in her presentation dress, with its regulation train depending from the shoulders. ABOVE RIGHT: Most debutantes, like Rosemary Wynn, were photographed in their presentation dresses, carefully arranged. All had to wear elbow-length white kid gloves.

An informal picture of debutantes Esme Harmsworth (left) and her sister Lorna, daughters of Lord Rothermere.

Esme Harmsworth was acclaimed as one of the two most beautiful debs of the year when she attended Queen Charlotte's Ball in May 1940.

Lorna Harmsworth, one of the few who chose a patterned dress for her presentation at Court in 1938.

Susan Meyrick was presented in 1938 and had a dance the following year.

OPPOSITE PAGE: Penny Woosnam, the daughter of one of England's great all-round athletes, Max Woosnam, was presented at a Court at Holyrood House during George VI's visit to Edinburgh in July 1937.

LEFT: Betty Shaughnessy, presented earlier in the Thirties, as a chic young married woman.

BELOW: The death of King George V in January 1936 meant that clothes worn at significant social events had to be in the mourning colours of black, white or mauve. Joan Stafford King-Harman, thrilled at the idea of wearing a colour usually reserved for older women, chose black for one of her dance frocks. She was presented later that season (when colours were permitted).

Denise Woosnam, older daughter of the athlete Max Woosnam, was presented at the garden party held by Edward VIII in July 1936 instead of a traditional Court.

Christian Grant and her mother, Lady Grant, about to leave for Court in March 1939. Debutantes usually carried flowers, their mothers ostrich-feather fans.

BELOW: Cynthia Denison-Pender, whose father was High Sheriff of Dorset, described herself as 'very much a country deb'.

Fiona Colquhoun, in a snapshot taken at her parents' home the year she was presented.

Sarah Norton went on to work in the highly secretive atmosphere of Bletchley Park, Britain's famous decrypting centre.

BELOW LEFT: Elizabeth Lowry-Corry was presented at the last Court of the Season, on 30 June 1939, just before her dance, and was at home in Suffolk when war was declared.

BELOW RIGHT: Rosemary Hodson, presented in May 1938, was the daughter of a hunting parson. Here she is photographed on her engagement in September 1940 to her future husband, Tony Trollope.

Isle of Man. All statuesque, beautiful girls who had volunteered the moment they could, to come over.'

~~~

For some former debutantes, life continued in an eerily normal way for a few months. Lorna Harmsworth, who had done a first-aid course, worked in the cottage hospital near Mereworth Castle in Kent, the country home of her father, Esmond Harmsworth, before going skiing in the winter of 1939 – the 'Phoney War' – with her great friend Diana Barnato. 'We drove across France in Diana's Bentley, to Mégève. There we met all the people who would normally have been at the Palace Hotel in St Moritz. We also met the Scots Guards, who were learning to ski for the purpose of going to Norway, and I skied with them. In the event, they didn't go there.

'We ended up at Monte Carlo for Easter – really, we'd been completely disregarding the fact that there was a war on. Then I got a message from my father: "Come back at once" [Russia had already overrun Finland and German troops had invaded Norway]. I went to Paris and got in a train there to come home.'

Mary Toulmin was another almost caught in France. Her American mother and English father – who had fought in both the South African War and the 1914–18 war – lived in Switzerland and also owned a house near Dinard in Brittany. Mary, who had been presented in London by a cousin of her father's, returned to the family home in Switzerland after doing the 1939 Season. 'Soon after the war began we went to the house in Dinard because my father thought it would be safer than staying in Switzerland. One day in the spring of 1940 I was out cycling with a girl friend and we passed a farmer I knew. "Don't go any further," he said. "The rumour is that the Germans have started to cross Normandy and are on their way here."

'I rushed back to the house and told my parents. "Well, in that case," my father replied, "we must pack a suitcase each and get a car to St Malo [the nearby ferry port] and see if we can find a boat." We found one, packed with British soldiers and wounded and a few refugees, and sailed across the Channel, calling at Jersey to pick up more people. This was just before Dunkirk.

'It was a Sunday and as all my mother's jewellery and money was in the bank we had to sail without them. The next day a friend managed to persuade the manager to hand over the jewellery by pointing out that otherwise it would be taken by the Germans, now only a day away – our friend got a fishing boat and came to England with it. Otherwise all we had were our small cases, our two dogs and our budgerigars. Everything else was left behind and we never saw it again.'

After staying for a short time in the Royal Court Hotel in Sloane Square, London, Mary and her parents left for America, where Mary's mother's family lived.

Lorna Harmsworth's friend Diana Barnato, after a conventional start, did one of the most difficult and unusual female jobs of the war. She early manifested the same passion for fast machines as her father, learning to fly as a debutante. 'I began simply to get away – as a debutante you were never alone, always chaperoned and under someone's supervision. In the air they couldn't come with you.

'The place to learn then was Brooklands [near Weybridge in Surrey]. In the middle of the car-racing circuit was a flying club. It cost £3 an hour – in those days I was far too much of a snob to mix with the hoi polloi for 7s 6d an hour in the Civil Air Guard. I did six hours in a Tiger Moth before I went solo and I had no idea what I was doing. After I'd done ten hours I ran out of pocket money and my family wouldn't help me – they didn't want me to get away. So that was the end of my flying until the war began.

'At first I was a Red Cross nurse, based in France, and drove an ambulance. But friends of mine in the ATA [Air Transport Auxiliary] knew how I loved flying and wanted to get me in it too. I said I was very out of practice but they decided to arrange for me to get a test with the Chief Flying Instructor. They took me riding in Windsor Park where they knew, although I didn't, we'd run into the Chief Flying Instructor of the ATA. I rode very well and had a beautiful horse so they thought first impressions would be good. They persuaded him to give me a flying test.

'Pilots then had to be under twenty-five to join the Royal Air Force, so anyone older than that who could fly often went into the ATA. We also had people with impaired vision and lame people – derelicts who could not pass the medical and get into the war properly in the RAF or Fleet Air Arm. There were also eight women in the ATA.'

At this point Diana had only ten hours of flying experience, far short of the required level. Before taking the actual test she practised by driving her Bentley, with its windows open, on the Egham bypass at take-off and landing speeds, correlating them with the feel of the wind in her hair so that getting them right in the cockpit would become second nature.

Her test was postponed owing to a hunting accident but in September 1941 she was taken on by the ATA and later trained at their school. From then on her days were packed, pervaded with the fervour of those who had volunteered rather than been conscripted. 'Every time you delivered a flight, especially after a difficult one, you thought: This is my little bit towards the war. One in the eye for Hitler. You really did.'

The war had put paid to the practice of Mary Pollock's paediatrician father, since almost all his small patients had left London. He became the Medical Officer in charge of evacuees over a large area surrounding the family's weekend cottage in Surrey. But with little happening in the Phoney War, the family returned to London at Christmas 1939. By this time Mary had decided to train as a physiotherapist, starting her three-year training at St Thomas's Hospital the following May. 'I knew there would be a need for physical rehabilitation and with my father a doctor and my mother having been a VAD in the first war, something hospital-y seemed natural.

'And though I'm not a conscientious objector at all, I knew in my heart that I'd rather make people better than try and kill them.'

Chapter 6

FANYs

'Posh girls driving staff cars'

In terms of class, the FANYs were, *par excellence*, the chic wartime service for women. 'Rather posh girls driving staff cars, I seem to remember,' as one man put it. 'Widely regarded as sexually sophisticated but only available to officers of very senior rank,' from another. The long-drawn-out liaison between General Eisenhower, the American C-in-C Europe (and later President of the United States), and his driver, the beautiful Kay Summersby, formerly a fashion model for Worth of Paris, did nothing to dispel this notion.

The reason why fathers could nod benignly at the thought of a daughter joining the FANYs and mothers utter sighs of approval not unmixed with envy was not hard to seek: if their cherished offspring did contract an alliance with someone, he would almost certainly be of the officer class. And that, in those days, meant 'gentleman'. 'The Motor Transport Corps was the volunteer course that the debutantes and post-debutantes flocked to when war was declared,' said Kay Summersby. As one pre-war debutante, Sheila Parish, remarked: 'There was very little culture shock in joining the FANYs, as all of us were from the same background.' Or as the Labour politician Denis Healey later put it: 'The FANYs were the aristocracy of the women's services.'

After the general disbandment of the women's wartime

services in 1918 – forcing most of the rank and file back into the home or domestic service – two independent voluntary organisations remained. One was the Motor Transport Section of the Women's Legion, founded by Lady Londonderry in 1915. Gradually, however, this was disbanded as its members joined other organisations or returned to civilian life.

The other body, the FANYs, originally consisted of a group of well-to-do voluntary nurses who rode out on their own horses (hence the word 'yeomanry'), clad in red and blue uniforms, to help the wounded in the Boer War of 1899–1902. In 1907 they were founded as an official body and the service was awarded seventeen Military Medals and twenty-seven Croix de Guerre. They provided a first-aid link between fighting men and the field hospitals, drove ambulances and ran soup kitchens, often in conditions of extreme danger. Although subtitled the Ambulance Car Corps and later, officially, the Women's Transport Service, they were always known as the FANYs, a name they jealously guarded.

Because of their voluntary status and the financial independence of most of them, the FANYs were able to continue on their independent course after the war. They began serious peacetime training as early as 1921 and from 1934 onwards one of their main wartime functions, driving, became a focus for their activities.

Led by the kind of upper-class women who had first founded and then joined their organisation, the FANYs naturally enough recruited fellow members largely from their own tribe. Many of these were the kind of girls who, barred from taking any kind of job by the rigid social conventions of the time, longed to 'do something'.

As another war threatened, and after innumerable changes of mind on the part of both the Cabinet and the War Office, it was decided that the various voluntary bodies were to be united within the framework of the Territorial Army. The FANYs became a subsidiary organisation of the Auxiliary Territorial

Service (ATS) which was formed in 1938. But as FANY head-quarters was private property, owned and run by FANY money, it could not be closed down. The end result was that they agreed to join the proposed scheme, on the basis of a gentleman's agreement guaranteeing them their identity and a degree of autonomy.

Already notable for their *esprit de corps*, the FANYs had an equally strong sense of commitment. Despite their cloistered upbringing and their total subjection to parental rule, most of them possessed an innate, often almost subconscious, sense of confidence. Their backgrounds and the homes they came from were usually at least the equal of those of the officers they chauffeured. Even being able to drive – and, often, to afford a car of one's own – was a distinctive marker: unlike the vast majority of those in the women's services, the FANYs came from families that owned one or more cars (in 1939, only one in ten families owned a car). Most, too, had been taught their driving skills by a professional, the family chauffeur.

One of these was Cynthia Denison-Pender who had joined the FANYs with her elder sister just before the war. Soon after arriving at Bovingdon, Cynthia, aged 18 and a newly qualified driver thanks to tuition by her parents' chauffeur, was sent into Dorchester at the wheel of a lorry. 'I'd never driven anything except an ordinary car before but there I was driving a six-wheeler with a sergeant beside me and as we went down a steep hill, he said: "Put her out of gear." I did so – but I couldn't put her back in gear again. I wondered what he'd say but he just mopped his brow with a bandanna and laughed.'

Cynthia, at eighteen one of the youngest FANYs, was next sent to Bristol to work for the hospital's blood transfusion unit. 'We had to take another exam before we were allowed to drive the mobile transfusion units – great refrigeration vans. We drove these fridge vans to Dover to embark for Dunkirk but were sent back – they weren't taking anyone over.'

Unsurprisingly, when the ATS was formed the FANYs' first task was to raise and train 1,500 driver-mechanics, to be sent where necessary throughout the country. Right from the start, FANYs were conscious of belonging to an élite, prepared to work as hard as they knew how but often with the belief that day-to-day rules did not always apply to them. Lavinia Holland-Hibbert, like virtually every girl who came out just before the war, spent as much time in nightclubs as she could. 'I was pretty insubordinate, always losing my car and going to London and dancing all night and being late on parade. My attitude was that if I wasn't found out there was nothing wrong. I always tried to make whatever I was doing, or wherever I was, fit in with my ways.'

Their female officers were in many cases friends of their parents, perhaps even their own godmothers (thus doing what these women told them came naturally). As FANYs, they might have been part of the ATS but even their uniforms could be distinctive. Many of them had these made by their fathers' uniform tailors; they wore their lanyards on the left, yeomanry-style, dyed them in the FANY colours of blue and pink, had FANY flashes on their shoulders and wore straps over their caps. Later, when they were officially amalgamated with the ATS, these distinctions were forbidden, though often – with the connivance of their officers – worn. 'When we did anything official,' said Lavinia, 'we were made to remove all these things – and how we resented it.'

Their work quickly expanded although, for most, some form of transport work – from driving generals or ambulances to ferrying unexploded bombs to a place of safety – was their main job. Some, thanks to the languages they had learned in their pre-debutante years while being 'finished', were contacts for secret agents working with resistance groups; a handful with perfect French were trained as agents and dropped into occupied

France – twelve were caught, tortured and killed. Two thousand of them served with SOE (Special Operations Executive) in Europe, around the Mediterranean and in the Middle and Far East. Many, like Diana Quilter, came to the more unusual jobs via a circuitous route.

'At the beginning of the war we were all foraging for jobs. It was difficult to find anything then as they couldn't absorb everyone. Finally I got an interview at the War Office and joined Censorship and was sent to Gibraltar, where we censored the American mail that came through Gibraltar. Then when Italy joined the war [on 11 June 1940] I and the other fifty-odd people working for Censorship had to come back.

'To do so we had to wait for a convoy. The boat we were put on was small and rather battered – for years it had been taking pilgrims to Mecca and it was already loaded with Italian prisoners when it got to us.

'It was quite a hazardous journey, as we were the slowest boat in the convoy – so slow that U-boats underwater could travel at the same speed, about six or seven knots. After three days, when we were in the middle of the Bay of Biscay, France fell [on June 22] and our escort left us to take troops off from Brest.

'So there we were, undefended. We were promptly attacked and quite a lot of us were sunk – only one-third of our fifteen-strong convoy eventually got home. And because our tiny ship was crammed with so many civilians and the wretched Italian prisoners in the hold, we couldn't stop to pick anyone up. That was much the worst of it.

'In fact, as we were by far the slowest we had to break with the convoy and then we really were on our own. I don't know that one was terrified – in a way it was very exhilarating. In order to give us something to do we were given handbells and told to ring them if we saw a periscope emerging. Of course they were being rung all the time as people thought they saw one. Once we really did, and an attack was so feared that we were all put into lifeboats and lowered to within two feet of the water, with a rating in the boat with us, ready to pick up the hawser that would have released us into the sea if we had been torpedoed. But nothing happened – I think we were such a small target they must have decided not to waste a torpedo on us.'

Once in England, Diana joined the FANYs, driving a mobile canteen throughout the Blitz (which began on 7 September 1940). Her canteen was based just off the Mile End Road, in London's East End, and every third night she was on duty at the nearby shelters.

'Most of these were under the river, shared with Chinese workers and dray-horses. The smell was terrible, we almost had to put on gas masks to go in. We stayed in the mouth of the shelter, near the horses, which were last in and first out. Jock Colville [then Assistant Private Secretary to the Prime Minister Winston Churchill] was a great friend of mine and he brought Mrs Churchill along to see our base and go round the shelters. There was a smoked salmon factory in that street so we used to have wonderful parties.'

One of these was on 31 March 1941. In his diary, Colville recorded: 'We drank sherry and ate smoked-salmon sandwiches at Diana's First Aid Post and were then escorted to the crypt of Christchurch, Spitalfields; the Kent and Essex Hay-yard (which was deserted); the Tilbury shelter; the Arches, Watney Street; and Gooche's. They have greatly improved; some are even cheerful, though it is terrible to see human beings living in such cramped conditions.'

For Diana Quilter, the worst thing about that time was finding her way to her destination in the blackout while driving her canteen, often with the route blocked by a bomb. 'In the cold of winter I remember trying to feed firemen with their hands literally frozen to the hosepipes as they fought the flames. You would have to put the hot tea to their lips and the sandwiches into their mouths.'

FANYs, as the saying went, could not only cope but, as they

had no duties set in stone, were apt to turn up anywhere. One of Sheila Parish's strangest assignments was being detailed to meet the fleeing King Zog of Albania and his family in June 1940.

'I was stationed at Plymouth for Dunkirk and was told to go and meet some boats coming in, on one of which was the King and his family, and take him to London. I took the biggest car I could find, set off and found the King with his sisters and his baby son on the quayside. He told me that he would accompany his men in the lorry containing his crates of luggage and that we should meet at the railway station.

'There I took him to the ticket office to buy the tickets for his group of sixty and he was asked for the requisite sum of money. He said: "I have no money at all." The ticket collector said: "Well, if you've no money you can't travel."

'The King, a conspicuous figure with his flaming red hair and heavily waxed moustache, turned and ordered some of his men to open one of the crates. From it, he picked out great handfuls of jewels and handed them to the ticket collector. The poor man was horrified,' said Sheila, 'but he let them travel.'

(When they arrived in London, the Albanian royal family took a third-floor suite at the Ritz. Six strapping bodyguards were accommodated on an upper floor and the rest of their entourage at the Athenaeum Hotel, also in Piccadilly. When the hall porter at the Ritz asked if their exceptionally heavy luggage contained anything of special value, King Zog replied: 'Yes. Gold.' This was hastily transferred to the Bank of England, from which the King's secretary would withdraw £1,000 every week.)

Much more gruesome was Sheila's memory of driving ambulances to fetch the survivors of HMS *Arcadia*, sunk by a U-boat in the retreat from Dunkirk, the four hundred aboard her singing 'Roll out the Barrel' as they drowned. 'The men who survived were in a terrible state, their bodies and clothes burned with flaming oil when they jumped into the sea.'

Lavinia Holland-Hibbert, a fully-fledged FANY by the time war broke out, was stationed at Oxford, where she began by driving officers, mainly from the Oxfordshire Yeomanry. After returning from a day's driving she would hand over a signed work docket, fill the car with petrol, clean, it, prepare everything ready for the next day, then finally immobilise it by taking out the rotor arm. In winter, she would also drain the radiator (no one had any antifreeze). She was paid nine shillings a week and if out working for more than ten hours a day received a subsistence allowance of five shillings.

Her two favourite passengers were both Jewish, one a doctor and the other the author Robert Henriques.* In her diary Lavinia, who had wanted to go to university but had been let down by her poor mathematics, wrote of those early months:

'Anti-Semitism was taken for granted but was not vicious. Henriques was accepted, indeed liked, in the Yeomanry because he was a countryman but, as an intellectual, was different from the other officers.

'Long journeys in the car, often at night, were wonderful opportunities for talk. I ranked my officers by how interesting their conversations were. About level with Henriques was a Jewish gynaecologist with hairy hands and outrageous fascist views. I was always reading Aldous Huxley, D. H. Lawrence, C. H. Morgan and Evelyn Waugh. My driving period, at the age of nineteen, was my 'university' period and Henriques and the hairy-handed doctor were my tutors. How they tolerated my driving I can't think. Quite often I'd lost my radiator cap and the car boiled at regular intervals. Sometimes the big end went (a military sin) but the officers often took over, particularly in London.'

---

* Robert Quixano Henriques was born in 1905 into one of the oldest Jewish families in England. He served in the Royal Artillery, retiring in 1933 and beginning a second career as a writer. In 1939 he published *No Arms, No Armour*, a highly praised and best-selling novel based on his army experience. As a Territorial officer, he was immediately recalled to the Royal Artillery.

In those brief months of the Phoney War Lavinia, like many others, did not realise what a life-or-death struggle lay ahead. One night, driving Henriques, the subject came up.

'He is one of those people who really minds terrifically about the war. He says he wouldn't mind dying tomorrow if it wasn't for his wife and what's the point of doing anything about arranging a new world when everything is so awful now. He loathes Neville Chamberlain and says to fight a totalitarian war one must have a totalitarian government with conscription of labour and wealth, with Churchill as PM. He has a very poor opinion of members of this Government and thinks every week of Chamberlain means a month longer of war.'

In November 1939 Lavinia was writing: 'Henriques' new book, *No Arms, No Armour*, has just been published. He is rather shy about it. He looked like a thin bloodhound all evening.

'Next day a very nice job: taking Henriques to Newbury Racecourse. He was a minute late and was very apologetic, which was surprising, as usually they just stroll out after an hour and say "Oh, she's here!" He was very interesting and we talked non-stop about women, about which he knew a lot but I only knew about one.

'Then we talked about his book. He said he was sorry it was a popular success as that meant it wasn't a good book. He loved talking about it. On the way back we discussed the technique of book-writing. He writes from far-off memories, from nine until one and then again from eight until ten in the evening. When we got back he said he was going to have a party at his house the next night and would I drive him and his friends there.

'So the following night I picked up the General, another chap and Henriques. The General sat in front as he had the shortest legs. We arrived at Henriques' very nice house at Winson [near Cirencester in Gloucestershire], a converted farmhouse – quite big and full of lovely odds and ends, a rich man's house, at least a rich connoisseur's house. We had a lovely high tea with Mrs

H, an almost ugly person, *belle laide* but very charming. I read press cuttings about his book. Then we all went to a troops' concert and Henriques was quite tolerant about my driving when I had to back the cold Austin down a hill and turn, and I slipped backwards, stalled the engine and ground my gears. But we got to where we were going on time.

'He gave me a copy of his book. He'd written in it: "To Driver Holland-Hibbert, the Malcolm Campbell of this war – when she starts". The book contains the first reference to homosexuals I'd ever read.'

~

On the day that Churchill succeeded Neville Chamberlain as Prime Minister – 10 May 1940 – Germany invaded Holland and Belgium. All leave for Lavinia's group of FANYs was cancelled, there was a parade at 8.30 a.m. and gas masks were tested.

Then came Dunkirk. 'We met the men coming back and drove them to hospital. They were in torn, oily, wet uniforms – one officer had nothing on but a blanket and a monocle – and their faces were black and covered with oil. All the men said: "Where were our bloody planes? Never saw one. Don't you girls go out with an airman." On Sunday we talked to them all day, cleaned their buttons and belts, sent their telegrams, bought them stamps and posted their letters.'

Sent to Camberley as a driving instructor after this, Lavinia was told that she ought to become an officer. Although luxuries like having your bed made, rooms cleaned and tidied, under-clothes washed, laundry sent, personal teapot and a three-course dinner, waited on by orderlies, were tempting, the downside of a commission meant leaving the FANYs and joining the ATS. FANYs had officially ceased to exist on 12 April 1940, with their members becoming part of the ATS.

But thanks to strenuous efforts by the FANY commanding

officers, they largely managed to maintain their identity. 'Even after we'd been absorbed into the ATS a gang of us FANY officers would come up to London for lunch on Sundays,' said Sheila Parish. 'We'd go to Claridge's Causerie,* where you were charged according to how much you drank – we didn't drink as we were hard up so could just about afford the lunch.'

With their contacts, many FANYs could manipulate the system. 'By the time I became an officer,' said Lavinia Holland-Hibbert, 'I knew how to work the Army. My parents had so many friends in high places and I'd got to know so many generals through my driving that I usually got the sort of postings I wanted.'

After the Blitz Diana Quilter, too, began to look for another job. 'I got an interview at the War Office, where they tested my German and French. It was good enough for the purpose they wanted, though they didn't exactly explain what that purpose was.

'I was just told go on the Underground, on the Piccadilly line, and get out at Arnos Grove, where I would see a long, tree-lined drive opposite the station.† "Walk along it for half a mile," I was told, "and then go through a gate on the right." I walked along this drive, past people stationed at intervals, and someone showed me the gate to go through. "You will go past a swimming pool," he said, "and then you will proceed on hands and knees." Then I realised he was joking.

'But the work *was* extremely secret. We were none of us allowed to keep a diary and it took me ten years to talk about it after the war. I wasn't even told what I was working for, just that I had to do some typing – documents to copy. I'd learned to type in German, so "sch" came more easily to me than "sh".

---

* For a flat sum, customers could eat as much as they liked.
† This drive led to Trent Park, the former home of Sir Philip Sassoon. During the war it became a transit and interrogation camp for high-ranking prisoners of war.

'I didn't even know what the place was until my first night on duty there. In the morning I saw a couple of feet hanging out of a window and a voice said something in German. I found I was in a rather grand prisoner-of-war camp. It was a transit camp for high-up officers or officials and we had two German generals, who had to have a servant looking after them.

'The rooms were all bugged but the Germans knew this and spent the first few days saying nothing to each other. Then we put in stool pigeons to try and get them to talk a bit and they did – but always against the noise of the gramophones, which were going day and night. We had other Germans, mostly refugees, to transcribe what they said. So copies came to us and we knew enough German to make sense of what they said.'

The prisoners, she found, all believed that Hitler had made a terrible mistake in invading Russia. Most had also been instilled with a real loathing of Britain; Diana felt that, should they ever succeed in an invasion, 'our fate would be worse than that of the Poles.

'We ended up receiving Hess, who had just come from the Tower of London where he had been closely interrogated.* He was lodged in a caravan in the garden. After a week or so he was sent to the camp in Wales where he stayed for the rest of the war.

'There was a wonderful garden, with a nine-hole golf course that we were allowed to play on in our lunch hour. One of the translators told us that the Germans, seeing us FANYs play, had asked: "Can we have one of those or are they reserved for the Italians?"'

After a brief spell at an Italian camp (run by MI 19), Diana spent the year before D-Day at the Civil Affairs Staff Centre

---

* In May 1941 Rudolph Hess, deputy Führer of Nazi Germany, had made a solo flight in a ME 110 to Britain, landing in Scotland, with the object, he claimed, of seeking peace between Britain and Germany so that they could jointly fight Soviet Russia. He was to spend the rest of his life in prison.

('known to us as the Gauleiter Schule') on London's Putney Common where civilians were being trained to follow the Army in, after the invasion of Germany, to restore water, electricity and other essential services, to organise a police force and generally to re-establish a working administrative structure.

The younger FANYs preserved their pristine innocence for a long time. One, still self-conscious about the long-ago episode, told me anonymously that when a girl under her command was raped by a newly arrived American officer the case collapsed thanks to her ignorance. 'It went up to the very top, as it meant the death penalty if the officer was found guilty. So it was highly embarrassing that I was so ignorant I didn't know what the girl was talking about – I'd never heard of rape and I was completely hazy about the facts of life – and so couldn't take the proper description needed for the trial. In the end, the officer was simply sent back and it was all hushed up.'

Sheila Parish, as innocent as most other girls of her background, was inspecting one of the huts under her command when she found two girls in bed together in the middle of the morning. To her, it was simply a breach of army regulations but the Regimental Sergeant Major pulled her out of the room before she could say anything and said: 'They're doing nothing except keeping each other warm. They doubtless share beds at home.'

~○

Most FANYs were adventurous – Diana Quilter volunteered to drive an ambulance in war-torn Greece ('I felt there must be more that I could do than sitting in Liverpool doing censorship work with a lot of elderly people') and Lavinia Holland-Hibbert fixed herself a posting to Italy. Few were frightened except by V-1s (doodlebugs) and V-2 rockets.

Many girls on the east coast had near misses. Sheila Parish was lecturing to three hundred ATS girls in a Nissen hut when a doodlebug went over, so low that they thought it would hit the roof and cause maximum fatalities. Fortunately it only hit a tree a hundred yards away.

Diana Quilter, by then in the ATS and stationed at Seven-oaks, was in a house that received a direct hit from a doodlebug. 'We were in the direct line of fire from Boulogne until the barrage balloons got them and Spitfire pilots learned to tip their wings and bring them down in open country* – though that didn't happen until quite late. Anyway, we heard this thing coming, its engine getting more and more laboured. Then it cut out. We all knew what this meant. There was an almighty explosion and when it cleared I found I was standing against the only wall that still remained upright. I lost four ATS that night. My husband – I'd married in 1942 – then in charge of London District, knew that the place where I was had had a direct hit but he didn't know whether or not I'd survived.'

For Lavinia Holland-Hibbert, brought up on the hunting field, fear was an unknown. 'I absolutely was never frightened. I don't think for one moment I ever thought that I or anyone I knew would be killed. I can't even remember feeling fear when we were being bombed in Italy.

'Partly it was because we were doing interesting jobs which we were good at because we were properly trained and we were given lots of responsibility and had lots of people to admire.

'But really, we were so young, we couldn't imagine we weren't going to have a lot more life.'

---

* The maximum speed of V-1 rockets (at launch) was 410 m.p.h. but they were considerably slower when they arrived over England – the first was fired on 13 June 1944. Maximum speeds of Spitfires ranged from the Mark I's 374 to almost 460 m.p.h. By flying in the same direction as a rocket, just beside it, a gentle touch beneath one wing would roll it over, out of control, to crash near by.

Chapter 7

ATS

'We were the rough, tough ones'

Girls joined the ATS for a variety of reasons but the uniform was not one of them. It was not so much the colour, khaki, that was off-putting but the unflattering cut, guaranteed to maximise the deficiencies of any figure except the tall and willowy. Nor, unlike the FANYs, were the ATS already well known and appreciated.

Where the FANYs had had a strong peacetime presence and considerable experience, the ATS were virtually new. The original Women's Auxiliary Army Corps (the WAAC), their linear forebears, had had a comparatively brief life and had been largely disbanded after the 1914–18 war.

When the girls who were to form this early body first arrived in France in 1917 they were greeted with hostility. In the early years of the century, the prejudice against women doing any kind of military work save that of nursing was widespread and rampant. Even Lady Londonderry, with friends in every high place, was several times shown the tradesmen's entrance when she arrived in uniform at the houses of friends. Letters in *The Times* anathematised 'women aping men' both in their work and in their clothing – a number of the Legion's despatch riders wore breeches in an era when trousers for women were unheard of.

Some of this hostility was a hangover from the anger aroused by the campaigns of the suffragettes to win the right to vote which, to the hidebound, appeared to be an attempt to win a male prerogative; the idea of a female military force seemed to be taking this concept an unwarranted step further. Some of it was simply an unthinking expression of the belief that a woman's role was solely that of wife and mother and that no good could come of any attempt to pervert this natural order.

But the determined women who founded the WAAC were members of the upper classes who knew, or were related to, those in power, including the generals, and who made the most of these contacts, persuading them to allow the first members of the newly-established Corps to arrive in France in 1917. This did not stop salacious rumours immediately finding their way home: the WAAC was a cover plan for a system of army brothels (its Chief Controller actually had to sign an affidavit to certify that no recruiting for prostitution had ever taken place) while jokes like 'Would you rather have a slap on the face or a WAAC on the knee?' did the rounds.

After the war (and the achievement of a first, limited franchise) women were thrust back into a home setting, be it as wives or as domestic servants. Men, as the breadwinners, believed that any jobs going were rightfully theirs and the Government co-operated to the extent that any woman working in the public service had to leave on getting married.

As another war loomed during the thirties, the Government thought again. The service was re-formed, coming into being as the Auxiliary Territorial Service (the ATS) by Royal Warrant on 9 September 1938. Recruiting for it followed a simple pattern: female County Commandants were appointed and they in turn selected officers and, through them, enrolled women for the companies raised in each county.

At the outbreak of war this new 17,000-strong service (914 officers, 16,000 other ranks) had little experience. The officers were scarcely trained, uniforms were at first in short supply, and there was a general sense of confusion as everyone learned 'on the job'. But only three months into the war their numbers had doubled and their value had become so obvious that in April 1941 the Secretary of State for War announced that 'the whole Service will be given full military status'.*

By far the largest of the women's services (by the end of the war its numbers totalled over 200,000), ATS members were cooks, waitresses, telephonists, drivers, clerks and storekeepers as well as being active on gun sites or in overseas bases. With such a wide range of functions and responsibilities, it soon became clear that there was an urgent need for recruitment, which continued virtually throughout the war.

One of those responsible for this task was Denise Woosnam, asked by the Cheshire Commandant to join the service when war broke out and then, after a course, to recruit a company. 'You met some very strange types in that first week's course. A lot were wearing collars and ties as a lot of rather butch types had been asked to come and start it all off and that was a real shock to me.' In January 1941 Denise was posted to the Department of Recruiting at the War Office and was living in her father's house in West Eaton Place, Belgravia.

'My sister Penny was working as a VAD at the Royal Masonic Hospital in Hammersmith and my brother was in the RAF. My work involved travelling to different enrolment stations in the South-East several times a week, speaking in cinemas after war films were shown, enrolling recruits (one was Mary Churchill, a great coup that she had chosen our service) and helping with new organisations such as the Girls' Training Corps, which was a form of pre-ATS and had Joan Vickers at its head.†

---

* After the war, and demobilisation, the decision was taken not to disband the ATS but to convert it into a regular Corps, with a corresponding Territorial Army section, on a voluntary basis. In tribute to its excellent wartime service, it was awarded the word 'Royal'. Thus, on 1 February 1949, the Women's Royal Army Corps came into being.

† Joan Vickers, later Dame Joan Vickers, a former welfare and social worker, became Conservative MP for Plymouth Devonport in 1955, remaining in the House of Commons until 1974 when she went as a life peer to the House of Lords.

'Quite often one or two of us would be asked to go down to the big Underground stations in the East End at night, where hundreds of people slept in sleeping bags or on any bedding they had been able to carry – if they were regulars they left this bedding there by day. There was no stealing and no disorder but a lot of singing, in one station led by a dwarf whose courage was an inspiration and who held everyone in thrall. Nobody knew, when they emerged each day, whether their homes would be razed to the ground and all their possessions lost. It was considered a comfort for them to be joined by members of the services.'

Later in the war a Schools Liaison Unit was formed by the War Office and twelve ATS officers, together with twelve army officers convalescing from wounds, were posted to areas in England and Wales to visit schools with a film unit, to talk about their war experiences and to help young people make up their minds which service they wanted to join when they left school. Denise, as one of the ATS team, spent two years touring the London District and the South-East. 'It was the idea of Colonel Boyd-Rochfort, from the War Office, and it was most effective. Each one of us ATS officers was accompanied by an officer who had been wounded and was convalescing. We showed films, and talked, at boys' and girls' schools. The army chap would explain how he had been wounded, and what fighting was like, and we would describe how women had backed up the men's services.'

Not everyone needed such expositions to attract them. Judy Impey, from a family that had been 'army' since the Indian Mutiny, knew without question that her destiny was the ATS. She was only eighteen when she joined up as a volunteer in 1942, to be sent straight to a training camp in Yorkshire.

'The first thing was to go and have a medical. We were shoved into a cubicle and told to take all our clothes off. When we got to the barracks there weren't enough uniforms to go round, so we were all issued with overalls and we lived in these for a week.'

Before joining the ATS, women had their mouths and feet checked by the Medical Officer, followed by a four-week training course in which they learned to march, obey orders and salute like regular soldiers. On-duty uniform was trousers, brown leggings, brown boots, a greatcoat and a tin helmet; for off-duty it was a khaki skirt and jacket. Pay was two shillings a day (plus, of course, food and accommodation).

Despite Judy's youth, it was perfectly clear to the authorities that here was embryo officer material. 'I was kept on at the end of the first three weeks and given a stripe and told to instruct the next lot that came in. They all came from Newcastle and it was just like having foreigners. I couldn't understand a word they said – not only the accent but they used different words. They thought it was hysterical but although none of the others spoke like me they didn't tease me because of my voice, I think because I laughed and made a joke of it.

'There were thirty-four of us in that barrack room and life was hard. We got nine shillings a week. I saved mine up and spent it on food and swapped my cigarette coupons for sweets. I knew little of the outside world but because of having gone to boarding school I wasn't frightened. And because my family had moved around the world a lot, new things were a challenge not a threat to me and I made a point of enjoying it.

'I have a strong Christian faith and I remember thinking the first night: Am I going to kneel down and say my prayers or not? I knew it was now or never. And I did. Looking back, I think I got a bit of respect for that. Another embarrassment was that when I left home my father said he would paint everything yellow, including my bicycle, to prevent it being stolen.

'Coming from an army family we'd been taught to have a pride in our appearance, whereas other people from my background who had had everything done for them possibly found adjusting more difficult.

'I learned so much about the ways of life the others had. I

learned that you ate fish and chips in bed, you smoked in bed, and if you went out you picked up a boy.

'I'd been taken out a lot by the young subalterns before I joined the Army. So I knew about boys, but not to pick them up out of the street which is what the others all did. If they hadn't picked up a boy, their evening was wasted. They didn't ask me to go with them. But I remember walking through the streets of the nearest town and looking through windows and thinking, I'd love to just be allowed to go in and sit in a home, in front of the fire. That's what you missed, a home.

'But I had a lot of outings here and there. We had barrack dances. The sergeants were wonderful dancers, especially at the tango – to dance the tango with a sergeant was bliss. I didn't really go out with them – well, there wasn't much opportunity. We worked jolly hard and a lot of our time off was in the daytime. But I'd go and have a barrack-room meal, in the Naafi, with them and I danced a lot with them, and I would take part if there was an entertainment, perhaps do some acting.

'After I'd been there some time I got two stripes although most of the others were much older than me. A little later I went for a selection board. They said, "Why do you think you'll make an officer?" I said: "I don't know, but I come from an army family."

'I went to OCTU [Officer Cadet Training Unit] in the latter part of 1942. There I met Mary Churchill. I remember being on night duty with her one night. We talked a lot about our home life, as you do, being on all night. I said, "How do you manage at meal-times?" and she said: "Oh, we all talk at once." She was very nice looking in an absolutely English way, light hair and rosy cheeks and smart as a button, and she came top when we had our IQ tests. I liked her very much.

'I was at OCTU for three or four months. Because I'd been kept on to train others, I was often given a leading part in barrack-room square duties. I'd done quite a lot of acting, so when it came to drill I was able to throw my voice. Another test was taking part in a show. All of which was to see if you were suitable to become an officer.

'I was well aware that we in the ATS were the rough, tough ones – we got all the dregs. They would come in, ragtag and bobtail in civilian clothes, no table manners – you didn't have to teach them that but you hoped it brushed off a bit – and some of them hungry. One of the awful jobs was delousing them. Also inspecting their feet. They had to have baths in disinfectant and they were given coarse underclothes.

'Some didn't want to go home when they had a weekend pass because they knew their father would take the strap to them, simply as a pastime. A lot of them came from violent homes where the father would take his big leather belt off and beat them, and probably abused them as well.

'The FANYs were jolly lucky that they didn't have this harsh beginning. They never had to rough it in the ranks like we did. Often they brought their own cars and simply said: "We will drive for the Army."'

Another girl made an officer after only a few months (in March 1940) was Lady Margaret (Meg) Egerton. 'We were told we were to become officers and we were sent up in front of Dame Helen Gwynne-Vaughan,* who was about a mile high, with straight grey hair and gaiters – really, she was a man and very terrifying. Another on the panel was Lady Maud Baillie,† very smart in kilt and uniform jacket.

'I was terrified but I could always laugh. I marched in. "Sit

---

* Dame Helen Gwynne-Vaughan had been the WAAC's Chief Controller (Overseas) in the 1914 war and had made such a success of this that she was appointed to take charge of the WRAF (Women's Royal Air Force). When this was disbanded in December 1919 she returned to her scientific career. When asked to return as head of the WAAF (Women's Auxiliary Air Force) in 1939 she refused on the grounds that she was sixty, but she agreed to become Major-General of the ATS.
† Lady Maud Baillie was the eldest daughter of the ninth Duke of Devonshire. Her husband, Brigadier the Hon. G. E. M. Baillie, died on active service in 1941. She served with distinction in the ATS from 1938 until 1945.

down, Egerton. Do you play hockey?" "No, ma'am." "Did you go to school?" "No, ma'am." "Are you a Girl Guide?" "No, ma'am." They were absurd questions but I found myself answering "No" to all of them and thinking: Please let me say "Yes" to *something*.

'"Well, what are you? Are you a clerk?" "Before the war, no, ma'am. I find clerk work very difficult. I spend the whole morning typing and the whole afternoon rubbing it out." They roared with laughter.'

Nevertheless, Meg Egerton's obvious intelligence, quick responses and initiative got her through and she and the other potential officers – who included her friend Cecilia Sprot – were sent to Brighton, to be billeted at the Ocean Hotel, Saltdene. 'We were marched along the Brighton road, with little boys throwing stones at us. We were taught everything about military life and there were five lectures a week on VD.

'Then we had to give a lecture ourselves. I lectured on my yachting trip [in April 1939, Meg had returned from a five-month cruise on the Duke of Sutherland's yacht as far as Tahiti] and that went down well. Most of the day was spent on parade. As a child I used to march along the Mall with my spade on my shoulders and I loved my drill, so I was always made to take the parade. When the war ended I led the ATS contingent in the Victory Parade in Scotland, for which we marched three miles.

'I would have loved to have been an operational AT [Auxiliary Territorial] but by the time this came in it was too late for me, so I was always on general duties. We trained people, drilled them and then posted them all over the country. I took a lot of parades.'

After officer school, Cecilia Sprot was posted to Edinburgh to teach new recruits. 'Each company had about thirty-five girls who stayed for three weeks. The ones who had been Girl Guides were much easier to cope with as they were used to drilling and being given orders. The most difficult thing was trying to learn thirty-five new names every three weeks.'

In 1941 Meg Egerton was sent to Glen Cross, near Pennycuik, the Royal Scots barracks, as adjutant. 'The Royal Scots had left behind a pioneer corps to look after the camp. At the camp concert I had to sing in front of the troops – I drank a lot of pink gin to give me courage. "Here comes Salome!" they would say.

'I had only one pip and really I was far too young to be an officer. I hated that job because I wasn't qualified enough for it. We got the conscripts then, the slum dwellers from Newcastle and Glasgow, who were fairly dicey.

'The ATS were issued with sanitary towels, paid for by money provided by Lord Nuffield. But we had to teach them to be clean. At Glen Cross we had a "head hut" where their heads were deloused. With a new intake we used to have a sweepstake on how many dirty heads out of a hundred there would be. Yes, we cleaned them up but when they went home on leave they got nits again.'

Nits (head lice) were a considerable problem in the first years of the war, affecting anything between 25 and 50 per cent of every intake in the ATS and WAAF. The standard treatment was to soak the head in a mixture of coal tar, cottonseed oil and paraffin, followed by shampooing and combing with a special steel-toothed comb to remove the remaining eggs. Often two or more treatments were needed, so those girls found to have nits were isolated until cleared, eating at special tables and sleeping apart from the others. By contrast, the incidence of venereal disease in the ATS was only 5.3 per thousand at the beginning of 1943, after which it fell steadily to less than one per thousand – far lower than in civilian life.

As with the other women's services, pregnancy was the only valid reason for leaving the ATS. Sometimes it seemed that the authorities were doing everything in their power to prevent a wife being lost to the service for such a reason.

Cecilia Sprot, stationed at Bagshot Park, a senior officers' school, as adjutant, got married at Bagshot in 1943. 'My husband-to-be [Willie, later Lord, Whitelaw] was very nervous when he met all these tough ladies in red tabs. When I asked to be posted near him in the Midlands I was sent to Perth. You couldn't ask to be moved for three months, so after three months I asked again and was promptly sent to Bournemouth.

'Then I managed to leave the ATS proper and went to an ack-ack battery in Lincoln, quite near him, when I became pregnant. It wasn't very long before he went abroad, so I had a little house in the village near my home. Then he didn't really come home for a long time. He would come back for a week, and then he was sent to Palestine. Next he was going to go to Japan, so I was relieved when the atom bomb ended the war.'

Judy Impey, newly commissioned, was sent to train to work on a gun site. 'I was quite good at maths and I happened to pick up the training well. I think it was one of the first times the Government started using IQ tests and they tested two of us to find out who to send on the courses.

'I took my yellow bicycle with me. The soldiers were very naughty; they knew we'd just got commissions so they would salute us when we were on our bicycles, guessing that we'd salute back and watching us wobble. Nobody had told us we didn't have to salute back.

'In October 1942 I was sent to a gun site outside Cardiff, where I had an amazing time. It was the first time they'd had a woman officer who was supposed to do what the men did – Churchill decided there weren't enough men to go round. Our Major was an old diehard who didn't approve of women so if ever I got into trouble I would turn to the sergeants. I was nineteen and reasonably good-looking and they would do anything for you. I learned to fire a tommy-gun and a sten gun. They loved teaching you how to fire a rifle – they had to lie down close beside you, you see.

'It's the sergeants who run the Army. I was lucky and got on with them all, they were like magic uncles who put things right.

If the girls lost some of their belongings and someone high up was coming down, the missing object would miraculously be there for inspection. I was never allowed to ask where it came from. If the men didn't like someone they would slip spirits into his beer. I remember seeing the Major pass out cold one evening, which shook me.

'It was hard work. We had lots of guns, 525s, Oerlikons [both types of anti-aircraft gun] and we did fire a lot at the enemy at night. You never really knew if you'd hit them or not when a whole lot came over; the point was to stop them, to put up a barrage. They came constantly. Once we went up to Anglesey for a holiday because we hadn't had one for ages. But the minute we got there they turned us round and sent us back again because Cardiff was being bombed.

'For quite a while I was in a tin hut with five men, on the edge of the cliff, and we got on splendidly. There was one bathroom, with no lock on the door – if one was in there one sang or whatever. We got on famously for eight or nine months until the authorities from above came down and were aghast and thought the situation highly immoral. So they made me sleep by myself in a broken-down hut right on the cliff edge, with broken windows, saying it was safer. I was much more frightened there.'

One of the most difficult things for a girl on her own to deal with was the monthly period. It was a subject never admitted in mixed company, much less discussed, and most girls would suffer agonies of embarrassment in chemists' shops should a man happen to be standing near when they wished to buy sanitary towels. Tampons had not been invented and the large and clumsy packets of STs, as they were called, were difficult to smuggle unobtrusively into a barrack room or, in Judy's case, hut.

'It wasn't the easiest thing to cope with. But the war was so all-pervadingly important – it was the one important thing in life – that somehow nothing else mattered and everything else became subsidiary. So that things that might have been embarrassing in normal times you just got on with.

'I have to say that being young and attractive helped enormously. Enormously. One never lacked for companionship or someone to escort one. On the whole they behaved well. It was when someone was tight that it got difficult. You never argued with a drunk man, you got out of it some other way. I saw a lot of drunkenness on the gun site, we lived so closely with the men. We shared the same Naafi,* where the men, several hundred of them, drank at night.'

~~~

Meg Egerton found herself in an even more desolate posting. 'After a year at the camp I went back in 1942 to HQ at Craigmillar, Edinburgh, with two pips. There we had Dame Baxter Ellis,† who was a lesbian but who had a heart of gold, with her girlfriend, Tony – they were known as Dick and Tony. That was a nice job except I had terrible hay fever. We got an hour for lunch and I had to race to the hospital for injections – you ran everywhere because otherwise the war would not be won.'

After two happy years as a captain with the Headquarters Company Meg was given the choice of going to Hull or the Orkney Islands. As a good Scot she settled for the latter.

'I set off for the Orkneys in 1943 with a lunatic AT as my batwoman – one day she painted all the furniture in my hut

* Navy, Army and Air Force Institutes: an organisation that runs canteens and shops for service personnel and their families.
† Mary Baxter Ellis joined the FANYs in 1915 and served in France and Belgium until 1919. In 1932 she was appointed Commandant of the FANYs, filling this position until her retirement in 1947. In 1938 she became a member of the Advisory Council of the ATS, serving with them from 1939 to 1945, when she was appointed their Senior Controller and Deputy Director at the War Office.

Ricketts blue [a particularly lurid shade] when I was away on leave. We arrived at Stromness, in Orkney, the worst crossing in the British Isles. The troopship took five hours and everyone was sick.

'There were eleven men and me. My title was against me. Did they try and take the mickey out of me – they were absolute shits, although some without an 'h' to their name were sweet. The Officers' Mess waiter used to apologise to me for his officers. They would say filthy things to embarrass me but all I would do was laugh when they tried to shock me off the face of the earth. They resented me largely because I was a female – I was never mocked because of how I spoke – and because I wouldn't respond to a pass.

'There was nowhere to go, no club anywhere and no transport to get there. A month after an officers' club was finally formed, the war ended. On the mainland you had various comforts but in Orkney officers didn't even get a leather jerkin although the troops did and they would lend us theirs.

'It was a terrible mess, this company. All the girls were in debt. The girls were pretty tarty. There were 10,000 men on the island in two ack-ack brigades, so there were a lot of para IIs – para II in the rules meant that you were pregnant. After a bit I pulled a string and they posted me a wonderful corporal I knew and she saved my life.

'I had a company in four different camps. I had to pay them all on pay day. The Commanding Officer, always known as the Draper's Bitch – she was the wife of a draper in Aberdeen – wore high heels with her uniform and was completely idiotic. Invariably she would send for me on days when there was no transport so I had to walk the three miles there and back to see her.

'One evening we heard a girl screaming in one of the huts. I asked what was wrong and was told: "I think she's got constipation – chronic constipation." She was taken to hospital, where all the doctors were drunk but not too drunk to say:

"Chronic constipation my foot, she's having a baby." And she had it in five minutes flat.

'I heard that one girl in one of my huts was pregnant and I had to find out – but how? It was often difficult to tell if a girl was pregnant as they had such funny shapes anyway, and big bottoms, and the jacket stood out rather. And I couldn't just accuse her or she might have me up for libel. So I started by asking: "Are you feeling all right?" "Yes, ma'am," she said. "Well, I don't think you look all right," I said. "I'm not happy about you and I'd like you to see the doctor." Then she burst into tears and it all came out – she was seven months pregnant. So of course I took a lot of trouble getting her fixed up.

'My worst moment was when I was asked by one of the grandees in Orkney to inspect a body of women in Kirkwall on a day well ahead. It was a life of such monotony that the days meant nothing. I was working away in this dark, freezing hut – it got dark at three in the afternoon – when the telephone went. "Weren't you coming to inspect us?" said a voice. I'd clean forgotten. I nearly died. It was too late to do anything about it as Kirkwall was twenty miles away."

Pregnancies also caused headaches for Judy Impey at her ack-ack station near Cardiff. 'As the only ATS officer I had to deal with the ones who got sent home pregnant – yet I still didn't know *how* you became pregnant. I was far younger than most of them and I literally had no idea. I had lots of boyfriends and I knew that if one of them wanted to go farther than the usual kiss and cuddle, particularly below the belt, instinct said no. But that's all I knew. I don't think I really found out about the facts of life until I got married.'

The innocence of the pre-war debutante's upbringing also enveloped Denise Woosnam. 'It was a great shock to find myself in a position of responsibility. I didn't find it easy giving orders and I agonised over decisions but I had wonderful older, nanny-like women in my company who helped greatly. All sorts of sex offences were reported and I didn't know what they were.

Luckily, one was shielded from them and others worked out the punishments.'

Denise was sent to work at an ack-ack station near Uxbridge, arriving there in September 1940 just as the Battle of Britain was beginning. It was a posting for which she had applied as her fiancé, Peter Pease, was a fighter pilot posted to Old Sarum (he flew, almost without respite, until 15 September when, with many others, he was killed on what became known as Battle of Britain Day).

That summer, German aircraft were constantly overhead, with sirens wailing their warning. Denise arrived at her new billet in the local rectory at Vange to find a note left in the hall to greet her: 'Dear Miss Woosnam, we are in the Village Shelter. Please join us, unless you don't mind being left alone. There is a gun in your room.' She remained in the house, more frightened of a bat that flew in through the window than of any bomb.

It was a traumatic posting. Denise saw people killed every day. But she felt real, gut-wrenching terror only once. 'We had to take the transport – the army lorries and so forth – out of garages and hangars and disperse it to prevent it being bombed. I was out once on my own when there was massive ack-ack fire and the sky was filled with white puffs, which I mistook for parachutes from the mass of German planes above me. I thought: Oh boy, I've had it – there were so many of them. That was my introduction to ack-ack fire.'

Ursie Barclay, who had originally joined the ATS in 1939 because she was told to do so by her mother, and was now running her own company, began as a storewoman and clerk in the company offices. 'Then my mother sent me to the Sergeants' Mess to be a waitress. One day she found me sitting down having tea with the sergeants instead of waiting on them so she took me away quick – she must have thought: "She's obviously going to fall in love with a sergeant", and she wasn't having *that*. So I was made clerk to one of the officers.

'Life went on like that for the first eighteen months of the war. When I was twenty I went up to Craigmillar to learn to be an officer. I remember being shown to my room where there were three mattress squares,* one on top of the other. "That's how you arrange your biscuits [mattress squares]," I was told. Then I had to lay out my kit. I got into such trouble with my kit – living at home I'd never heard of biscuits, never been shown how to lay out ATS kit.'

After the month-long Officers' Training Course came several postings, including one at Shoeburyness on the Essex coast, measuring gun trajectories ('the other girls were all extremely clever'). At twenty-one, the earliest age at which, with parental permission, it was possible to go overseas, Ursie, with her mother's reluctant agreement, set sail on a troopship for Italy in mid-1942.

'Before we went we were given a lecture by Lady Maud Baillie, in her kilt and uniform jacket. "If you get asked out to dinner by twelve young men on the same night when you get wherever you are going," she said, "it's not because you are popular. It's because you're scarce."'

It was a roundabout route as the troopship was delivering and picking up service passengers from a number of destinations.

'We had to go via Iran and with submarines in the Mediterranean it took us three weeks to get to Iran. There we met some lovely young men going back to the desert. When we had to get on a train to Cairo they said – gallantly, we thought then – "You have the padded seats and we'll sleep on the wooden ones." So we had the padded seats and were bitten to such distraction by the bugs that we had to sleep in the corridor.

'The train kept stopping and all along the line there were orange trees, with ripe fruit, and we kept getting out and picking oranges all the way to Algiers. None of us had seen an orange for ages.

'In Italy the older ones would try it on. They had come

---

* Laid in a line, they formed a mattress.

straight from the desert into headquarters, perhaps not having seen their wives for three years, but I don't think there were any divorces because of us.

'I was sent to Eisenhower's headquarters – all the generals, including Alexander, were there. I was a Staff Captain and kept the Order of Battle for the REME [Royal Electrical and Mechanical Engineers] General – I moved the little flags about. After about three months Rome fell and we flew to Naples in Dakotas that took off one after another, like trains. You sat in hollow seats all down the sides, facing each other.

'We were stationed at Caserta Palace. We had lovely parties there – that's where I met my husband. This glamorous young man – I learned later he'd been brought in by submarine – asked me: "Could you possibly tell me the way to General Alexander's office?" I looked at him and said: "Better than that – I can take you."'

Chapter 8

Fun in Wartime

'Boyfriends were more important than bombs'

However hard and austere the times, the young and single managed to have fun. Girls who a few months earlier had dropped evening dresses on to the floor when they returned from balls at 3.00 a.m., knowing that a servant would later pick them up, mend anything torn, deal with stains and return them fresh to a cupboard, and that breakfast would be served at a civilised hour in the morning in the comfort of luxurious surroundings, now caught crowded, smelly Underground trains in the uniforms they had worn all day to dance for a few hours in a basement nightclub.

For those who had to bring up small children during the war, life was, by contrast, frequently difficult and usually drab. While for single girls, particularly those in the services, surrounded by other single people of roughly the same age, it might often be dangerous but was full of vivid, exciting and enjoyable moments, the highlight of many a young mother's day was when she was sent a few eggs by an aunt living in the country or managed to procure a piece of (unrationed) offal to supplement the meat ration. For those in the country – where most mothers tried to take their children in the Blitz – petrol rationing meant that social life was restricted to those within bicycling distance.

'It's so much easier to have a war when you're not married,' said Diana Quilter. 'I had the time of my life but my married sister moved from horrible cottage to horrible cottage following her husband in the Army. And after Dunkirk he never returned to front-line fighting.'

Those who had employed servants before the war (which basically meant everyone who could afford them) soon saw them disappear, either through volunteering or, a little later, through conscription, leaving behind only those too old for either. By September 1940 the rich MP and diarist Henry 'Chips' Channon was noting that his 'depleted staff' was six instead of its former fifteen. Many, too, was the large country household, formerly staffed by nine or ten, maintained throughout the war by two elderly women (the mistress of the house and Nanny, who had according to custom stayed on after the children had left home), with possibly a daily help who spared several hours from looking after her own husband and children.

In London, the rich had a simpler option. Some simply closed their houses and lived in one of the large hotels where, cared for by the hotel staff, often surrounded by their own furniture and entertaining frequently, life continued as nearly as possible as they had formerly known it, dining, dancing and drinking champagne. Others appeared in their favourite hotel after their own houses had been bombed – as happened to several of the mansions in Belgrave Square – or came in after fire-watching to change for one of the large and merry dinner parties now held there.

The Dorchester, supposedly London's most impregnable building thanks to its construction of reinforced concrete, had a loyal coterie, as did Claridge's, the Ritz and the Savoy. With all meals limited to three courses at a cost of no more than five shillings by Government decree, lunches and dinners at these establishments were little more expensive than anywhere else. As Chips Channon pointed out in his diary: 'Ritzes always thrive in wartime, as we are all cookless. Also in wartime the herd instinct rises ...'

Countless others used these grand hotels as meeting-places,

particularly the Ritz with its central position in Piccadilly. As the war drew on, its downstairs bar became so much the unofficial rendezvous for homosexuals that eventually the Brigade of Guards put a ban on it for their officers.

Despite the bombs, London hummed. With petrol rationed, and friends scattered around the country or abroad, the capital was a magnet. For anyone in the armed services with enough leave to reach it, London was the place to make for, offering the best chance of seeing friends. The bars of the big hotels became almost like clubs: young officers, unexpectedly home on leave, would be certain of finding people they knew there.

Few of those who headed for the metropolis worried about anything as trivial as missing a night's sleep, often coming off duty late, travelling to London, dancing all night and then returning for duty the following morning. 'On London leave days I'd come up from Hamble, on the Solent, where I was stationed, and change into a long dress at my father's flat, to be taken out to dinner and a nightclub,' said Diana Barnato.

'In the early hours of dawn it would be back to the flat, change back into uniform and taxi to Waterloo for the 0420 train back to Eastleigh, the nearest station to Hamble – I had a weekly arrangement with two brothers from the Hyde Park Corner taxi rank to pick me up. Whatever was going on, from bombs to shrapnel pouring down, one of the brothers would always be there, sitting in his tin hat in his taxi.'

There were certain recognised meeting places, certain preferred restaurants and above all certain favourite nightclubs. The most popular of these was the 400, which had been opened in 1935 in the cellars next door to the Alhambra Theatre in Leicester Square. Dark, glamorous and intimate, its walls were covered with red silk and lined with deep red plush banquettes, red velvet curtains hung in draped folds down to the wine-red carpet, gilded standard lamps threw soft light upwards and its tables were lit only by one small candle. Members kept their own bottles of gin or whisky at the club, marked to the level

to which they had drunk when they left (and scrupulously untouched on their return, be it after five days or five years).*
It was run by the immensely efficient and popular Luigi Rossi, and was packed every night with officers and their girlfriends, swaying dreamily cheek to cheek on its small, dark, reflective dance floor. Nothing put them off – neither the difficulties of getting there nor the air raids. As Sarah Norton put it: 'Boyfriends were more important than bombs'.

Some restaurants, like the Mirabelle and the Savoy, also offered dancing but most tended to close early, especially with the rapidly escalating shortage of staff (one restaurateur, the owner of the White Tower in Percy Street, who lost his whole staff, allegedly kept up appearances by shouting orders down the lift shaft, running down to cook the dinner, running up again and ordering the food to be sent up, then hauling it up himself). Nightclubs, on the other hand, boomed. Immensely popular, they stayed open until dawn, couples in uniform trancelike and almost stationary in each other's arms as they put in a last request for 'Let there be love'.

'I went up to London every other weekend, straight to nightclubs and then back by train,' said Val Canning. 'Very often we were stuck in tunnels and I'd miss the last bus and have to walk the four miles back from Guildford. But I was never worried by this – there were never any nasty people about then.'

As a nurse, Penny Woosnam got some evenings off. 'When I wanted to go to the 400 I took a train at night – our hospital was about twelve miles away. If there was a raid all the lights would go out and one would be stopped for about an hour, probably in the middle of a field. Of course there was no way of letting one's escort know – he just had to wait hopefully.'

Suzanne Irwin used to get to London by hitching a lift. 'We'd stand on the main road that went through Bagshot, outside a

---

* When it closed (to become a discotheque) in 1965, three hundred members still had bottles there, some of many years standing.

pub called the Jolly Farmer. Then we'd go to the 400 or the
Florida. We were in the ATS by then but off duty we could
wear our FANY uniforms, which were much nicer. Our ATS
uniforms were rather nasty – the jacket, the hat and those thick
lisle stockings. FANYs had webbing ties, suede shoes, a Sam
Browne belt and a much nicer hat and shirt.'

The comforting presence of Rossi, who ran the club with
warmth, friendliness and supreme tact, made everyone feel
secure.

'We always felt safe in the 400, as we saw all our friends,'
said Betty Grenfell (née Shaughnessy). 'The minute the siren
went we would dive into Leicester Square Underground station
where everyone was sitting with their blue tin teapots. "Oh,
hello Miss, come and have a cup of tea," they'd say. There was
such a sense of camaraderie.' Everyone joined in the bursts of
song: 'Roll out the Barrel', 'Run, rabbit, run' or – most popular
of all – 'Hitler has only got one ball, the other is in the Leeds
Town Hall', sung to the tune of 'Colonel Bogey'.

Air raids did not stop the nightly excursions of those in search
of fun; in fact, the bombs often seemed more of a threat once
home again. 'One of the lodgings I had was down a little cul-
de-sac at the corner of Cadogan Square,' said Anne Douglas-
Scott-Montagu, a nurse. 'I had a tiny little narrow room with a
huge plate glass window and the thought of those windows
shattering and cutting me up really worried me. My mother
lent me some enormous tins of Ronuk polish, so I put the bed
on top of them, put an extra mattress on top of it and slept for
months on end on another mattress on the floor under the bed.
I reckoned that if the glass blew in or the ceiling came down I
was protected.

'I loved being there, though, as I led a very gay life. It was
always nightclubs. Somebody would come back on leave and
say "What about dinner tonight?" The 400 was the great place,
with Ted Heath and his band, also the Florida. And you certainly wore a long dress if you went out to a party.' So entrenched

was the (upper class) custom of changing for dinner – not only if you were dining out or going to a nightclub – that it persisted well into the war.

The importance of the Ritz as a rendezvous was so well known that the few, intermittent, buses running along Piccadilly would pull up opposite it, although it was not an official bus stop. The conductors would speed the girls who sprang off on their way with a cheery 'Have a good time, darling'.

Another great meeting place was the Berkeley Hotel* – either at its entrance or in the bar, both invariably packed with uniformed officers and their girlfriends. 'We were not allowed to leave barracks other than in uniform,' said ATS girl Suzanne Irwin, 'so we had to go to nightclubs in our uniforms. I remember once in Edinburgh putting on an evening dress, with its skirt tucked up, and my greatcoat over the top to hide it. Because I was "other ranks" I had to report to the sergeant before leaving and she said: "Irwin, undo your coat." So I had to, and down fell the skirt of my evening dress. That was the end of my evening out as I was punished by being confined to barracks for twenty-four hours.'

Pre-war debutantes had long dresses left over from their Seasons, which could be lent or borrowed to give variety, while mothers confined to the country often handed theirs over to daughters who could make use of them. As the war progressed and life became tougher, the chance to climb into a pretty dress and put on a pair of hoarded nylons was morale-boosting after long days in uniform, as was anything that smacked of frivolity and femininity, such as Elizabeth Arden's velvet-covered gas-mask cases which had a little silk-lined pocket for cosmetics on top. (The rule that gas masks were to be carried at all times was not always followed: some girls, like Sarah Norton, left theirs gathering dust under the beds, using the case for purse, make-up and the obligatory identity card.)

---

* Then on the corner of Piccadilly and Berkeley Street.

Fiona Colquhoun, as a FANY who drove around London, spent much of her time enabling others to enjoy themselves. 'A lot of smooching went on in the back of my car. I used to have to take officers and their girlfriends out to dinner and then when I picked them up and drove them home there was smooching in the back. If a doodlebug had landed there was more smooching still. One man always started at a certain roundabout, regular as clockwork. I never found out what it was about it. They never asked me out – I don't think they were allowed to. Also, being married, I went straight home. But we used to be given drinks at the Ritz bar if we'd driven an officer anywhere. We got them half-price because we were in khaki.'

The main hazards of London life were bombs and the blackout. Between 7 September 1940, when a force of around thirty-five German bombers, escorted by six hundred fighters, advanced on a twenty-mile front along the Thames and turned London's Docklands into an inferno, and the end of November 1940, three million London houses were destroyed or damaged. By the time the main Blitz ended in May 1941, one in six Londoners had been made homeless (in all, there were 60,595 civilian casualties in the UK as a direct result of enemy action).

With bombs raining down, few serious repairs began until 1943, so that anyone out at night on the pitch-dark roads and pavements might not only lose their way but encounter unexpected obstacles. Sandbags filled doorways; piles of rubble, invisible in the blackout unless someone had dabbed a splash of white paint on them, made sudden hazards on pavements. The railings which had edged parks and squares and which might have served as guides had been melted down. Walking through Hyde Park, one might encounter a flock of sheep, ghostly white in the darkness (watching them being sheared was a popular summer spectacle). Sometimes there was a sudden smell of gas

(gas pipes broke under the impact of bombs, whereas the more flexible electricity cables often survived). Worst of all, after a heavy raid when the emergency services were fully stretched, was the possibility of stepping on a dead body. Often the air was thick with dust, powdered plaster and debris, so that oncoming pedestrians made their presence known by continual coughing. All was made worse by the thick fogs that were a feature of pre-war and wartime London winters.

The blackout, introduced on 1 September 1939, was at first so severe that road casualties doubled and 20 per cent of the population damaged themselves in one way or another – tripping over kerbs, stumbling into the path of an oncoming car or, in the country, falling into ditches or cutting themselves on barbed wire. Modification was essential: soon Council workers were painting white bands round lamp posts and other obstacles and picking out kerbs and crossings in white; large white spots were painted on the backs of buses, policemen wore white gauntlet gloves and men were encouraged to sport white handkerchiefs in their breast pockets.

To counter the gas attacks, of which everyone lived in fear, the tops of pillar boxes were painted with yellow gas-detecting paint (various qualified chemists had been recruited into Gas Identification Squads) and Air Raid Wardens were issued with special gas masks with a speaking box and a charcoal filter that soaked up poisons such as mustard gas. All vehicle lights were of course kept to a minimum, with brown paper or some other shielding material pasted over headlights with only a narrow cross cut in it to allow some light to escape, so that traffic crawled.

A torch was a regular item of personal equipment. Sarah Norton's friend and flatmate Osla Benning, as invincibly ignorant on sexual matters as Sarah herself, caused a mild sensation in a nightclub when she complained loudly that it was very inconsiderate of her boyfriend always to carry his torch in his pocket as it was so uncomfortable when dancing. ("Grow up!

That's an erection," hissed an older woman near by. But Osla was still none the wiser.)

'I had a very gay life socially but it was quite dangerous walking about in the blackout,' said Diana Quilter, stationed at Trent Park in Hertfordshire. 'I'd been lent a little house in Grosvenor Cottages for the nights when I wasn't on duty in my mobile canteen in the East End. I'd get as far as Sloane Square by Underground. If I was unlucky, the alert would already have gone and I would have to stay in the station but if I was lucky I could run and join my friend Caroline and drink port and lemon under the kitchen table.'

Bombs were everywhere, but the drone of German bombers overhead and the sound of British anti-aircraft guns did not stop the chatter and laughter in London restaurants. People became adept at distinguishing between different types of bombs – the thud of incendiaries (which left curtains motionless) and the crump of high explosive, when windows rattled, or shattered, and curtains blew inwards.

'I don't think it occurred to one to be frightened,' said Suzanne Irwin. 'Once there was an air raid while we were standing in line in Leicester Square – queuing to get in to the 400, it was so popular. But we didn't think of giving up our places.'

When Pamela Joyce had her twenty-first birthday party at the Berkeley Hotel in March 1943 bombs were falling all around. 'My parents were worried sick but we were enjoying the delicious dinner and dancing merrily. I suppose it was being young but we were quite impervious to it.'

Some girls were in nightclubs when they took a direct hit. On the brilliant moonlit night of Saturday 8 March, 1941, London had its heaviest air attack for some weeks. At the Café de Paris, busier than ever with a Saturday-night crowd, Val Canning and her escort were sitting on the gallery floor looking down at the dancers circling below them to the strains of 'Oh, Johnny', played by the famous Snakehips Johnson and his band, and trying to spot friends.

Suddenly, at 9.40 p.m., a bomb crashed through the roof of the building, dropping between the two staircases straight on to the band below. Johnson and the entire band were killed instantly. All but one of the lights went out and the restaurant was filled with dust and smoke. People searched for their partners with torches, cigarette lighters and matches. The cabaret girls, sitting in their make-up room waiting to be called, were some of the few who escaped unscathed – altogether thirty-four people were killed and a further eighty taken to hospital injured.

Val and her partner, horrified, stared at the bodies lying below them. 'I saw men running about and bending over the dead and wounded. At first I thought they were feeling for a heartbeat but they'd come in from the street and were taking their wallets and money.'

Sarah Norton recalled being really frightened only once – that same night. 'An air raid started just after we arrived at the Mirabelle. We had dinner there and then, as all seemed quiet, we left.' They emerged into a silent Curzon Street, found one of the few taxis braving the bombs, and set off for the 400. On the way they spotted an incendiary bomb, stopped the taxi, and helped firemen put it out with a bucket of sand on the pavement.

'That bomb actually saved our lives,' said Sarah. 'Stopping for it meant we just missed the devastating one that landed on the Café de Paris [close to Leicester Square]. It was terrible, but we felt we shouldn't let ourselves be daunted by anything the enemy did and that we had to continue. So, feeling very shaken, we went on to the 400.

'While we were dancing another raid started and we soon had to stop – it was like trying to balance on a ship's deck in a storm. Sitting down was almost as difficult as the seats rose up and then crashed down again as bombs fell. The bottles and glasses fell off people's tables and rats came out from behind the red curtains round the walls. By this time I was motionless with terror – I couldn't eat, speak, drink or smoke. It seemed to go on for ages and then suddenly there was an enormous explosion right beside us and an Air Raid Warden staggered in to say that the whole building was on fire and we must leave.

'Outside, the pavement was so hot that it scorched through the thin soles of my shoes and the broken glass cut me round the ankles. Suddenly it was quiet again and all you could hear was the roar of burning buildings and the crackling of smaller fires.'

Even on one of wartime's cheapest, most serene joys, a quiet country walk, danger from the skies could intrude. 'We saw so many German parachutists coming down during the Battle of Britain and the raids that at one time I wasn't allowed to walk the dog alone in case there was a German parachutist hiding in the bracken,' said Mary Pollock, then based at the family cottage in Surrey. Sarah Norton, whose mother had rented a cottage in nearby Leatherhead, in the notorious Bomb Alley that formed the flight path of the German bombers heading for London after they had crossed the Channel – and on which they often jettisoned their bombs when returning to lighten their load and save fuel – nearly lost her life one autumn day in 1940 when out for a walk on the Downs.

A spectacular dogfight had begun above her, with planes weaving about in tight circles, guns blazing and engines screaming. 'At one point one flew down towards me and to my horror I saw the black swastika painted on its side. It was a Messerschmitt and the pilot had his guns aimed at me! Shaking, I ran for the nearest clump of trees and threw myself into a pile of leaves. I could hear the bullets plopping all round me. It was then I began to hate the Germans.'

There were, of course, plenty of bombs elsewhere to destroy the enjoyment of a 48-hour pass. A cousin of Lady Moyra Ponsonby, in the RAF, came down to their grand and comfortable house, Stansted, for a rest one weekend ('one way and another, my parents had servants all through the war'), five miles from Portsmouth as the Messerschmitt flew. The city was then under heavy air attack, and departing bombers would jettison their bombs as they fled (a hundred fell on the estate altogether), possibly believing that the size of the house meant it was of military importance.

At six that evening there was a dogfight above Stansted and bombs fell in succession all down the two-mile drive, culminating in the bomber itself crashing near by. Moyra went up on the roof to see if an incendiary bomb had fallen and when she came down found that her cousin had gone to find the crashed German plane.

'He tore across the former Sussex cricket ground by the front of the house and just as he got close to the plane it blew up. He was carried back in and put on a bed until an ambulance came for him. He was admitted to my hospital, where I saw him. A lump of metal had perforated his bowel in several places and he died two days later. After that people would say: "I'll come and stay if I'm feeling brave".'

Another who came was Jock Colville,* taken by Moyra to look at the wreck of the crashed Ju.88 – he had told her, half seriously, that his motive for coming to stay was to see one of the great aerial battles that so often took place above the house. His diary for Sunday 18 August, 1940 records:

'... we were sitting on the terrace looking towards Thorney Island with the Portsmouth balloons just visible over the trees to our right ... Then to our left, from the direction of Chichester and Tangmere, came the roar of engines and the noise of machine-gun fire. "There they are!" exclaimed Moyra and, shading our eyes to escape the glare of this August day, we saw not far from us about twenty machines engaged in a fight. Soon a German bomber came hurtling down with smoke pouring

---

* John (later Sir John) Colville, always known as Jock, was Assistant Private Secretary to the Prime Minister, Winston Churchill, in 1940–41 and 1943–45. After the war he became private secretary to Princess Elizabeth before she became Queen and in 1948 he married Lady Margaret Egerton. He later became known for his books and diaries.

from its tail and we lost sight of it behind the trees. A parachute opened and sank gracefully through the whirling fighters and bombers. Out of the mêlée came a dive-bomber, hovered like a bird of prey, and then sped steeply down on Thorney Island. There were vast explosions as another and another followed and my attention was diverted from the fight as clouds of smoke rose from the burning hangars of Thorney aerodrome. In all, the battle only lasted about two minutes ... presently, standing on the terrace balustrade, I saw four of the barrage balloons at Portsmouth collapse in flames.' After tea he and Moyra played tennis until she was summoned to deal with casualties at the Royal West Sussex Hospital in Chichester.

It was this combination of the deadly struggle above and ordinary, sometimes frivolous life on the ground that often produced an effect of the surreal. 'We were sitting on the terrace at Mereworth,* having tea one sunny afternoon, with the butler in white gloves serving us,' said Lorna Harmsworth. 'And above us a dogfight was raging.'

~~⌒

The luxury of a few hours off and the heightened emotions of war made even the simplest pleasures seem meaningful and exotic. One of these was the lunch-hour concerts at the National Gallery.

When war broke out the Gallery's priceless contents had to be stored well way from bombs in the right atmospheric conditions. Music, fortunately, could still be enjoyed. When the (British-born) Dame Myra Hess, an acclaimed concert pianist who was touring America when war broke out, heard that all live music performances had been stopped, she cut short her tour and returned to England to inaugurate the highly popular series of lunch-time concerts. Dame Myra, who knew everyone

---

* Mereworth Castle in Kent, home of Esmond Harmsworth.

Diana Quilter worked as a censor in Gibraltar before joining the FANYs in the late summer of 1940.

Lavinia Holland-Hibbert follows just behind Princess Mary, the sister of George V and ATS Commandant-in-Chief, as she inspects some ATS military police trainees of South-Eastern Command in December 1942.

Denise Woosnam, who became an ATS officer, recruited a company of ATS from Chester, near her family's home.

LEFT: Judy Impey, from an Army family, joined the ATS in 1942 and became one of its youngest officers. RIGHT: Penny Woosnam joined the Red Cross in 1938 ('all I ever wanted to do was sew or be a nurse'). Her first serious wartime job was as a VAD in Chatham.

ABOVE LEFT: Suzanne Irwin, who had joined the FANYs in 1937, was on her way to the Portree Balls in Scotland in September 1939 when she was called up. ABOVE RIGHT: FANY Lady Barbara Legge met her Polish officer husband in Italy in 1944. BELOW: Nursing was a popular choice for many debs. Lady Moyra Ponsonby, here on ward duty, became a VAD in 1938, then nursed at the Westminster Hospital.

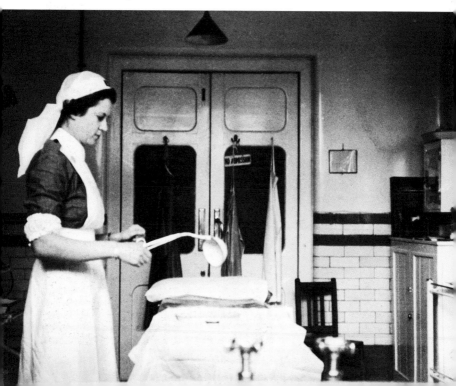

Lavinia Holland-Hibbert shows her squad of ATS how to immobilise a vehicle.

Fanny Gore Browne joined the WRNS in January 1942, and was commissioned two years later, three weeks before her 21st birthday.

Lady Elizabeth Scott in February 1945. She joined the WRNS in 1942 and during the autumn of 1943 she worked as a decoder on the Cunard liner *Mauretania* (then a troopship). She was commissioned in 1944.

COUNTRY LIFE

Vol. XCVII. No. 2510   FEBRUARY 23, 1945

LADY ELIZABETH SCOTT

Lady Elizabeth Scott, the elder daughter of the Duke and Duchess of Buccleuch, who is now a cypher officer, joined the W.R.N.S. in March, 1942, and was a rating until August, 1944, when she received her commission. For some months Lady Elizabeth served as a coder in a troopship crossing the Atlantic

Below: In the week before VE-Day, Sheila Parish, serving in the FANYs, provided the last wartime alternative to *Country Life*'s regular 'girls in pearls'.

Opposite page TOP LEFT: Daughter of an Admiral of the Fleet, Daphne Brock inevitably became a Wren. Despite her insubordination in her first week (refusing to eat her breakfast porridge) she received accelerated promotion and was quickly commissioned. TOP RIGHT: Daphne Brock (sitting at the front, on the right) in Malta, 1944, with other Wren officers. BOTTOM: Frances Campbell-Preston (back row, right), whose husband was a prisoner of war and who lived with her mother-in-law on the west coast of Scotland, became an Immobile Wren stationed at Oban.

COUNTRY LIFE

Vol. XCVII. No. 2520   MAY 4, 1945

MISS SHEILA PARISH

Miss Parish is the second daughter of the late Lieutenant-Colonel Francis W. Parish, The King's Royal Rifle Corps, and Mrs. Parish, of Crowcombe Barton, Taunton, Somerset, and is a great-granddaughter of Mr. Gladstone. She is serving in the F.A.N.Y.

Diana Barnato, here with her dog 'Peanut', was one of the 'Attagirls' – ferry-pilots flying for the Air Transport Auxiliary.

who was anyone in the musical world, persuaded other performers to appear for a mere pittance, while herself playing at a great many of these concerts without a fee. 'She looked like a Wagnerian soprano or a harpist with her flowing sleeves, large arms that seemed mighty but were used for dainty precision work, agreeable feathery runs, delicate attacks on the piano nerve centres,' wrote one admiring concert-goer.* 'I never hear "Jesu, Joy of Man's Desiring" without thinking of her,' recalled Joan Stafford King-Harman. 'You always went away feeling better.' The admission fee was only a shilling and there was a strict rule that no sandwiches could be eaten during performances. Londoners flocked to them, and by the autumn of 1944 more than 1,300 of these lunchtime concerts had taken place.

Yet there was the ever-present possibility of horror. Pamela Joyce, when working in London at the Admiralty's Meteorological Department in Lansdowne Row, off Berkeley Square, would go down to the National Gallery in her lunch hour, catching a bus to Trafalgar Square at Green Park. 'One day we were whistling round Eros in Piccadilly Circus when a bomb fell on the Regent's Palace Hotel. The bus swung and swerved but nothing more because its momentum carried it on and its rubber wheels clung to the road, and the wire mesh all over the inside of its windows protected us. But there were people lying everywhere, all over the road, because the glass in all the shops had blown out and sliced into them. And when I came back after lunch, there they still were, all these dead people lying across the road.'

Sometimes the sight of a devastated house was almost as bad. 'We always came up to London on days off,' said Joan Stafford King-Harman. 'I remember once going to see a friend and when I got to her house it was nothing but a heap of rubble. I was panic-stricken until I found that mercifully she and her mother

* Dawn Powell, in her diary for 1939.

had been sleeping somewhere else that night – she hadn't been able to get in touch with me.'

All communication was difficult even in peacetime. There were often lengthy telephone delays at peak times and in wartime, with most telephone lines kept busy in the business of the war and fewer operators than before, telephoning was more difficult still. 'If you had a date in London and the car wouldn't start you couldn't ring up and say: "I'll be late".' It was the same if a lift by car was slow in coming or if a train was delayed. All three were common occurrences.

'We'd always go to London on our days off,' said Jean Campbell-Harris, who worked at Bletchley Park (see Chapter 12). 'After night shift a group of us would go up in the morning and have lunch at Claridge's – none of us drank and as no restaurant was allowed to charge more than five shillings, we could just about afford it. We got paid three pounds a week and thirty shillings (half) went on your billet. We'd spend the afternoon at Keith Prowse at the bottom of Bond Street, listening to gramophone records – all my money went on them, mostly Charles Trenet.

'There was one called "J'ai ta main dans ma main" and whenever I used to arrive at my favourite restaurant the band leader would play it when I walked in. We'd have rung up friends before coming, then I'd change into a dress in my parents' flat and then we went on to nightclubs, generally the 400 but sometimes the Embassy. Not being in uniform, I needed clothes and my mother was wonderful in giving me coupons.* Also I had a friend, Lady Jean Graham, who was the same size as me so we would swap clothes for variety.

'One evening when I went to the 400 one of my brothers was at one table with a girl, another brother and his girl at another table, then me and a boyfriend and then, at the fourth, my

---

* Clothes were rationed from 1 June 1941, each (new) garment being worth a set number of clothing coupons, issued annually.

father with a girlfriend. We were so cross with my father for this that we ignored the people we were with and just sat and glowered at him until he left. Later, one brother, who was in the Horse Guards, liberated the family of Rossi, who ran the 400, in the invasion of Italy. After that he was never allowed to pay another bill there.'

For girls in the services, money was often a problem but seldom insuperable. 'I had fifteen shillings pay a fortnight,' said Fanny Gore Browne. 'We were all short of money. We got a set number of free travel warrants but otherwise we often hitch-hiked. We seldom had trouble, though a couple of times there was a try-on.

'We all learned to drink beer because it was cheaper. I joined the Players Theatre Club,* and used to go there with boyfriends. It was very good value as you got something cheap on a plate.'

Hitch-hiking was practically *de rigueur* – if only because few young men and women in the armed forces could afford rail fares if the sudden chance of a day or two's pass came up. With the whole country anxious to help them, and with all drivers aware that every precious drop of petrol might have been bought with the life of a merchant seaman, travelling with a full car became a patriotic duty and – as far as female safety was concerned – a uniform rendered them almost as inviolable as a nun's habit.

'As long as I had my nurse's uniform on I'd hitch,' said Anne Douglas-Scott-Montagu. 'I'd go to Osterley Park station, up to the main road, cross it to get to the right side and wait until I saw a reasonable-looking car. I never had any trouble at all, of any description. My parents were quite happy about my doing this. But I wouldn't have done it without my uniform.'

Her uniform also served her well for an extraordinary and

---

* This was tucked away under the arches in Villiers Street behind London's Charing Cross Station. The actor Leonard Sachs was the Master of Ceremonies.

unofficial jaunt on the Saturday before D-Day. 'I had a friend whom I knew quite well on the aerodrome at Beaulieu. I'd come down to Brockenhurst station and he said he'd meet me and take me up in an aeroplane. "Be sure and wear your uniform," he told me. We got into this little Cessna, which was used for staff people, and flew off, all quite openly.

'We flew parallel with the sea, the whole way from Lymington airport towards Southampton. And there we saw the D-Day fleet. It was a most unbelievable sight. I can see it now – the whole of the Solent was packed with ships like sardines – if you had dropped a stone you could hardly have avoided hitting a ship. Naval ships, transports, every sort you could think of. We flew round in a circle and then flew back. How we were allowed to go up I can't imagine but nobody objected and we never heard anything about it.'

Pilots were often a law unto themselves. Sarah Norton, staying with her grandmother in East Lothian during the early part of the war, acted as pony despatch rider to the village two miles away, armed with a 410 shotgun to repel any airborne raiders ('the idea of a seventeen-year-old girl bringing down a Heinkel with a rabbit gun did not seem strange at the time'). The young Hurricane pilots stationed on the airfield at the other side of her grandmother's woods, who often came to dinner, would invariably fly low and drop their thank-you letters, weighted down with two pennies, on the front lawn.

~

Though a surprisingly high percentage of trains ran on time, the longer the journey the greater the chance of disruption. As the war progressed, the deep fatigue felt by so many showed on these journeys, where both civilian and service men and women fell asleep as soon as they sat down. Often, trains were so crowded that the only option was to stand in corridors that were too packed for reading or smoking to be possible ('at least,' said

Sarah, 'this meant that falling over was equally impossible'). For Joan Stafford King-Harman, the occasional visits back to her home in Ireland were difficult and, once there, the contrast with conditions in England were a sharp reminder of what life had once been like.

'We had horrible journeys. First there was the train from Euston to Holyhead, in the blackout and with carriages and corridors crammed. Everyone was terribly friendly and handed round whatever food they'd brought. A soldier would go to sleep on your neck and you'd go to sleep on the next person. You never knew when the train would halt miles from anywhere because of an air raid.

'As soon as you got on to the mail boat you were given your lifejacket, which you had to wear the whole time. The ship was blacked out too. We usually got a cabin and tried to get some sleep but it was pretty noisy as they'd be potting away at mines every few minutes. Before you left the cabin to disembark you knew you were in Ireland by the smell of turf wafting over, which the Irish were using for fuel as they were so short of coal. When you came on deck the blazing lights were extraordinary after the blackout.

'The food was very good and, after England, so rich, with lashings of butter and cream and meat and game that we'd get "Irish tummy" – one's stomach was so used to wartime rations that one would quite often get violently sick.

'After England the lavishness seemed extraordinary. I remember going down to the stables one day and seeing that the foals were being given eggs with their feed. I gasped and said: "We're only getting one egg a month!" My mother simply said: "Oh, eggs are very good for their coats." But she'd send us things over – eggs and tins of Irish spiced beef packed in wooden boxes and sometimes game after a shoot. You could put a brace of snipe in a bag with a label round its neck, send it off that evening and it would arrive in London the next morning.'

Wartime shifts were usually long. Diana Lyttelton, working

at the Air Ministry, did two twelve-hour days, followed by two twelve-hour nights, followed by two days off. 'So after the second night, you didn't bother to go to bed, you just staggered home. I would go back to Eton [where her father was a housemaster] on the Green Line bus, so tired that I remember falling asleep on the drawing-room carpet one afternoon.'

Esme Harmsworth, not yet called up, stuck like everyone else to pre-war sartorial habits. Everyone – old, young, rich, poor, male or female – still wore hats. Esme and her friends went out to dinner in long evening dresses and high-heeled shoes, adding a stylish note to the sea of uniforms around them. 'One young man took me to the Mirabelle in Curzon Street and while we were there the bombing started. "We can't stay here," he said, "it's got a glass roof. We'd better go to the ballroom at the Mayfair [near by in Piccadilly] as it's underground."

'When we ran out it was as bright as day as the whole of that part of London was lit up by searchlights. All the windows had been blown out so the whole place was covered in fine glass that sparkled like a frosty day in winter, a most beautiful sight. He sped ahead of me – soldiers didn't like the bombing – up Lansdowne Passage and into Berkeley Street, me following holding up my long dress and trying to skip over the glass in my thin shoes. We'd just got down into the Mayfair ballroom when a whole lot of people collapsed down the stairs. A bomb had landed in the doorway and killed the doorman. We'd missed death by seconds but funnily enough I wasn't even frightened.'

Christian Grant's diary of a packed weekend in January 1942 gives a flavour of the frantic urgency to cram as much gaiety as possible into the hours not spent working or on duty.

'*Fri Jan 2*. Worked. Out with Pip in evening to see Appointment for Love and on to dinner at Quag's – just for a change! We had our special table for the umpteenth time and Château d'Yquem. Black dress, sequin bolero and fur coat.

'*Saturday 3*. Stayed in bed pretty late and then went down to food office to get emergency ration card as the cottage at Fulmer [in Buckinghamshire] is still very wet and I may be in London some time. Prue Blake and Bronwen Williams-Wynn to lunch. Sewed my dress most of the afternoon. Out with Bobbie Miller, drinks with Bobby Hobart in his rooms at the Berkeley then dinner Lansdowne where we saw Mig with Ann Scott. On to the 400, which was packed. We didn't get a sofa table till it was practically time to go home, and practically packed up entirely with hunger waiting for eggs (can still get eggs occasionally in niteries). Got taxi right away too. Fur coat, Hawaiian dress, low-heeled sandals!

'*Sunday 4*. Lay in bed and felt luxurious for hours. Johnnie came round about 1 o'clock and we went out to a very good lunch at the Mirabelle. Car packed up on a short circuit and we spent most of the afternoon getting it fixed, so there really wasn't time to do much else. We went back to 32 Walpole Street [her mother's house, rented for £200 p.a.] and sat around and talked until it was time for him to drive down to Windsor. Johnnie rang up later from Windsor. Red dress, blue jacket.'

Christian and her escort would have been another couple in the Café de Paris on the night it was bombed but had got bored and left for the 400 just before the disaster.

Some missed death by inches as well as minutes. At 9.30 on the evening of 22 August 1940, the first German long-range shells landed on the southern counties of England. From then on, the guns that fired them, hidden in tunnels on the French coast between Calais and Boulogne, hurled their 1,500-lb shells 40,000 feet into the air, so that they fell with virtually no warning – only a distant flash on the far side of the Channel heralded the explosion that would follow about a minute later. The area around Dover soon became known as Hellfire Corner.

Fanny Gore Browne, working as a Wren in Dover, was

narrowly missed by one of these monsters. 'I'd been up to London with a girl friend on a 36-hour pass. We would come off night watch, take the 9.00 a.m. train to Charing Cross from Dover, walk to the flat, get on the telephone and make assignations. We did without sleep a great deal.

'We came back to Dover Priory in the morning as we were on watch again at 1.00 lunchtime. As we walked up from the station we were quite unaware there'd been a shelling warning – this was a double siren.

'We were crossing this garden by the church and a shell dropped and exploded just in front of us. We were blown flat and covered with dust. When we got to our feet we saw a crater just in front. We looked at each other, then brushed each other down. We both knew that if our train had been a minute early we would have been killed. But of course we never told anyone.'

Nor did the shells, with their threat of an approaching invasion, stop normal activities in Dover. Although on a clear day those with binoculars could actually see German tanks and trucks, people still queued in an orderly fashion for the cinema, 'Business as Usual' signs went up on boarded-up shop windows, and the *Dover Express* carried a notice which read: 'The enemy is but twenty miles away but dances will be held every Monday'. Social life became important in every way, perhaps most of all as a morale-booster.

One girl even left nursing because of the impossibility of seeing friends. 'I realised I would never get to meet anyone or do anything unless I could have evenings off,' said Penny Woosnam. 'All my friends who were soldiers, with a few in the Navy, couldn't get off during the day and I couldn't get off at night in time to get to London.'

Fanny Gore Browne, a Wren officer, was sent to France in early September 1944. 'We landed at Arromanches, north-west of Caen, which was very exciting, and went straight into quarters that the Germans had just left. My father had told me that anything occupied by the Germans always smelt, the reason being that they eat so much meat, particularly pork. So when we went into this totally empty house we opened the windows and washed the floor – a packet of nightlights, a baby pillow, a rug and a bottle of Dettol was my equipment for war.'

After three weeks in Normandy, Third Officer Fanny was sent to Saint-Germain-en-Laye (to the west of Paris, where General Eisenhower had his headquarters).

'We went into Paris all the time and got very good at doing without sleep. Paris was an American zone then and as I had an American boyfriend who had his own jeep I'd got it made.

'In Paris you noticed the women immediately. We'd all got dowdy by that stage of the war but they were beautifully dressed and coiffed, thin as rakes because there wasn't much food except for the appalling black market – and of course Paris, unlike London, hadn't been bombed. The first thing we did was window-shopping. We went down the Faubourg St Honoré, into all the wonderful parfumiers, being sprayed as they do – to smell scent was wonderful, after Britain. I was taken to Maxim's, a senior officers' restaurant, where I had *pâté de foie gras* for the first time in my life.'

The greatest celebrations were, of course, for V-E Day. Fanny, at home on leave when one of her brothers, a prisoner of war, was released, realised she would miss the celebrations in Paris and went back a day early. 'Somebody produced a clean shirt for me and I was away – life's very easy when you wear uniform. We had a marine band at Saint-Germain and they played outside the chateau. We all got into cars to go to Paris; ours had a great White Ensign behind it and we sat on the roof. There was dancing in the Place de la Concorde and we all ended up in the Naafi Officers' Club, in the Rothschild house in the Faubourg St Honoré, after walking down to the river – it was a beautiful warm night. Next day we had to go back to work and clean up.'

In England Lady Moyra Ponsonby, back at the Royal West Sussex Hospital in Chichester and working on the afternoon shift, heard a rumour that the war might be over but by the time she set off for home at four thirty nothing had been said. She left feeling 'a little deflated', to listen anxiously first to the five o'clock and then the six o'clock news, ready to dash for a train if there was an announcement. At nine came the longed-for announcement, proclaiming that the next day, Tuesday 8 May, would be V-E Day, with two days' holiday for everyone and a broadcast by the Prime Minister at 3.00 p.m.

'So this is it!' Moyra wrote in her diary. 'But one cannot feel frightfully excited as we have been expecting it for so many days now that it seems a bit of an anticlimax, particularly as we have to wait until tomorrow to celebrate.'

Early on Tuesday morning she set off for the hospital with her toothbrush in her bag. 'Find everyone wandering round with red, white and blue belts and rosettes. Decorations going up everywhere but everyone depressed and disgruntled and not knowing how to celebrate. The service patients are disgruntled because it looks as if they are not going to be given a late pass and the nurses are bad-tempered because we have not yet been told of any extra off-duty. I feel frightfully depressed, the weather is hot and thundery and I have a headache. Sister is in an awful temper and if it weren't for D [her boyfriend, later her husband, the eminent surgeon Sir Denis Browne] having rung up at lunch-time to confirm about plans for tonight, I might quite easily have decided to go home to bed instead.

'But from then on I never looked back. At three o'clock Winston broadcasts the cease-fire and we are told of the crowds in Whitehall, Piccadilly, etc. and around BP [Buckingham Palace]. At 4.30 I raid the drug cupboard for aspirins and dash for the train.

'D meets me at the station, the jubilant atmosphere of London gets one. D has been reconnoitring London on his bicycle all afternoon and so has the altered bus routes taped. We join a very friendly crowd on a bus to Victoria when we walk via Pont Street to Sir Neill's. His champagne is delicious and lots of it. I am past thinking anything dreary now!

'We listen to the King's speech and then D and I move off to see crowds outside BP. On our way down Eaton Gate we see lights on in the Reas' house so bang on the door. With apologies for our merry state we go in and talk for a bit. At 10.30 we resume our course towards the Palace and arrive just in time to see the King and Queen and Princess Elizabeth appear on the balcony. I must say I like this sort of party.

'We then wander about among the crowds who are in extreme good humour. We walk into St James's Park where one gets the best view of the floodlighting. Coloured rockets going up everywhere and bonfires on all open spaces. We see the King and Queen appear for the last time at 12.30, after which the floodlighting is turned off and the crowds slowly move off to bed.

'Sink into a rather drunken stupor to wake at 5.00 a.m., get no more sleep and at 6.30 ring Kitty [fellow nurse] to see if she is coming back on the same train with me. Tumble into a cold bath and while I am dressing the saintly Lorna gets breakfast for me. Go off on foot at 7.15 to catch my train feeling in a far better mood than when I came up. Find Kitty on train, also with somewhat of a hangover. Back at the hospital at 10.30. Wouldn't have missed it for anything.'

The celebrations went on all night, with doors and posts from air-raid shelters flung on to bonfires, Claridge's and the Ritz lit up until the small hours, flags planted on lamp posts and constant singing and dancing. The greatest war in history was over.

Chapter 9

Factories

'We were working too hard to flirt ...'

Without the factories that produced arms and munitions, the war would have ground to a halt almost within days. As speedily as possible, engineering works were turned from the production of cars to that of army vehicles, tanks or aeroplanes, chemical and paint works made anything from explosives and demolition charges to safety fuses, while small factories that had once produced anything from sewing machines to windscreen wipers were welded together (by means of vehicles shunting between them) into assembly lines for machine guns.

One of the most extraordinary transformations was in the furniture industry of north-east London, where carpenters changed from making chairs and tables to producing a wooden aircraft, the Mosquito: sheets of paper-thin plywood and balsa-wood were glued together, heat-strengthened and then sawn, shaved and shaped into the plane's components. The result was a very light, fast, highly versatile fighter-bomber that could carry the same bomb weight as a conventional bomber at a greater height – 21,000 feet – and if you wanted it to go faster you gave it a good wax with furniture polish.

With more and more men needed for the fighting forces, the great reservoir of labour for the factories now working at full pressure was the nation's women. At the beginning of December 1941 conscription for women (for all the unmarried between twenty and thirty, an age band later revised upwards first to forty, then forty-five and eventually to fifty) was introduced for the first time in British history, those women to be directed to work where needed. Because of the number who had already volunteered for the women's services, the majority of these were sent to work in factories.

Among those who volunteered for factory work were several of the girls who had had a sparkling debutante season in pre-war days. Without any of the compensations of life in the women's services – the chance of meeting some glamorous officer, possible service abroad, a good posting, time in the open air – factory work was not the first choice for any but the most dedicated and patriotic. The two things everyone knew about it was that it was both extremely hard work and vital for winning the war.

Sarah Norton and her great friend, Osla Benning, working respectively at an ARP (Air Raid Precautions) centre and as a typist in the War Office, felt they should be doing more. Momentarily tempted by the Wrens ('the uniform was so pretty'), they decided to try for work in an aircraft factory, a high priority for the country after the destruction of aircraft in the Battle of Britain. In early 1940 they were taken on at the factory of Hawker-Siddeley at Colnbrook, near Slough, where Hurricanes were made.

A greater contrast to their former life as debutantes would have been difficult to find. First they were sent to the factory's training school to learn to be Aircraft Mechanical Fitters. It was an exhausting life. Work – standing all the time while learning drilling, riveting, countersinking and filing – started at 8.00 a.m. and finished at 6.00 p.m., with an hour for lunch and two fifteen-minute tea breaks. But the shop steward was kindly; and everyone there, whatever their background, character or ideology, was united in their determination to produce aircraft to the highest standards.

After three months, Sarah was a Qualified Semi-skilled

Mechanic and on the way towards working on Hurricanes. She and Osla lived with her father (a director of Pinewood Studios) in a small cottage near Farnham Common (her mother was away, also working in a factory which made 4.7-inch naval guns). Light relief in the evenings was provided by some of the young men they knew who were stationed only five miles away at Victoria Barracks, Windsor, before being sent abroad.

Every eighth day was a day off: time so precious that Sarah, heading for London, friends and the 400, like the rest of her debutante generation, would go straight to the Slough road to hitch a lift, overnight bag in hand, the moment she left the factory gates that evening. In London she would stay at Claridge's ('£3 a night with breakfast, a lot of money but worth it') where she would arrive in her filthy boiler suit spattered with steel filings. There the famous hall porter, Mr Gibbs, who had known her since the days of childhood tea parties, would pass on messages – telephoning was often interrupted for long periods by bombs – and tell her who else was staying in the hotel.

After three months at the Hawker-Siddeley factory, by which time both girls had settled into their training, a directive suddenly arrived. It ordered them to report, without hope of appeal or contradiction, to a small parts factory on the Slough Trading Estate where semi-skilled workers were urgently needed.

It was a horribly different world. Even their reception came as a shock. The manager told them that their carefully acquired skills were futile before sending them off to the Medical Room, to be asked aggressively by the Sister: 'Have you been treated for venereal disease? How many men do you sleep with? How many times a week do you have a bath?' Soon Sarah realised that her abrupt answers to questions she saw as insulting had unwittingly antagonised both manager and Sister. 'I clearly had the wrong accent, which made me appear out of place and foreign, presenting some kind of threat.'

Their work was repetitive, dull and tiring, in an atmosphere so choked with dust that often it was difficult to see what was going on. 'After an eight-hour shift my eyes, nostrils and mouth were full of scratching metal dust and even the regulatory three-inch bath did little to relieve the irritation,' she wrote in her memoir of that period, *The Road to Station X*. 'The canteen food was repellent and competed with the rest of the factory in an attempt to undermine all effort and sanity. But the women and girls we worked with were angels from all walks of life; they were kind and reassuring, with an indomitable sense of humour that no mean management could suppress.'

Over them hung what Sarah described as the sword of Damocles. It had been spotted immediately by their workmates that somehow they were 'different' from the others ('I suppose it was our funny voices') and although their technique for deflecting interest was asking and listening avidly to stories about the lives of their workmates, sooner or later the question would come: 'What did you do before the war?' – and what to say then? Admitting to their debutante life might have meant a breakdown of trust with their new-found friends and caused them to be ostracised.

When the question finally came, unexpectedly, both girls were thrown and, in an effort to play for time, asked their workmates – four women on the same bench, of whom they were very fond – to guess. 'Mannequins at Selfridges!' shouted one triumphantly above the din of drilling and over-loud music. 'Don't be daft,' said another, who had worked in the store. 'I'd 'ave 'eard about it in Corsets and Suspenders'.

Suddenly Osla had a brainwave. 'To tell you the truth, we were fan dancers,' she told them. 'How many fans do you use?' asked one of her interlocutors. 'Three, of course,' said Osla promptly. Asked the same question, Sarah lost her head and said, 'Two.' A hush fell over the workbench as they digested this – then decided it was simply an outrageous fib and roared with laughter.

But the deception could not last. One day, eating baked beans in the canteen with their four friends, they confessed, praying inwardly for forgiveness. 'We told them that we had done absolutely nothing before the war except dance and play around London as debutantes, wearing long frocks every evening and, what was worse, my father was a Lord and my mother a Lady – the latter's status hopefully mitigated by the fact that she also worked in a factory,' wrote Sarah later. 'Waiting for the axe to fall was painful but the anguish did not last long.'

Their friends did not know exactly what a debutante was, but they did know they wanted to meet a Lord – so could they all come to tea next Sunday? The tea party was a great success and Sarah's father was instantly christened Lordie.

What was not so happy were the effects of their workplace on them. Both Sarah and Osla became so tired and anaemic that they had to take days off, a weakness aggravated by the terrible food, the airless working conditions, the damp floors that even soaked through everyone's wooden working clogs and, worst of all, the bullying of the manager.

Only Osla and Sarah had the courage to do something. They decided to go straight to the top, in this case the Ministry of Labour in London's St James's Square.

They drafted an appeal and, armed with a lucky horseshoe charm lent by one of their workbench friends, arrived for their appointment in their grimy working boiler suits. They were received by a charming, courteous man, who listened to them carefully. Two weeks later the unpleasant manager disappeared as if in a puff of smoke, to be replaced by a fair and decent boss who caused a transformation for the better in the lives of all who worked in the factory.

But Sarah and Osla's life there was coming to an end: soon afterwards, they were told to report to a Labour Exchange near Lincoln's Inn. It meant bidding a sad farewell to their friends and making a fresh start somewhere else.

Others arrived at factories with previous work experience. Frances Grenfell, whose husband Patrick Campbell-Preston had been captured in 1940, had been an Immobile Wren in Scotland, living at his family home. When this category was abolished, she came south to look after her father, living in a cottage at Bucklebury, just outside Reading, with her baby and her old nanny who joined them. After a brief spell in the WVS she went to work in a factory.

This was the old-established Reading firm of Huntley & Palmer's biscuits, where modern working practices had considerably ruffled the workforce. In contrast to Scotland, where Frances had frequently encountered friends of her father or her husband's family who had overridden the barrier of rank, in the factory the 'us and them' barrier between the equivalent of officers and rank and file was strong. 'It was extraordinary. You really were on the other side of the line.'

Huntley & Palmer had been one of the first to take up the Bedaux scheme, now called time and motion, which had caused immense resentment.* Most of their workers were female, though the heavy work was done by men. Since the scheme had begun, many of these women had left to marry and have children but when the war came Huntley & Palmer pleaded with them to return to the factory. When the Bedaux inspectors came round, recalled Frances, these girls would quite deliberately stop working and just sit on their chairs and smoke.

'One was in a completely Labour trade union world and it was fascinating. I remember one of the directors walking through after lunch, at about three o'clock – we only got an hour – with a buttonhole and we'd been hard at it. And the feeling! There was tremendous resentment, and I felt exactly

---

* Charles Bedaux, an American, was the originator of time and motion studies, designed to improve productivity largely through the eradication of time-wasting practices. It made him an immense fortune – and earned him equally immense dislike among those subjected to it.

the same. That man – what the hell does he think he's doing? You became on their side, passionately.

'Yet the real joke was almost the opposite. I went to the factory with two very rich friends that I'd rather talked into coming with me – I thought it was time they did some war work. They used to embarrass me hugely. One day they wouldn't turn up and when, the following morning, the other girls asked why they hadn't come to work, they'd say: "Darling, I couldn't *possibly* come in, the nursery maid was away" or "The chauffeur couldn't bring me". And I'd be sitting there and thinking: "God, don't talk like that, for goodness' sake."

'The last straw was when both of them became pregnant and said they couldn't lift the heavy trays and I'd have to do it. But to my fury the rest of the workforce only said admiringly: "Isn't it wonderful of them to come in when you think who they are!" By this time I was seething. When the other girls had asked me who looked after my baby I'd said: "My grandmother," and when they asked me about my life I frankly lied – I wasn't going to let on. But my friends went on about the second footman and the others loved it.

'What struck me most about the others was how awfully nice they were and how brave. I really loved them. My friends and I weren't mocked at all because of our voices – they took the attitude that it was awfully nice of us to go and do the work and were frightfully kind to us. They were as interested in us as we were in them. The thing is we were all on the same side. But this didn't happen everywhere – a friend of mine who had to work in munitions factories in South Wales found it very difficult, with a tremendous communist feeling and people going on strike a lot.'

Christian Grant began to work in a factory at the suggestion of her brother, who thought it was the most useful thing she could do in the war. 'It was the Handley Page aircraft factory in Cricklewood, in north London – a neighbourhood that until then I didn't know existed. The wonderful thing was that there was a direct Underground line to Green Park – the great meeting place was the downstairs bar at the Ritz, which was directly opposite. *Everybody* was there at drinks time. So after clocking off I would dash out to the Underground, whiz down to Green Park and straight into the Ritz and down the stairs on the right. I'd still be in my heavy khaki-brown boiler suit and I'd spend the evening like that, often at the 400. I still danced all night all the time – one went out every night. All those lovely boys who came home on leave somehow managed to find out where one was.

'Our factory made heavy bombers called Halifaxes. You could just hear *Music While You Work* over the general banging and crashing and slamming – some of the machines were very noisy. When I got home to my little flat I had to do fire-watching rotas once or twice a week. The refugees from Germany who lived in the same block, being suspect, weren't asked to. During the day they sat in the sun and at night they went to bed. I thought it most unfair!'

Christian Grant's diary vividly records the difficulties and exhaustion. The first thing she had done was to take an eight weeks' training course in aircraft engineering, the necessary preparation for the job she was offered by Handley Page. A day or two before the date she was due to start work, her call-up papers arrived from the Ministry of Labour.

There followed one of those all-too-common bureaucratic muddles, exacerbated by officials who stuck rigidly to the rules. To be taken on by Handley Page, she needed a card from the Labour Exchange – but, as she was now a conscript, they refused to issue her with one. 'Seems damn silly,' she wrote on 16 January 1942. 'They want to get girls into jobs and I have the qualifications and the job is waiting but they won't let me go into it. Hardly slept a wink.

'*17 Jan.* Back to Labour Exchange. Still no change. Practically burst into tears. Most human of the harpies relented and gave me a card. Have a feeling it is illegal so fled from Exchange and up to H-P to get taken on without a second's delay.

'*21 Jan*. Up to YWCA, off Maida Vale, in snow and slush. Have cubicle, very plain, bed, dressing table, wardrobe, chair, washstand with basin and tin jug. Other girls seem friendly and helpful. I wonder how this life will turn out. Feel pretty confident but definitely wary. Here we go on something rather different. Wish myself luck.

'*22 Jan*. Through dark and snow to H-P by 7.45 a.m. Dark grey sky, light grey snow, hurrying grey forms and the red rosy glow of fire-buckets – beautiful in a weird unreal way. First sight of real bits of aeroplanes gives me a big thrill. Other girls and men on benches near, very helpful. Put on to sawing and filing ends of hundreds of anonymous bits of aluminium. Have to stand all day but it isn't as tiring as I thought it would be. Very surprising at first to see men carrying huge bits of aeroplane with one hand until one realises it's aluminium. Huge lunch in canteen. Back to YWCA. Mig [the man she married a year later] called in and made a scene and made me miserable. Had a cry. Went to bed.

'*23 Jan*. Made 243 anonymous bits today – did 240 in seven hours which was "bogey time". Must beat bogey to get bonus. Lunched in upstairs canteen. It was so packed I had to queue till nearly one before I got food. There was a small band playing, it was strangely moving – a mixture of bravado and pathos. An old man was sitting opposite me: he had a thin, tired, sweat-damp face and sat leaning forward. At the end of the table a girl put her head down where her plate – roast beef, Yorkshire pudding, two vegetables – had been, and went to sleep. Later, the man on the bench behind me warned me against working too hard. "Why do it?" he pointed out. "You don't earn any more." A girl said that if one worked hard it put the others in a bad light.'

On Saturday 24 January Christian was writing: 'Believe I beat bogey by five hours on an eight-hour job this morning.'

It was the start of an unpleasant period with her workmates.

'During the time ahead I got a lot of persecution through working hard. Everyone I knew and loved was in the forces, fighting, and I felt the least I could do was to work as hard as I could and this was extremely unpopular.

'They were awful to me. If they talked to me at all I was mocked. The girls were bitchy but the men actually did worse things. We had these billycans for tea with our names on and someone would come round with a load of billycans filled with tea on their arm. They would put engine oil in my tea – we used this stuff called Flux, that you oiled capstan lathes with, which looked like milk but was in fact an oil compound. The men would put this Flux into my billycan with the tea instead of milk, so that I couldn't drink it – and after several hours' work you really longed for your tea.

'There were all sorts of petty ways they were spiteful. We were each responsible for our own small personal tools, kept in a drawer with a padlock in front of our work stations. At night we'd clean our tools, put them in the drawer and then padlock it. I would find they had picked the padlock and either taken all the tools or substituted awful old bent rusty things for mine.

'Then, round the edge of this dreadful factory there was a little bit of grass about four foot wide. I longed for something pretty, so I used a bit to make a small garden. But everything, pansies, lettuces, and so on, was always ripped up and never survived.

'More than anything else, there was a turning their backs on me. Until, eventually, there was a breakthrough, when one girl asked me: "Why do you talk that silly way?" I said: "I'm sorry, I can't help it – it's just the way my family talk. I'm not doing it on purpose." Then they were friendlier, and gradually I got included in the giggles and jokes.'

At the same time as Christian was being bullied and tormented by her fellow male workers, some of them made advances. 'We were working too hard to flirt, but they used to ask me out. I was rather surprised because of the awful initiation

I'd had to go through, with nobody talking to me because they thought I was stuck-up as I didn't talk the way they did, so I'd sometimes go with them on the backs of their motor bicycles for the same reason.

'But I just didn't fancy the chaps. I was used to dear darling upright people, straight from Eton into the Grenadiers. The truly awful thing also was that they were so smelly. Not even us sort of chaps used deodorants then, and certainly not factory workers.'

Christian found the work so tiring, on top of getting from her home in Chelsea to Cricklewood in fog and blackout early in the morning, that she was determined to get a small flat and live nearer the factory. Her mother resisted this but Christian pointed out that she was now twenty-one and able to earn her own living. Part of her mother's objection, she discovered, was not simply that she did not wish her daughter to live away from home – unusual in those days – but that Maida Vale, Christian's choice of location, had the wrong sort of aura 'as it used to have pretty little houses inhabited by kept women'.

The following day Christian's resolve was strengthened. 'It seemed a very long day today,' she wrote. 'I was drilling the whole day and when 6.00 o'clock came I really wondered if I could stand upright another minute. I wear the wide 8th Hussars belt and find it very comforting to strap it in tight – it seems to support the small of my back. I went for a wander round the whole factory in my lunch hour – somehow it is a lot smaller than I thought but there is a lot to see and learn about. Pip picked me up at 5.30 and we sat in the car and then had a very filling supper at a little French café. He gave me a quaint little seed pearl brooch and showed me the lovely diamond ring that might have been mine. [Pip was one of several young men who wanted to marry Christian.]

'*27 January.* Still drilling holes in bomb-rack pipes. Was going to post office in lunch hour but simply too beat to budge from table. Was given masses of advice by an old hand on almost every subject – including to beware of the factory Romeos! Was paid another visit by a dashing individual who told me I ought to try drinking – perhaps a little port in a nice saloon bar (he thinks I am a complete country mouse). Am amazed at the candour with which everyone talks – they don't exactly swear, they just use amazing words, like "trollop" for instance, in their ordinary conversation. Bed at 8.00 p.m. as very tired.

'*29 January.* The men all play darts in the lunch hour – there are darts boards hung all over the place. Dinner with Pip at Quaglino's. Feel strangely cold, perhaps it is tiredness. Wore black velvet and Pip's seed pearl brooch.

'*Feb 2.* Moved to new flat, 132a Wellesley Court, Maida Vale. Flat is on fourth floor, rent £102 p.a.

'*Feb 9.* My new boiler suit is black. My brown one is all ingrained with little metal grains so I sort of sparkle under a bright light.

'*Feb 10.* Was ticked off for reading newspaper in tea break. (Tea breaks are very strictly only ten minutes. We hardly had time to put down our tools and pour some tea out of one's billycan, brought round by a boy with about a dozen slung over his arm before it was time to start work again.) Law says women have to have ten minutes so why we can't do what we like with it I can't think. Anyway there it is. It was suddenly light this morning – the first time I have been able to read the headlines of the paper on the way to work.

'*15 Feb.* Mig gave me his automatic to take back to flat with me because I must confess I am slightly shaken with all these murders.

'*16 Feb.* Lots of new girls coming in. Have visions of night work. Loathe the idea but someone must do it and as I am young and healthy there is no reason why it shouldn't be me. In fact it should be. Am still appalled by idleness of men around me at work – they seem to work entirely and absolutely for money and money alone. I don't feel sure enough of my ground yet to take a stand on the subject but I am definitely warming up. I have so far only said anything to the other girls and even then one has to watch one's words or they think they are being preached at.'

In March 1942, she wrote to a magazine called *Flight*. Her letter was printed in its issue of 2 April and deserves quoting in full, partly for the spirit of determined patriotism that so infused Christian and her friends, and partly because it shows that the attitude that relegated so many women to subsidiary jobs had not yet been eradicated by the war:

'Sir, I was one of the first girls in London to train as a fitter under a Government training scheme, and now I am working, with about 20 other girls, as a detail fitter for a well-known aircraft firm.

'What we all desperately want to know is – how can we learn more? Are we doomed to work for the rest of the war at routine sawing and filing jobs? I asked our charge-hand how we could learn more about our jobs and he replied, somewhat vaguely, that we would learn in time. This is all very well, but the amount we learn in the shop can be judged by the fact that I found that one of the girls, who had been there for over a year, did not even know the name of the metal she handled daily!

'We are young, alert, intelligent girls, eager and anxious to work and learn and be useful. How can we learn? There are no night-classes to teach us the science of aircraft production, we don't know what books to read, and though we study papers and magazines like your very excellent one, our basic knowledge is so limited that we cannot fully understand or appreciate the articles.

'The men we work with seem mostly to be interested solely in making money – they don't care in the least about what part the job they are doing will play in the performance of the finished aircraft; they only care whether or not it will earn them more bonus.

'I, for instance, am 21 years old, gained seven credits in my School Certificate, including one in mathematics, and am filled with a burning desire to place all my energy, not only my mechanical physical strength, at the service of the country.

'I and the other girls at the factory don't ask to be given easy jobs for nothing – we would be perfectly willing to give up our evenings to study if it would lead us forward to intelligent jobs; jobs which perhaps we could keep after the war, and to which we could devote our lives.

'Can't the "stuck-in-the-rut" jobs be left to people who *like* ruts (and there seem to be plenty of them at the factory)? Can't our energies be directed to something our brains can get a grip on? All day long we do the same routine jobs – I know someone has to do them and we stick to them for that reason, but can't our brains have something to do as well?'

Christian signed her letter 'Brains Rust' (a tribute to the popular radio programme, *The Brains Trust*, run by Professor Joad).

This heartfelt plea resulted in the offer of a tempting job from another aircraft firm which she had, regretfully, to refuse, as she was newly engaged and planned to marry shortly. Yet, even so, she was not allowed to go on holiday alone with her fiancé when he had a week's leave – they spent it in Salcombe, with her mother as chaperone.

Later, also as a result of her letter, Christian received a second offer, this time of a technical training course, which resulted in a job as a technical adviser at a small branch of the Ministry of Production, in the West End of London.

From the moment she joined it at the end of 1942 she found the work fascinating. 'We were exchanging radar information with the Americans so as not to duplicate research, which meant knowing which centres in the US were researching which aspect, obtaining information from them and passing it on to their opposite numbers in England. We really had to know what we were doing, and there I really felt I was using myself.'

All the same, there were massive discrepancies between the amount that men and women were paid. It was not so long ago – about four years – since men had gone on strike because married women were being employed and thus, it was thought, taking the bread out of the mouths of those whom society deemed to be the breadwinners. The average wartime pay for skilled women in factories was £2 15s od a week and it was not unknown for an unskilled man to earn more than a skilled woman.

As resentment at this inequity rose, female workers in the Rolls-Royce factory in Glasgow went on strike. At first, they were pelted with tomatoes and eggs (presumably rotten, as eggs were strictly rationed and often unavailable) but these protests stopped when the protesters realised how little the women were being paid. Their strike succeeded in improving their position but only marginally: they returned to work with their pay increased to that of a male semi-skilled worker – but not that of a male skilled worker.

Another girl who worked in an aircraft factory was Lady Grenfell (née Betty Shaughnessy), who spent all day making wireless parts for Mosquitoes (wooden fighter-bombers) while her mother looked after her children. 'I went up every day from Windsor to Tottenham Court Road and back again at night. *Music While You Work* blared the whole time, as you passed these bits constantly down the assembly line until it was time to go back by train in the blackout – you arrived at Paddington Station in pitch dark and had to find your way to the train. Often you did not see daylight the whole day. I did this for eighteen months. What struck me about all the others was their marvellous patriotism.'

Cynthia Denison-Pender was one of those who left the FANYs because she did not wish to become a home-based ATS officer. She had been sent to Senior Officers' School at twenty, but at this age she was too young to be allowed to go abroad 'and therefore the only thing I could do was become an

ATS officer. I didn't want to be one. I never saw myself as driving a lot of randy officers – and they *were* randy.

'I really wanted to do something more for the war so in the autumn of 1940 I joined Westlands Aircraft in Yeovil as a trainee draughtswoman, drawing specifications for the jig and tool department. Your pencil had to be so accurate it had a chisel point rather than an ordinary one. I clocked in at 8.00 a.m. and clocked out at 6.00 p.m. and went home at weekends on a motor bike.

'If you were a draughtswoman you went through the machine shops first. There was snobbism in that factory but it wasn't class-based, it was between the workers and the staff. We, the draughtsmen, were staff, the others were workers. When Stafford Cripps came and talked to us, he said: "Hail, Comrades."* I worked there for two years until my health gave out.'

~

Health could be a problem for all but the very strongest. The long hours, the lack of fresh air, the canteen food that had been cooked for so long that its vitamin content had disappeared, and the grinding monotony that ate up day after day of youth, all combined to wear down the system, no matter how patriotic the intent. Eighteen-year-old Pamela Joyce, called up in January 1940, was directed into a factory, under the aegis of the Admiralty, that had been built into the South Downs behind Brighton. Here, at this secret location, heads for naval gyroscopes were made.

'We had to clock in at 7.00 every morning and work

* Sir Stafford Cripps, an ardent socialist, was ambassador to the Soviet Union from 1940 to 1942. After he returned he was appointed Minister for Aircraft Production. He was later Chancellor of the Exchequer in Attlee's postwar government.

compulsory overtime until 7.30 in the evening. I was paid £5 a week. Canteen lunches were 1s 6d, stew, rolypoly pudding, a cup of dishwater coffee. At the end of the day I just came home and collapsed straight into bed.

'I had no means of getting to this factory as I hadn't got a car – couldn't drive, and anyway there was no petrol – and the public service transport didn't start until 7.00 a.m., the time I was supposed to be there. So every morning I would get up at 6.00 a.m. and stand on the pavement outside my parents' flat at Preston [on the outskirts of Brighton], where I was living, and hitch-hike. There was never a moment's bother. You felt as safe as houses. Nobody touched you.

'People then were incredibly decent. Once I dropped my brown suede clutch bag on the way home, in the blackout. It had all my treasures in it, including a week's wages, and I was worried sick. Next day I went to the police station and sure enough it had been handed in, nothing touched, everything there.

'It was extraordinary working in that factory. Bombs flying about all over the place, *Music While You Work* on all day very loud – that did drive me mad – all sorts of incredible people working on the lines. One never let on anything about oneself and luckily nobody ever said: "Where do you come from?" The answer was you just got on with whoever was working next to you. One was fairly anonymous – we were all in overalls, which we picked up at the door, and we had our hair tied up in these protective caps because of the machinery. Everybody was nice, there was no aggro, there wasn't a dividing line between anybody. We were all doing the same thing, we were all involved in rations and so on, we all clocked in and out and we all went our own way outside.'

After three years Pam was switched from the Brighton factory to one in Acton, London – with the same exhausting conditions. 'It was originally the Siemens factory, which we'd taken over. I was in rather ghastly digs, a bedsitting room, where I had to look after myself and of course I'd never cooked before – luckily one had a canteen lunch.

'At this point my health gave out and I had a slight break-down – I think it was just sheer exhaustion and strange food.'

She had six months off on medical grounds and was then transferred from munitions-making to the Meteorological Department in the Admiralty proper, in Lansdowne Row. 'That was very civilised and I began to have a social life. When boyfriends rang up, one whizzed off to Hatchett's [in Piccadilly] for dinner – 7s 6d – and then on to the 400.'

Again, Pam never thought twice about walking across Hyde Park in the depths of a winter night and blackout to catch her Green Line bus back to Richmond, where her parents were now living. 'When the Americans arrived they were worried, I think, about some of their soldiers. Their military police, who always patrolled in pairs, wore white-painted helmets and white spats – they were known as Snowdrops – and we were all issued with whistles, like Girl Guide whistles, to blow if we had any prob-lems and the Snowdrops would come at once. I never had to blow mine.

'One horrendous night when I'd been out with a boyfriend we couldn't get home. Bombs were flying around and all the tubes had stopped because the electricity had been cut off. We got ourselves to Piccadilly Underground, which was the deepest, where there was a whole pile of mattresses at the entrance. You just grabbed one, and snuggled yourself down into it.

'Then, next morning, such a nice thing. The first tube into the station from the East End came in about 6.30. And there, on it, were some wonderful old biddies rather like Norah Batty with wrinkled stockings and hairnets, holding flasks of sweet tea and saying: "C'mon, ducks, have a cup of tea." And you got up, shook yourself and went off. It was all sheer goodwill on their part; they just appeared, like fairy godmothers.

'That was the wonderful thing during the war, the feeling of friendship.'

Chapter 10

Nursing

'Sometimes the ambulance bells never stopped'

Nursing, like the FANYs, was one of the branches of war work that historically had drawn the daughters of the upper classes – in fact, the Voluntary Aid Detachment was the oldest of the women's services. In the ranks of this organisation were many of the wives, sisters and sweethearts of the officers fighting in France in 1914–18 who had volunteered to drive ambulances – often paid for with their own money – as near to the Front as they were allowed.

The Red Cross itself had originated in 1859 when a young Swiss traveller, horrified at the carnage resulting from the battle of Solferino between France and Austria ('every fifteen minutes I have seen a human being die in unimaginable agony,' he wrote to a friend), published a book urging that volunteer relief societies be formed to care impartially for the wounded of both sides.* His book became a best-seller and the Red Cross was the result.

In 1909 the War Office initiated a scheme for the organisation of voluntary aid, whereby the British Red Cross was given the task of providing supplementary nursing aid to the Territorial Forces Medical Service in the event of war. For this purpose, the county branches of the British Red Cross organised units

---

* *Un souvenir de Solferino* by Henri Dunant.

called Voluntary Aid Detachments, of which the members (who quickly became called VADs) were given a training in nursing and first aid. Within a year there were 6,000 of them, a number which rose when the First World War broke out in 1914 and they were combined with the units raised by the Order of St John of Jerusalem.

This – later known as St John Ambulance – had an even older history. Its origins dated back to the capture of Jerusalem in 1099 by the Crusaders, who found a small colony of Benedictine monks there, devoted to caring for sick pilgrims to the Holy City. Because of the need to defend their patients, these evolved into soldier-monks and then into armed knights, taking their name, the Order of St John of Jerusalem, from that of their hospital, the Hospital of St John. The knights and their work spread all over Christendom – during the Middle Ages they built numerous hospitals for the poor – but their wealth and property was seized by Henry VIII and the (Catholic) Order suppressed. It continued to operate in Europe and after the loss of its headquarters in Malta in 1798 some members of the Order decided to revive the British branch.

During the Industrial Revolution, conditions and machinery were so hazardous and workers so exhausted by the long hours that accidents were frequent. Victims rarely saw a doctor in time and death or disability from untreated injuries were commonplace. Members of the British Order wanted to find a way to help. They decided to train ordinary people in first aid so that accident victims could be treated on the spot. In 1877 they set up the St John Ambulance Association to provide this emergency medical care in an organised way and it was granted a charter by Queen Victoria in 1888. Through local branches, it quickly spread over the entire British Empire.

When the eminent nurse Sister Agnes Keyser became one of King Edward VII's greatest women friends and was permitted to name the hospital she had founded in 1908 in Beaumont Street, Marylebone, after him, it put a social patina on a profession that was already admired for its selfless dedication and humanitarian work. There was also, possibly, a further subliminal factor: brought up from birth to believe that caring for a husband and children would be their future, for most young women caring for patients was perhaps just one step further.

In any case, the Government, anticipating a far higher rate of casualties from bombing than actually occurred, had begun building hospitals several years earlier and was anxious for nurses to fill them.*

Like many who later trained to nurse professionally, Fortune Smith began her nursing career as a VAD, soon after the start of the war. She first worked in the hospital in Horsham close to where she lived but was soon sent to Chailey Hospital (also in Sussex), originally a home for the disabled, which had expanded into a large children's hospital.

'It was an open-air hospital. We nurses slept in huts. The front was open throughout the year, so we had sleeping bags and a little flask to keep us going. It was very cold, with no heating in this country house and there was snow on the ground when we went there. At night you had a dim torch to undress by. The children were in open wards and the babies were bathed in the open air, even in the middle of winter, though there were arc lamps overhead for that.

'It was during the time of the Battle of Britain. You could see the fleets of bombers going over, then you saw these tiny fighters going up. Every single day we saw the fighters go up and we could see pilots from the ones that were hit parachuting down, or the plane itself coming down. It was extraordinary – though these dogfights happened so regularly that after a bit they

---

* (Their fifty-casualties-per-ton-of-bombs rule of thumb was extrapolated from casualties sustained in the First World War, when many of those casualties were people who had stood in the streets gaping at enemy planes above rather than seeking shelter. The bombing of Guernica was also fresh in many minds, as too was Baldwin's dictum that 'the bomber will always get through'.)

Third Officer Lady Anne Spencer in October 1943. She joined the WRNS in 1942, was involved in plotting convoys and was commissioned in 1943.

ABOVE: The Café de Paris, a favourite place to spend an evening and dance, in January 1940. BELOW: The aftermath of the bomb that fell through the roof of the Café de Paris on the night of 8 March 1941, killing the entire band and many of the dancers.

ABOVE: Sandbags – the great protection against the flying glass produced by bomb blast – around the ballroom entrance to the Dorchester in Park Lane. The Dorchester was a popular wartime rendezvous. BELOW: Watching the cabaret in a nightspot in 1941, girls still wore long evening dresses but their escorts were generally in uniform.

Christian Grant and a 12th Lancer boyfriend at the Nut House, a nightclub that stayed open even later than the 400.

'Right Dress.' ATS recruits in training, August 1943.

Hyde Park. As food rationing began to bite, growing vegetables became a priority and parks were dug up.

Dining and dancing in wartime London, 1941.

TOP: ATS girls Lady Margaret Egerton (left) and her friend Cecilia Sprot changed out of uniform to dance whenever they could manage. ABOVE: Suzanne Irwin's wartime marriage to David Woodhouse (later Lord Terrington) took place at St George's, Hanover Square, in November 1942.

Bletchley girl Joan Stafford King-Harman married her husband George Dennehey in June 1943. Both came from keen racing families and the results of the Derby were announced to cheers at their Claridges reception.

Val Canning married Lt Anthony Philip Wellesley Colley in January 1941. He was killed on D-Day.

BELOW LEFT: Lavinia Holland-Hibbert at Fiesole, above Florence, in February 1944.

BELOW RIGHT: Denis Healey at Positano, 1944. 'We drove in a jeep to all the famous towns,' recalled Lavinia Holland-Hibbert. 'Denis really educated me.'

seemed almost impersonal.' (The heaviest day's fighting was on 15 August 1940, when the Luftwaffe sent in 1,800 aircraft against Britain's air defences.)

Anne Douglas-Scott-Montagu was another who began her nursing career with the Red Cross, wearing its uniform of dark blue coat and skirt, black stockings with flat black shoes, white shirt with black tie, and Red Cross insignia on the shoulder. Her mother was president of the area round her home, Beaulieu Abbey, and Anne was a divisional secretary. 'I did clerical work and organised the flag days, which were quite unusual then.'

When the war broke out she went to work in Lymington Cottage Hospital, on the edge of the New Forest, for which she was given a special allowance of petrol. 'Going through the forest was awfully difficult. Your headlights were just slits, pointing downwards, so you had no beam at all. Everyone drove terribly slowly, hanging on to the verge.

'The First Aid Post for the whole area was in our front hall at Beaulieu. My grandmother organised a sewing association where material was ripped up to make bandages – a Hospital Supply Depot – and then the boudoir was turned into the headquarters of the ARP [Air Raid Precautions] for the whole area. So we had three major things going on in different parts of the house.

'I was at home ill for a year during the war and then, in January 1945, went off to work in one of the Red Cross headquarters in London, in Wilton Crescent – the other house was in Grosvenor Crescent – as a secretary. It was the part of the Red Cross that did all the training.

'We did the evacuation of children whom the Government scheme didn't cover – they would only take children who were fit and well, schoolchildren, without mothers. There was also an organisation called the ICAA – the Invalid Children's Aid Association. We used to find places for them in the country and I used to see them off at the station, see they'd got their gas masks and so on. So you can imagine there was a lot of correspondence, finding people who would have them, and sorting out trains and so forth.

'Sometimes I'd have to comb the nits out of the evacuees' hair. I also learned how to put a hot-water bottle in a bed and when all the fleas had collected there in the warmth, wet a bar of soap and catch them on it. We also took turns to be on duty on the roof – there was a stirrup pump for incendiary bombs.

'I used to go round London by bicycle. It was very difficult to get hold of batteries for bicycle lamps then and I managed to find a wonderful little paraffin bicycle lamp. I remember bicycling back past Cadogan Gardens, where a lot of American soldiers were stationed, with a stream of smoke pouring out of my lamp and a trail of wolf whistles following me.

'Twice a week I was on duty in the Underground – the very deep station at Knightsbridge. People were allowed in at 10 p.m. and had to be gone at about 7 a.m. It was fitted with three-tier bunks and we had a first-aid post in the corner.'

~

In the first years of the Blitz, the Government had distributed 1.5 million of what were known as Anderson shelters – basically curved, corrugated iron huts with steel plates at either end, measuring 5ft 6in by 4ft 6in, to accommodate up to six people. Once dug into place in the garden, these shelters were half-buried in the ground with earth heaped on top.

But Anderson shelters proved cold and damp – besides, not everyone had gardens. As bombs rained down, people began to seek safety in the deep basements of public buildings and the crypts of churches. When 100-odd people burst into the Savoy Hotel on the evening of 15 September 1940, eight days after the Blitz had begun, it was clear that the pressure for deep, secure shelter was unstoppable. The Government had hitherto forbidden the use of the Underground but those with no other refuge simply bought a ticket and stayed on the platforms all night. Soon selected stations were equipped with bunk beds and toilets and, nightly, around 60,000 would convene in these havens.

Underground shelters such as those at Holborn, Knightsbridge and Notting Hill Gate all had their own first-aid post, manned by the Red Cross, which arranged concerts, games and film shows. As raids continued throughout the war there were also night classes, programmes of gramophone music, and books that could be borrowed from fifty-two lending libraries. Sometimes trains brought in refreshments for sale.

'One night a woman started having a baby,' recalled Anne Douglas-Scott-Montagu, on duty at Knightsbridge Underground. 'We had to get her to Queen Charlotte's Hospital in Goldhawk Road and there was an air raid going on. We got her up the stairs – the escalators stopped at midnight – and I was sent with her in the ambulance to look after her. The raid was in full swing with all the guns in Hyde Park going off and searchlights roving.

'Suddenly the woman said: "Oh dear, this baby's going to come, do you know what to do?" The people with me, both professionals, panicked and said: "No, no, we don't know what to do, we've never had anything to do with babies." I thought this was crazy – so terrifying for the poor woman – so I said: "I know what to do." Of course all I knew was what I'd read in Red Cross books, about tying the cord with string, but I pretended I knew absolutely what to do and she calmed down. Mercifully we got her to the hospital before the baby arrived.'

So rare were babies born to single women that the imminent arrival of one sometimes took even nurses by surprise. 'I was on night duty with two other nurses,' said Fortune Smith, 'when the one standing by me asked: "Do you think that after the war there will be a different view about illegitimate babies?" I'd actually never heard of one, so I hadn't the faintest idea.

'Then, to my horror, about two weeks later this girl had a baby. We weren't meant to know – she was rushed away and it was put about that she'd had a sudden appendix, and that was that. Of course if I'd known I'd have befriended her. The father was someone in the RAF, who was subsequently killed. It was desperately sad, she was completely cut off by her parents and her family.

'I remember the Matron came down from Great Ormond Street and I overheard her saying to the Sister: "Sister! Where were your eyes?"'

Blackout precautions were of course just as stringent for hospitals as for private houses. There was also the need to protect against flying glass, should a bomb fall near by. In Fortune Smith's hospital all the cots were moved away from windows into passages, lit by a few dim lights, like miners' lamps, on the floor. Penny Woosnam and her fellow nurses had to heave mattresses up against the enormous windows of the wards in which they worked so as to protect the patients and themselves.

Fortune and the great friend with whom she shared a hut at Chailey, Lady Bridget Guinness, soon decided that they would be more useful if they were properly trained. 'So both of us embarked on the three-year nursing training. You had to have School Certificate, buy your own uniform, and were paid £33 a year. Bridget went to St Thomas's and I went to Great Ormond Street because I wanted to nurse children.'

The perils awaiting pretty young women walking alone through dark London streets seemed non-existent then. 'All the girls who were nurses at Great Ormond Street walked there from Russell Square Underground in total darkness, and we weren't in the least nervous – nothing ever happened,' said Fortune Smith. She herself, when part of the hospital was evacuated to Tadworth Court, near Epsom, would hitch-hike home on her day off (wearing civilian clothes rather than the protection of her uniform). 'I'd stop any lorry and sit in front with the driver. It never so much as crossed my mind that it could be risky.'

∽

Nursing was a hard and physically demanding job, involving much of the kind of labour that is now done either mechanically or by contract staff. In most hospitals, Matron inspected the wards twice a day: they had to be immaculately clean, with everything spick-and-span. 'We held Matron, and the ward sister, in great awe,' recalled Fortune. 'All the cleaning was done by the hospital cleaners or the nurses. I can't recall a single mistake – a major mistake – nor do I know of a single case of infection picked up from the hospital during those wartime years I spent nursing.'*

As the lowest in the nursing pecking order, VADs were usually given the dirtiest jobs to do. At St Bartholomew's, for instance, where four rows of fifteen beds made up a ward, each bed close to the next with no curtains in between, the VADs spoon-fed the disabled, made all the beds, warmed bedpans and emptied them when used ('I learned not to breathe through my nose until this was done,' said one girl) as well as sterilising equipment and making tea.

Their treatment as – often – glorified ward maids was exacerbated in many cases by professional nurses suspicious of those from privileged backgrounds.

'I was always sent to do the dirty things,' said Penny Woosnam. 'The other nurses took it out on me. The first day I was at Chatham Hospital, in Kent, a senior nurse said to me: "You see that man over there – he's got glass in his penis.

---

* In spite of a shortage of doctors, the potential for pollution of bomb-damaged water mains or sewers, and the stringency of the wartime diet, there were no major epidemics such as typhoid although – in London – the incidence of tuberculosis rose.

Bandage it." So of course I bandaged it like a stump, didn't I, with the bandage going over the top, not like a finger, round and round. He was too embarrassed to tell me – I remember he was pink in the face – especially as by this time it was stiff. I'd never seen a penis before, let alone an erect one.

'The most nerve-racking moment was after a man had died. We VADs weren't allowed to lay him out – the nurses did that, crossing his arms on his chest and putting him on a trolley to go down to the mortuary in the basement. I was told to take him and at first I didn't think anything about it.

'But when I was halfway through the tunnel leading to the mortuary one of the crossed arms of the corpse suddenly flung itself outward. I was scared stiff – I thought he must still be alive. Then his other arm flung itself out. By the time I'd reached the mortuary I was a shaking, gibbering wreck. The man in the mortuary looked at me and said: "Where's the orderly?" I said: "Nurse didn't give me one." He created. "*Nobody* is allowed to bring a dead person down alone. There *has* to be two people and one of them *must* be a male orderly." I think there were red faces upstairs after that.'

Penny, an exceptionally pretty girl, was unlucky enough to have her looks as well as her class held against her. At the Royal Masonic Hospital in Great Queen Street her popularity with patients secured her most of the dirty jobs. 'The men would always greet me "Hello, Nurse Sunshine" so I got given the enemas instead of the broken legs.'

After a young nurse or VAD had proved herself, she was accepted – the busy life of the wards left little time for resentment – although class differences were still noticed, albeit good-humouredly. 'I got mobbed up by the housemen about my voice and my name – my nickname was "Nurse thank-you-so-much Forbes Adam",' said Virginia Forbes Adam. 'They couldn't place where I'd been to school – they eventually thought it must have been Cheltenham Ladies' College. But it was good-natured teasing.'

Esme Harmsworth was sternly told by a senior ward sister to be careful when dealing with any patient who had a pink overall folded at the end of his bed – but not the reason why. Later, she learned that these overalls were dealt out only to those patients suffering from venereal diseases. But Esme had one consolation: she returned each night to the Ritz, where she was living. 'I left every day as the cleaners arrived, catching the Underground at Green Park and changing at Holborn for St Paul's. It was like emerging from a luxurious cocoon to bare hardship each day – I went from one extreme to the other.' (The Ritz, like other grand hotels, was more affordable then than it is now, even in real terms: rooms could be had from 25 shillings a night upwards.)

Patients were quick to spot the young and untried. 'Come and look at my scar,' the older male ones would shout; invariably it was in a very private place. Younger men tended to be more bashful, carefully covering themselves up when being washed.

Mockery from most patients was friendly. 'One day I was in a ward where they were short, and I was given a broom and told to sweep the floor,' said Ann Reid. 'I had no idea how to do it. I saw an old girl in bed doubled up with laughter. She looked at me and said: "I bet you've never swept a floor." I said: "You're right – but you're going to tell me how to do it."'

Child patients often had little hesitation in correcting the young VADs. Fiona Colquhoun worked as a VAD at Harefield Hospital near Watford. 'I drove there every day, often with only half a light because the battery had run out. It was terribly hard work but I loved it. One day I was in the children's ward and I went to take a little boy's temperature. I was trying to put the thermometer in his mouth and he said: "Excuse me, Miss, I think you've got the wrong 'ole."'

Ann Darlington was one of those who had already joined the Red Cross when the war started. 'All I knew was how to bandage somebody's sprained ankle and I was terrified of being called up to the Front with no nursing experience as I might have put people's lives at risk. My uncle, William Hirst, was Chairman of the Board of Governors of Huddersfield Infirmary, which was a teaching hospital, so he asked them to take me on. Matron said she would send me to a ward where there was a Sister who was very difficult but an excellent teacher.

'I went straight there and on my first day Sister came in and said: "Oh dear, that boy who died last night, his parents want his shirt changed – two nurses will have to go down to the mortuary and do it." She turned to me and said: "I suppose nurses like you don't do that sort of thing." I'd never seen a dead body, let alone touched a corpse, but of course I stuck my nose in the air and said: "Of course we do." So down we went and did it.

'The other thing I remember there was when a chap who'd been in a coma and come out of it after a lorry accident was put in the main ward and the terrifying Sister told me to give him an enema. So I got the bowl of water, drew the curtains round the bed and asked him to take his trousers down. Because he'd just come out of a coma he was in a completely dotty state and he started leaping about in the bed and shouting: "Mates, mates, here's a tart come to rape me!" It made the day of all the men in the ward but I was getting more and more flustered as I thought Sister would come in because of the noise. Suddenly I saw a medical student looking over and laughing, so I said, "You bloody well come and help me." So he came and literally lay across the chap and I managed to do the job. After that, Sister gave me all the most ghastly jobs to do because she thought I was ready for anything.'

Nursing in the Blitz was doubly tiring because virtually every night was broken. Fortune Smith managed to get away with staying in her room, strictly against orders. 'You were supposed to get dressed and go down and sit in the basement but I secretly stayed in bed as I reckoned that other people were going through worse.'

Not so for Virginia Forbes Adam, another who had begun as a St John Ambulance VAD and then decided to take up nursing professionally.* Taken on at King's College Hospital in Denmark Hill, Camberwell, after three months at the nurses' training school in Banstead, Surrey, she was living in the hospital's nurses' home when the raids were at their height.

'The nurses' home had three floors of which one – mine – faced north, so you looked straight over the rooftops to St Paul's. When the bombs were really bad the first thing I did on waking was to look out and see if St Paul's was still there. There were raids every night and even if we weren't on duty we still had to get dressed and go down to the cellars if there was bombing. Even if one was so exhausted one longed just to bury one's head under the bedclothes it was no good, somebody still came round and drove you downstairs.'

Her day started with the clang of a bell at 6.00 a.m., followed by breakfast at 6.30. Then came the long-drawn-out bedpan rounds, with a coffee break of twenty minutes between 9.00 and 10.00 a.m. There was a four-hour off-duty period during the working day, which ended at 10.00 p.m. The wards were kept warm by coal fires at each end – the coal brought up by porters – but the corridors were unheated; nurses scurried down them in their cloaks.

Virginia worked on several wards in turn: first on the Matthew Whiting Ward for gynaecological cases, where a week of major operations alternated with a week of recovery. 'The ones who were operated on were immensely grateful for anything done for them. It was very touching the way they would suddenly give you an egg if a relation visited them from the country. Us pupil nurses did all the bedpans – everybody was kept in bed for about three weeks after a hysterectomy or a hernia. Patients came straight back from the theatre to the ward, heavily sedated. The anaesthetics used in those days made people very sick. I was able to take that in my stride but the one

---

* By 1942 there were only 6,000 VADs, no doubt because so many had decided to take the full-time nurses' training.

thing I never got used to was emptying sputum mugs – one of the complications of an operation was bronchitis.

'There was one terrible operation which I used to hate, for cancer of the colon. They did this two-handed, with one surgeon starting from the abdomen, the other from the rectum and they would be so pleased when they met in the middle that they shook hands with each other.'

In King's, new nurses spent a minimum of two months on each ward, possibly returning to the same ward several times. One of the least pleasant, Virginia Forbes Adam found, was the military ward for the skin diseases, such as erysipelas, that were rife in the Army. 'I was a junior staff nurse in the men's medical ward – mostly heart failure and pneumonia – followed by a stint in the men's surgical ward. Sometimes the ambulance bells never stopped. People would be brought in who had to have both legs amputated, or terribly badly cut with glass. They were all so incredibly brave. One person was so badly damaged that my friend, a night nurse on casualty, couldn't tell if they were man or woman.'

For the professional nurse, some of the most heart-rending cases were the soldiers and pilots who had suffered devastating burns. When Jean Falkner, who had done her nurse's training at the Radcliffe Hospital in Oxford, later went to work for the famous plastic surgeon Sir Harold Gillies at Park Prewitt Hospital (on the outskirts of Basingstoke), she was posted to the Burns Unit. 'I can never forget the terrible smell of burnt flesh. In those days we used to have to wash the bandages by hand before they were put into a steriliser. The work involved the operating theatre and putting the patients in saline baths and dressing their wounds – even fifty years later, I could hardly bear *The English Patient*.

'One day, just after D-Day, walking into the ward, I saw rows of stretchers, each with its label, of desperately burned young men. Their courage and spirit were extraordinary. One particular body had no face, only eyes and a hole with four teeth where the mouth and jaw should have been. Yet as I passed I heard a loud wolf whistle. I managed some kind of reply and then had to run outside to cry.'

Occasionally, there was a kind of grisly light relief. 'Once, when I was on night duty with another nurse, a whole convoy of burned soldiers came in, carried on stretchers with labels to identify them – often, they had no faces – and we were alerted that Sir Harold was driving down from London to operate.

'I prepared everything, instruments laid out, patients wrapped in green operating robes, lights ablaze, theatre nurses scrubbed up, when the great man appeared at the door of the operating theatre with a roar, wearing only long white cotton underpants and vest. I had prepped everything except his operating gown. Luckily, he laughed.'

Jean's work brought her into contact with Professor (later Sir) Alexander Fleming, the discoverer of penicillin. 'I'd met him at the Radcliffe because he did his first penicillin experiments there. Later, at Park Prewitt with Sir Harold, we often had sandwiches together – I had a friend who worked in the path. lab. I gave a lot of those first penicillin injections to patients.'

Lady Moyra Ponsonby, nursing at the Westminster Hospital, found it 'unbelievably strict. One lived in the nurses' home and you had to be signed in at 9.00 p.m. and not a moment later. There were four nurses to a ward, including the sister, with one always off duty. Each ward had fifteen men and fifteen women, which is harder work than thirty men or thirty women. We nursed and washed up at least one main meal – a ward maid did the other. I found night duty the most shattering – you were never on it for less than a fortnight. During night duty you had two nights off.'

Her diary for New Year's Day 1943 records: 'Received my first and last raspberry from Matron this morning, with two other nurses, for walking over to the Home without our cloaks on. She was extremely angry! I'm very pleased to have seen her in this mood. After last night's gin-drinking am not able to face this morning's meal.'

As an earl's daughter, Lady Moyra encountered considerable suspicion but her determination to prove herself paid off. On 13 June 1943 she was writing: 'Am thrilled! Matron asks me to special a nurse who is to have a radical amputation of breast. No more scrubbing and sluicing, this will be real nursing. I feel quite flattered. This should make Sister Jones feel rather silly after asking me if I had ever done a blanket bath!' A fortnight later she believed she knew the reason for the difficulties she encountered. 'I think the reason why Sister Jones was treating me so oddly was probably because Matron said I must be treated more strictly than any of her nurses. Memo: not because of any insubordination on my part but purely for my own good, to prevent any chance of anyone saying that I was treated differently from the rest.'

Ann Darlington, transferred to King's College Hospital, parts of which had been moved to locations all round London in 1940, owing to the Blitz, found herself in Leatherhead, where she had been sent to cope with the rush of wounded after Dunkirk. The temporary hospital to which she had been transferred had originally been a school for the blind, and a number of Nissen huts had been quickly erected in the grounds to serve as makeshift wards.

'The first day there was the most terrible experience. The retreat from Dunkirk was in full swing and all sorts of patients were arriving who needed operations. Because the place had never been used as a hospital there were no directions on the walls so the confusion was immense. People were saying: "Nurse, take this man to operating theatre Number Five on the trolley," "Quick, get a blanket for this chap!" and one had no idea where the blankets were kept or where the theatres were.

People were running round like rabbits but once we'd got it sorted out it was okay.

'The other thing was that the blind school, which was a vast building, had tall windows like a Gothic church which we couldn't really black out. So one had to nurse at night holding a tiny torch – which meant that you had to go and check with your torch to see if anyone had died. We were incredibly busy because there were so many serious cases. I remember when one man, in a single room rather than the main ward, rang his bell, I dropped everything and ran, only for him to say: "Oh, nurse, can you help me with my crossword?"

'The Battle of Britain was going on over our heads. There was no air-raid shelter at the bottom of the school and if a bomb had been dropped on the building we'd all have been killed. The authorities didn't really know what to do but someone said that there should be an extra mattress for every patient and that we should put these on top of them in a raid, so that it would at least stop injuries from shrapnel and broken glass. So every time the siren went we solemnly put thirty mattresses on thirty patients. During the height of the Battle they were going on and off every twenty minutes. In the end we went on strike because we said that we couldn't do this *and* nurse the patients. So we were allowed to stop doing it, though the patients all said: "Where's my mattress?"'

Later Ann was transferred to Bath Royal Hospital (VADs were expected to be as mobile as nurses). This hospital, divided into an ordinary and a military section, proved a hideous experience. 'I was on the military side, where the sisters were all army sisters and there were army nurses and Red Cross nurses like me. The reason it was so dreadful was that the Red Cross nurses were organised by the local Red Cross commandant and she had no idea how to organise a complete hospital wing.

'It was that cold winter of 1941. Six of us were put to live in the most awful, abandoned house, where the walls ran with water, there was no heating except an old coal range in the kitchen – by the time it got warm after we'd lit it in the morning we'd gone off to work – and nowhere to put anything. Our bedrooms were cold and wet and our clothes damp. What saved us was that one of us was the daughter of a consultant and when she became ill through the conditions he came down from London, took one look, and had a go at the hospital until something was done.

'By this time I was getting fed up. The military nurses were far more conscious of rank than all the other ones I'd met. Once, when I was with a sister, a doctor and a consultant, the doctor asked me to fetch him a patient's X-rays. I trotted off, got them, and handed them to him, only to get the most frightful rocket from the Sister afterwards – she said correct procedure was to hand them first to her so that she could hand them to him. The whole atmosphere was so hierarchical. The nurses were always trying to make us train as full-time nurses and I utterly refused – in those days if you were training you were treated like a fifteen-year-old and had to be in at 9.00 p.m. I was twenty-seven and I just wasn't going to do that sort of thing.

'So in 1942 I decided to stop nursing and I went and trained as a speech therapist at the West End Hospital for Nervous Diseases. It was very interesting. You were dealing with children from the East End who'd lost their speech from shock in the Blitz. They'd seen their parents and houses bombed. We had to get them to talk.

'I worked with a very good psychiatrist. We had a great sand tray, with little toy fire engines, ambulances, soldiers, policemen and aeroplanes and the children played with these. We sat and watched. After a bit, we would ask them a question. At first they wouldn't answer but after a bit they'd suddenly say a word. The psychiatrist would sometimes do it by getting something deliberately wrong – he'd point to a horse and say: "Is it a cow?" and they'd say: "No. Horse." He managed to get most of them talking.

'We had one man who'd completely lost his speech. When

he regained it he spoke with a broad Welsh accent, to the astonishment of his wife. It transpired that as a child he'd lived in Wales, then his family moved out and he'd gone to school and university in England, and when his speech came back it was as childhood speech.

'I got my qualification as a speech therapist but by that time I was pregnant with my first child so I never practised.'

Mary Pollock's work as a physiotherapist at St Thomas's Hospital focused on the body rather than the mind. 'There were many more electrical treatments then. We had diathermy and short wave, all of which had to be done in large mesh cages, otherwise the radio waves would go up and could be picked up by German aircraft, who would then know where we and they were.

'At St Thomas's we got mostly the dear Lambeth people. I had to give a back massage to my first patient, so I told her to undress, pulled the cubicle curtains round her and then came back. There she was, stark naked but for her hat. I said: "Well, you can remove your hat, too, while you're about it." She said: "Oh, no, dear, I couldn't do that!" and as I put a rug round her I asked her why.

'She lifted it up and it was full of cigarette stubs, all stuck in her hair. She used to go along the streets, pick up the cigarette ends that people threw down, take them home and roll them up into proper cigarettes that she could smoke. Her whole hair was full of these stubs.

'Another woman told me proudly that she always had as much Guinness as she liked to drink – she'd been given a whole cask. "You see," she said, "one day I got something stuck in my teeth when I was drinking a Guinness. I pulled it out and it was the claw of a cockroach!" So Guinness gave her this great cask as a reward for keeping her mouth shut. She was frightfully pleased.'

Part of Mary Pollock's training was at Queen Mary's Hospital, Roehampton, in south-west London, then as now known

for its work with the wounded, disabled and those with pros-
theses. 'My work here ranged from teaching amputees to walk
again with an artificial leg to training TB patients in their
sanatorium in a new posture.

'In those days they treated TB patients quite differently –
they used to remove the affected lung. This made their bodies
very crooked so I used to have to teach them in advance how to
straighten up their heads and necks and how to stand.

'You couldn't do the operation for removing a lung with an
anaesthetic, so patients had to have a spinal injection. It was a
long operation and they all hated the idea of it – they'd all say
"Come in and hold my hand," because they were awake the
whole time. I almost passed out with the first op, because as
you sat by the patient, holding their hand and talking to them,
you could see their body being opened up and everything
inside – heart beating, everything.'

Any German patients were naturally given similar treatment
to British servicemen. At first some could not be persuaded to
accept it. 'A lot of Germans from a U-boat sunk by a destroyer
were brought in to my hospital,' said Penny Woosnam, nursing
in Chatham. 'If you came within ten yards of them they would
scream and we couldn't understand why – of course, they only
spoke German. We'd try and reassure them – "Look, it's only a
thermometer!" Finally we discovered they'd been told that if
they were caught by the British we would kill them.'

Lady Moyra Ponsonby had a similar experience at the Westminster Hospital. 'A Balkan Beam was a structure over the bed
to give an extension, to which a broken leg can be attached. It
looked a bit like goalposts at the head and foot of the bed. A
German soldier we were taking towards it thought it was a
gallows and that he was going to be hanged. He was absolutely
terrified.'

Virginia Forbes Adam, at King's College Hospital, found
that on the whole she preferred nursing women to men 'because
they were basically cleaner. There always seemed to be a mess

of tobacco round men, and they had more coughs, with more of the dreaded sputum.'

~⁓

In 1944 Cynthia Denison-Pender, who had joined the Red Cross, was working for the War Organisation, which combined the Red Cross and St John's, at 14 Grosvenor Crescent. 'We drove ambulances, private cars, vans, lorries, everything. We did a mass evacuation when the V-1s and V-2s came. When the V-1s started, the petrified East End people went down to the Chislehurst Caves in Kent – mostly young wives with children – and we took them sandwiches and nappies and saw that they had hot water and blankets.'

These caves, seven miles south-east of Greenwich, consisted of twenty-two miles of tunnels, supposedly hewn out under the hills by Druids two thousand years ago. Some of the galleries, over thirty feet high, were used by the War Office for the storing of explosives, but their real fame was as shelters. Around 7,500 people lived there during the 1941–4 Blitz. Everyone had to be in their place by 9.00 p.m. and silent by 10.30. Each 'pitch' was numbered and, if left unoccupied for four days, was considered vacant and free for anyone to take over.

In the first days of the Blitz, everything was comparatively organised, with 'permanent' residents bringing their own beds, sheets, tables, chairs and even stoves. But as the caves became more and more crowded, people were packed together sleeping on the rough floors and those who wanted to relieve themselves often had to walk a mile or more to reach the outside of the caves, picking their way by the only light available, that of candles.

As more and more people were rendered homeless and des-titute, conditions in places like the large Underground stations where thousands sheltered every night, and the notorious Tilbury shelter in Stepney where 12,000 regularly took refuge, were even worse. With cold, damp, dirt, discomfort and appalling sanitation, not surprisingly, they were a hotbed for the passing-on of scabies, impetigo, lice and bronchitis.

By the time of the bombardment by V-1 and V-2 rockets in 1944 almost 15,000 people a night were sheltering in Chislehurst, and the caves were so popular that a notice had to be put up at London Bridge Station saying: "Chislehurst Caves full. No room for newcomers." It was not surprising: from packed, squalid conditions, the Government, the owner of the Caves and the occupants themselves had together produced a well-organised community with amenities that most people who lived there – for 6d a week – could never otherwise have afforded. The tunnels were lit with electric light, there was an underground concert hall, a church, a barber's shop and a gymnasium where boys could learn boxing. Two dance bands provided music every evening and there was a weekly dance. Carts drawn by pit ponies cleared away the rubbish.

'Usually you were called to places to fetch people,' recalled Cynthia Denison-Pender. 'I always slept in the garage so as to be ready. Worst of all was going to these derelict old ladies to take them out of London because of the V-2s. You had to carry them down, two of you making a chair with your hands. What I remember most is the masses of urine – there were always countless pots of pee under the beds and the rooms stank – I hadn't realised what the slums were like before.

'We much preferred the V-1s. If you were driving you could guess by the rocket's trajectory where it would land and you could steer away from it – once, when I was had up for going too fast, I said I was avoiding a V-1.'

For those who were not driving, the sudden cutting-out of a V-1's engine meant that an explosion was imminent. 'The only time I was frightened during the war was when a buzz bomb came over the hospital at Basingstoke in the middle of an operation and the engine cut out,' said Jean Falkner. 'Sir Harold Gillies, who was operating, said: "Everyone get under the table except myself and the anaesthetist," and I'm afraid we all did. But luckily it wasn't too close.'

The V-2s were another matter. Cynthia Denison-Pender was one of many who found them 'petrifying. They scared us all stiff. Once I was driving a whole lot of chaps who'd come back from the Japanese war, who had beri-beri and were yellow. Then a V-2 dropped about 30 yards in front of us and there was literally no road left – luckily, it was a hot summer evening and my windows were open so we didn't get glass blown in our faces but the van turned round three times. By the end the men were green rather than yellow.'

Chapter 11

Love and Marriage

'... and then we got engaged. Crazy, really, wasn't it?'

Wartime love has an urgency that speeds up emotion, over-leaps normal barriers and plunges those struck by it into a passion heightened by separation and fear of death – and, you would think, overcomes such trifles as class distinction. Yet of the forty-seven women I talked to, although most had made great friends across the class barrier – for barrier is what it was – only two or three had married someone from a different background.

'Of course I picked up boyfriends at the factory because they chatted you up, though I didn't actually take any of them home,' said Pamela Joyce, working in an Admiralty munitions factory and later in the Meteorological Department in London. 'I was quite sensible about it.'

Pre-war attitudes, lifelong in the case of many upper-class parents, absorbed almost by osmosis by their daughters, were hard to slough.

'If one met a boyfriend there was no question of shacking up,' said Pamela. 'The telephone went, one went to the theatre – I saw *Annie Get Your Gun* three times because I never let on that I'd been taken before – you were taken out to dinner, they sent flowers, they rang up again. That's the way it was.'

Even the pre-war custom of chaperonage, overt or implicit, was hard to shake off, sometimes hovering once more over girls who returned to the parental home on leave, no matter that elsewhere they were doing jobs on which the lives of others often depended.

'Once, during the war, when George and I were definitely walking out – all my family knew that – we were staying with my dear old Great-Aunt Helen,' said Joan Stafford King-Harman. 'My father, there for dinner, had said good night to us and we'd told them both we were off to the 400, where we had a bottle of gin.

'At about 3.00 a.m. Great-Aunt Helen rings up my father: "What shall I do? Joan hasn't come home!" He was furious at being woken up, so he just said: "Well, Aunt Helen, if she's got herself into trouble, she's got herself into trouble. Good night!" and put down the receiver.'

The knowledge that daughters were now meeting not only the carefully selected young men of good family who had surrounded them in their debutante Season but others – for whom it was not necessarily an axiom of faith that Nice Girls Didn't – rarely encouraged these mothers to break their long-standing silence on matters sexual and offer any more explicit guidance to their daughters than the occasional mumbled sentence of pre-war years.

'Don't forget even the nicest man will try to take advantage of you,' said Fanny Gore Browne's mother when her daughter went off to join the Wrens. 'In other words,' inferred Fanny from this vague warning, 'don't lead him on.'

The innocence of pre-war days constantly prevailed. 'My physical life was slow in evolving, I'd never been kissed with an open mouth before,' said Diana Barnato, then in her early twenties.

'When I got married, sex was still a bit of a mystery – my understanding was that it was solely for procreation,' said Sarah Norton. 'My mother had died so my aunt, Kitty Brownlow, was supposed to tell me the facts of life. But all she said was: "Don't worry if it hurts – it gets better."'

Cynthia Denison-Pender found that her very naïveté was a protection against unwanted advances. 'I was extraordinarily innocent, which meant that people treated one rather differently. Once one of our engine fitters came out when I was on my own and said "Miss Pender, it's lovely to get you alone because I love you passionately," but he never made a move. Our sergeant was a lesbian but at eighteen I didn't know what a lesbian was.'

Val Canning was equally innocent when she married her husband, Anthony Wellesley Colley. 'I'd had about thirteen proposals – I was good at dancing and chat – but I always knew that this was the man I was going to marry.

'We were literally childhood sweethearts – we met when I was eight and he was nine and I knew then. We always had last dances together. He was very good-looking. Both of us had a prime minister as an ancestor.

'Being Catholic I had a baby within a year of marriage. When I was expecting my second child I had a serious falling-out with my mother, who said I was completely stupid having another child in wartime. She went off in such a fury that I went to my mother-in-law in Lincolnshire, weeping the whole way. I had to work hard and it was very lonely there – not a soul around except for a few old people. If you went to a tennis party you had to bicycle there and bring your own tea.

'After a bit I went down to Woking where I had a beloved aunt and bought a house on the outskirts – my husband's uncle and my aunt's husband lent me two thousand pounds to do this. It was much easier for my husband to see me in Woking than when I was up in Lincolnshire with his mother and I thought it was time we had a proper home.'

Val's husband was killed on D-Day. 'He had survived all the other raids – he was in the first raid on Norway, No. 4 Commando, led by Lord Lovat. They were allowed to come and see their wives just before D-Day, which is how I knew something major was going to happen. They went over on 5 June. He managed to get on the beach. He was leading his men and as he got to the defence wall ahead he was shot by a sniper. They always shot the officers because they thought then the men would go to pieces but of course they didn't as they were just as well trained. He was twenty-five.'

~⌐

Love in wartime was a chancy business, with loss always at the forefront of everyone's mind. With poor communications, sudden cancellations of leave or despatch elsewhere, it could be difficult for those of either sex to know if silence meant that the affair had fizzled out – or something far worse. 'You lived from day to day in the war – that's my main memory,' said Anne Douglas-Scott-Montagu. 'You might suddenly hear that someone you were very fond of had been killed.'

'Although we got used to coping with death it was terrible if a boat was lost,' said Fanny Gore Browne, a Wren stationed in Dover. 'The naval officer in charge of us said: "I really think I'm going to stop you girls going out with the coastal forces – it's too distressing." And of course there were casualties from the Fleet Air Arm up the road, whom many of us also knew.'

For Lavinia Holland-Hibbert, always passionately interested both in things of the mind and in politics, love was literally an education. As a FANY serving in Italy, she had met Denis Healey ('a clever young sapper from the 8th Army') in the spring of 1944 and one day telephoned him to ask if he would drive her and a friend to a political meeting. On the way back they went to his room to look at his books.

'After this,' she wrote in her diary, 'the evening became different from any other.' He slept on a camp bed planted in the middle of a stone floor. All around were boxes with books laid on them – books of poetry and philosophy in German, French, Italian and English and a few modern novels, together with one or two first editions bought in Florence. 'Read this,' he said, handing her a poem called 'Leda and the Swan', and watching her closely. 'Um, yes,' she said as she read of Leda's rape by the Swan. 'You read it far too quickly,' said Healey. 'Stay to dinner.'

That night she described both Healey and the evening in her diary. 'Denis is a thickset dark young man with very thick eyebrows meeting over his eyes. He has an amusing laughing face and a slightly high Oxford voice with an under roughness. He's full of self-confidence, the right kind. He knows what he wants and it's worth wanting.

'There was no need to make conversation. We talked about ourselves or books so that I noticed neither the usual bad dinner at the Officers' Club nor the aimless wandering about in moonlit Siena streets afterwards. We discussed life for a third of the time, books for another third, and in the last third he told me what he was going to do – either be a don at Merton or a Labour MP. He went back to the 8th Army next day.'

When he reappeared it was the start of sightseeing expeditions, looking at pictures and art exhibitions, buying books and going to the cinema. He told Lavinia about his life and loves – he thought he was going to marry a schoolteacher called Edna. 'Denis has such vitality,' she wrote, 'it streams from him, wakes one up and makes one very good-tempered.'

They went to Perugia, to Assisi – he was going to give her a tour of as much of Umbria as he could cover – and sang 'The Red Flag' driving down to San Gimignano. 'We both thought the Left was the only future for Europe because they were the only ones who really opposed Hitler.

'We drove round in a jeep to all the famous towns. The best of the pictures from the Uffizi had all been put in the Sitwell castle of Montegufoni to keep them safe for the duration of the war and Denis persuaded the caretaker to let us look at some of them. We saw the *Primavera*, facing the wall, in a long underground gallery.

'Denis really educated me, both musically and artistically. He was a very percipient person. But he had certain habits. When I was going out with him I was not allowed to see anyone else. I rather kicked at that because I'd been used to seeing all my boyfriends on different nights.'

Denis Healey later discreetly described their love affair in his autobiography, *The Time of My Life*. Talking of their sightseeing, he wrote: 'On many of these explorations I was accompanied by a young captain in the Female Auxiliary [sic] Nursing Yeomanry, called Lavinia. We spent weekends at the medieval town of San Gimignano and later at the enchanting fishing village of Positano south of Naples. The FANYs were an exceptional lot, with much broader views and wider interests than I would have then expected.'

Lady Anne Spencer, a Wren stationed at Immingham on the Humber, met her future husband, Christopher Wake-Walker, almost by chance (in May 1943). 'Lots of ships came in for refitting. One knew people on them and they would ask the officers in for drinks. Christopher was the First Lieutenant of HMS *Pytchley*, a Hunt-class destroyer. The Pytchley Hunt* was started by my family, the Spencers, in 1760, so the Commanding Officer rang up and said would I go on board for tea – Wren officers were only allowed on board for tea [except for parties].

'And there was Christopher, covered with mud from playing rugger. That was the beginning of everything.'

As their feelings for each other developed, so did the dread and uncertainty of wartime romance. 'It was awful, wondering if the ships were going to come in. We kept in touch by letters, which took three or four days – you wrote to British Forces Post Office – and we met in London when we were on leave.'

Love did not often cross the barrier of rank, although the Navy took the sensible attitude that a good-looking Wren was always welcome, whether lower deck or officer. 'Pretty Wrens

* One of the most famous hunts in England, based in Northamptonshire.

always got asked into the wardrooms,' said one former Wren officer. 'There were endless drinks parties on board, especially Sunday morning drinks, in the wardroom – in the Mediterranean, these were on deck, under awnings. Only the captain had privacy, as he had a day cabin.

'You were never allowed to go on board ship alone – two of you was the minimum. But there were ways round that. Destroyers would usually tie up two abreast and if your boyfriend was the captain of the far ship, you and a friend would board the near one and you alone would go on to the far one. It was perfectly all right as the two of you had been seen to go on board together.

'As an officer, the situation of being asked out by someone of a different class did not occur.'

Rank as much as class was a barrier. Officers mixed with officers and other ranks with other ranks, though there was sometimes resentment when a well-born AT private or Wren rating was seen out with an officer.

Lady Barbara Legge's route to marriage with someone from a completely different world – a glamorous Polish officer – was as romantic as it was circuitous. 'My four years with the FANYs were up, at the end of which they had to give me a fortnight's what they called terminal furlough. At this point I left the ATS [into which the FANYs had been subsumed]. I wanted to join the Free FANYs, which meant that I had to be given a hush-hush job quickly before I could be called up at the end of that fortnight.'

She found herself in SOE (Special Operations Executive) and was soon sent to Amersham, from where Polish agents were being dropped into Poland. When the Germans discovered this route and began shooting them down, it was decided to move the operation first to North Africa and then to Italy. With them, in 1944, went Barbara.

She and the other FANYs were told to set up a holding station in Sidi Ferruch, near Algiers, in two small and filthy bungalows, preparing them for the Poles who would shortly be coming from England. 'All we had to clean these bungalows was two nail brushes, half a bath towel and all the sea water we wanted. But we managed it.

'We all got gippy tummies and the drains got blocked. We told the landlord and he said: "Until les mademoiselles arrived it was all right but now it is *Tirez, tirez, tirez tout le temps*." The only loo paper we had was leaflets that had been dropped on Algiers that said "Courage et espoir".

'Then we were moved to Italy in an Arab train that took two days and a night to travel two hundred miles. We finished up in Philippeville [in Algeria] where the last three ships had been sunk and where we were boarded on to what had been a French ship and taken to Brindisi, in southern Italy.

'Here we stayed for just over a fortnight. We were the only Englishwomen to be seen and we had a wonderful time – if my vehicle broke down I just sat and waited and a queue formed to help me.'

Barbara met her future husband, Adam Kwiatkowski, when sent in her truck to ask for some beds. 'The next time I met him he'd got appendicitis and another FANY who rather liked him wanted to go and see him and asked me to come with her. And I did and he was looking very pale and interesting, and from there it went on.

'We were married in the spring of 1945, in a little church in a village in the hills behind Fresano, in Puglia, by a Polish Jesuit priest, in Polish, with Adam's brother officers, my FANY friends and my sister there. We were very fortunate because in the SOE, once married, I should have been sent straight home. But the Consul in Bari said he couldn't do that because in Italy we needed a civil wedding to legalise our marriage, so we had the six weeks this took to set up.

'My sister and Adam's best man came with us as witnesses but when we got to the register office we were told we needed not two but four witnesses. "Have you got any cigarettes?" asked the man behind the desk. Fortunately we had. "Well, go and hold them up in the street," he said. Adam did so and a queue of witnesses quickly formed.'

Once home Adam was quickly accepted by Barbara's family. But there was one other person whose verdict mattered greatly: Nanny. 'She was terribly important in the lives of all of us and her opinions mattered very much indeed. I was really worried about how she would react to my marrying Adam. It was a huge relief when I got a letter from my mother saying: "Don't worry, darling, it's all right with Nanny. She's ordered him some name tapes."*

Girls who had been brought up with the tentative advances of young men fully aware that Nice Girls Didn't sometimes got a rude shock at the mating habits of others. One evening, a fellow nurse said to Ann Darlington, working as a nurse in Bath: 'I'm going out with my boyfriend for dinner and he's got a friend – will you join us?' How marvellous, thought Ann, a proper meal for once. But when they met the two airmen it transpired that 'a proper meal' was not on the menu.

'We went to the chaps' lodgings where we had a dreadful supper. After the meal we sat in the sitting room and it became obvious that my friend and her boyfriend were going to have sex there, so I and the other man left the room. He said: "Shall we go to the upstairs bedroom?" "No," I replied, sitting firmly on the stairs and he said: "Thank goodness – I'm a married man with children. Why don't we go for a walk outside for a bit?"

'No sooner had we gone a little way than there was an air raid – they were bombing the local airfield. So we flung ourselves in a ditch and lay there until the All Clear sounded and then we went back. By this time my friend and the other chap were sitting primly by the fire. They said: "Where have you been?"

---

* Name tapes were not just a boarding school essential; as there were no washing machines everything was sent to the laundry and, unless marked, could easily be muddled.

"Oh," I replied, "we've been lying in a ditch." It wasn't until they looked startled that I realised how it must have sounded.'

~~⌒~~

Lesbianism took several of the 1939 set by surprise. Daphne Brock was standing in her petticoat – 'black silk, I remember' – when she was assaulted by a fellow Wren. 'I was just looking to see if my hem was straight when this six-foot woman came in, chucked me over the bed and leapt on me. I was terrified. Although I was absolutely innocent in sexual matters I knew what she was after. I lost my cool and shouted and screamed. I was quite strong because I'd played a lot of tennis and swum but I couldn't move her. Then she heard someone coming and got off.

'I was so upset that I rang Geoffrey Moss, a novelist who lived near us in Sussex and who'd been terribly sweet to me after my mother died and had said: "You can always come to me if you have any problems." Because I sounded so down he asked me to come and see him.

'I went to London and told him all about it and he asked me if I'd reported it. I said: "Not yet." He replied: "Well, don't, because your First Officer is a well-known one." Then he took me to a club in Shepherd's Market where all the lesbians gathered and that taught me a lot. He put it in perspective for me – I'd never heard of lesbianism before.'

Lady Margaret Egerton, stationed in Orkney, had an even more unnerving experience. 'Off the boat got this ... *man*, with nicotine round her mouth, kitbag over her shoulder and an Eton crop. You had to censor letters in Orkney and it was obvious from hers that she was a roaring lizzie. As a corporal, she messed with the three male sergeants and would drink them under the table every night.

'Our lights went out at 11 p.m. and then you had a Tilley lamp if needed. It was so cold I had eleven army blankets on my bed. That night, through my dreams, I heard the distant sound of revelry and it seemed to be getting nearer.

'It stopped outside my door. In my half-asleep state I heard the door being opened. It was this corporal, drunk as a coot. It was pitch dark and I heard heavy, breathing getting nearer, until she bent over me. She stank of whisky.

'"It's your turrrn tonight, ma'am," she growled. "It's your turrrn tonight . . ."

'Then I came to. I said: "Get the hell out of here, Staff!" and she went, leaving me thinking: What do I do in the morning? But it was never referred to again. When I rang up our Commanding Officer next day to say that I'd had a lesbian assault she sounded puzzled and said: "What's that?"'

For girls who had been debutantes before the war, one of the factors that made wartime married life so difficult was that they simply had not been trained for it. In one sense, they had been trained for nothing else *but* marriage – but a marriage that promised a life similar to that of their parents. Educated to become cultured young women with a knowledge of the arts and music, fluent in at least one foreign language, everything they had picked up about running a house involved giving orders to (hopefully) well-trained staff who would see that rooms were always clean and that food, magically transmuted from raw to well-prepared, appeared on the table. Many had not so much as boiled a kettle and none had done any housework.

Mary Armitage, who married her fiancé Ian Freeland in January 1940, was one of them. She and her new husband lived in an hotel for several months because both of them believed she could not cook. 'We never talked about it, we pretended to each other and to the world that we couldn't find a house. I thought there was a great mystique about cooking – my father was a general so we always had a cook, chauffeur, batman, housemaid, parlour-maid, nanny and nursery maid and when I went to stay with my grandmother it was an even bigger household – footmen, butler, etc. – so it never occurred to one to make one's bed. In fact I still drop my clothes on the floor.

'Ian was stationed on the Island of Portland, in charge of fifty young recruits to defend fifteen miles of Dorset coastline. We lived in what was called a private hotel, with six or seven residents. Ian and I used to have rows in whispers in our bedroom. One of the residents complained to the proprietor that she'd seen us going into the bathroom together – it was *that* sort of hotel.

'It was the time we thought the Germans were going to invade at any moment, the summer of Dunkirk. I watched the first daylight raid from a hill above Portland Harbour – dive-bombers sinking a supply ship anchored there. To my amazement, they dived almost vertically, somehow straightening out at the end. One wasn't particularly frightened of the bombs but one was of the Germans coming – we were really convinced they were going to. Ian gave me a little revolver to kill a German – or myself.

'I didn't learn how to cook until I'd been married for eight years. In 1942 Ian was being sent all over the place and as Daddy had become ill and retired in September 1942 I went to live with him at his house in Lechlade. There I stayed for the rest of the war, with my two small children, and his housekeeper cooked for us all. Immediately afterwards we went to Germany to join our husbands where, again, I didn't have to cook.'

Anne Reid was another who had to learn even the simplest things by experience. 'It was quite a shock doing things for myself. Desmond adored junket so I decided to make him some. I knew you had to heat up the milk so I put some in a Pyrex dish and put it on the gas hob and was surprised when it broke. That was the end of our milk ration.'

'When I got married our first house was a rented one at Hatch End, near Pinner,' recalled Esme Harmsworth. 'We were married in January 1942 and it was one of the coldest winters you could imagine. This is really shaming beyond words but I couldn't understand why the house was so cold and why it was so cold at night – I slept in four or five jumpers. Of course it was because there was no central heating but I didn't know what central heating was then – I hadn't even realised my father's house had it.

'I didn't know how to make a cup of tea either. I said to my husband that I'd read in books that making a good cup of tea was rather complicated. He looked at me in astonishment and said: "No, it isn't. When I was a fag at Eton we all learned that sort of thing." So he taught me what he'd learned at Eton – how to make tea, scramble or fry eggs, and fry bacon if there was any. That's all we had to go on for a bit.'

∽

Weddings in wartime often relied on the generosity of friends and relations with both rations and clothing: clothes had been rationed from June 1941, with an annual issue of sixty-six coupons.* As a short dress cost eleven coupons and a nightdress six, it was not so much a question of having a trousseau as acquiring enough coupons to buy a wedding dress. Esme Harmsworth circumvented this problem with a wedding dress made of lace and net, neither of which was on coupons. Other girls, like Susan Meyrick and Val Canning, were able to use their former Presentation frocks; Val, who had made her Presentation dress, inserted sleeves and appliquéd lace over the train.

Lady Anne Spencer, who married her husband, Captain Christopher Wake-Walker, in Westminster Abbey in February 1944, did the same – but with her mother's dress. 'She had worn this white satin dress the night I was presented at Court – the night when Ribbentrop walked past the King and Queen and gave the Nazi salute.

'We got sleeves put in and a train put on by the clever dressmaker who matched up the satin. I had no bridesmaids or

---

* Growing children received an extra ten coupons.

pages or flowers – I just held a handkerchief – and two Wren officers as ushers. They brought all the gold and silver plate out of the cellars to put on the altar and the choir came back from where they'd been evacuated to sing. Christopher's father was Third Sea Lord at the time so we were allowed to have the reception at Admiralty House, which my mother decorated with forsythia she'd picked and brought up from Althorp.'

For those who wished to avoid wartime pregnancies, production of a wedding ring could be essential, as Christian Grant discovered. 'I went to a gynaecologist before I got married – still a virgin, needless to say – and asked him how not to get pregnant. It was the middle of the war and I didn't want a baby then. My wedding day was fixed and everything but even that didn't move him. I was an unmarried girl and that was that. His answer was: "Come back and ask me again when you are actually married."'

Everyone had time for a bride and groom. Passers-by would stop to watch: the sight of a bride, as well as giving a glimpse of the style and glamour that had disappeared with the war, offered a sense of normality and hope. Occasionally, for one of these debutante brides, getting married brought a brief return to the kind of life they had just begun to know before the war. 'My parents were wonderful about my wedding,' said Joan Stafford King-Harman. 'I'd decided to convert to Catholicism because the family of my husband-to-be, George Dennehey, was Catholic, so we got married at Brompton Oratory – with the reception at Claridge's. I'd never stayed at Claridge's before. We had a wonderful dinner party the night before and on my wedding morning I went to get my face done at Cyclax* just round the corner.

---

* The House of Cyclax, established in 1896 and famous for its 'English rose' look, produced the cosmetics used by Princess Elizabeth, continuing to supply her with make-up when she became Queen. They received the Royal Warrant in 1961. Today Cyclax make skin-care products and sun creams.

'As my parents lived in Ireland, where there was no rationing, my mother had produced a lovely piece of white satin for my dress. She took this and some navy silk to the dressmaker where she got her Ascot clothes, who made me a gorgeous silk dress, and my wedding dress. My parents gave us linen from Walpole's and my mother also gave me two beautiful satin nightdresses.

'We didn't have child attendants as the odd buzz bomb was still coming over but our best man cut the cake with his naval sword. We were very much in the racing world and our wedding was on Derby Day, a Saturday. As the wartime Derby was run at Newmarket we said to Claridge's that we must have a wireless and the result was broadcast at the reception, to great cheers. We honeymooned at Feniton Court, near Honiton, and when we arrived Kate, the old housemaid, started unpacking for me and said firmly: "You'll sleep on that side of the bed, Miss."'

Rosemary Hodson, who married her husband Tony Trollope in March 1941, had a wedding cake made from dried fruit and a tin of butter sent over by a friend from America. 'My brother David, who had been in a landing in Italy by the Volturno River, was staying in a farmhouse and when he said: "I've got to get back for my sister's wedding," the daughter of the house gave him a bolt of white silk which she had been saving for her own wedding. That made my wedding nightdress, which had a completely circular skirt.

'People gave us clothes coupons which covered a dress for me and our bridesmaids. At the beginning of June we had four days' honeymoon – Tony was only just back from France after Dunkirk.

'When we were first married he worked in the War Office, so we needed a flat. We only knew the Chelsea-ish bit of London, so when a very nice young woman wanted to rent her flat at the top of one of those houses in Cadogan Square we were delighted. We were rather astounded to find that her bedroom had mirrors on the ceiling but we soon learned why – her clients would come charging up the stairs, to be greeted by

Tony at the top. We left because the shrapnel from the shells fired by the guns in Hyde Park kept coming through our sitting-room ceiling – it was at the time of the Blitz – but fortunately missed the bedroom ceiling.

'When I married I couldn't cook at all. I was so worried the night before I first cooked our meat ration – a slice of gristly beef that would hardly cover a saucer – that I couldn't sleep. I cooked my first cake in a cocoa tin because there were no cake tins.*

'My predominant memories of married life in the war are cold and hunger. There was a time when every single one of my fingertips was poisoned and that was just lack of vitamins. Lots of people got spots, and their hair fell out and that sort of thing. For some, the wartime diet was healthier than they'd had before but it wasn't really adequate.

'Our first baby died and although I was supposed not to, I was determined to get pregnant again soon – Tony was going to be sent abroad. When he left for India we both knew I was pregnant – but he didn't see Joanna until she was four. She was born in December 1943.

'By then we were living in York, in a small all-electric house and the electricity was turned off between ten and five every day. The cold was absolutely awful. My mother used to send us a pound of sausages through the post when she could get them – she lived in the country and knew the butcher – because sausages travelled better than liver. I had nothing to put on the Christmas tree so I tied silver teaspoons on as decorations. Joanna and I had a miserable Christmas in the intense cold waiting for Tony to come home. All the sick had to come home first and there was very little transport. He eventually returned in 1947.'

Anne Reid became engaged to her future husband in April 1939. Just before their wedding in September he was called up and they were allowed only twenty-four hours' honeymoon.

* Such 'luxuries' would have used metal needed for armaments.

'Our married life started off in Windsor. We were always in the London area. I did a quick first-aid course with St John, and then worked in the Savoy garages where there was a Rescue Ambulance Unit, a Red Cross Mobile Unit, and a Heavy Rescue and Light Rescue Unit – a whole little world down in the darkness. When we weren't busy we worked in the Charing Cross Hospital across the road.

'We worked day shifts in the hospital, and at night we slept on stretchers in the garages. When the Blitz started we were really busy. I'd be terrified now but when you are young you never think anything's going to happen to you. I do remember it as bitterly cold and wearing layers of clothes under my uniform, endless vests and things called spencers, which had long sleeves.

'I worked there about three years. I got about mostly by bicycle. I had a little torch with a cover that gave a faint light for bicycling in the blackout but one night I got totally lost in a thick fog in the middle of Trafalgar Square in the blackout when my torch gave out. As there wasn't any traffic I didn't know which way to go.

'For the last six months before D-Day we were up in Yorkshire so I left my job in London and worked in a canteen there. When Desmond went to Normandy I was doing a job in London. He was wounded very badly in Normandy in August and flown to a hospital near Cardiff. He was on the danger list for quite a long time, so I went down there. He was in hospital for nearly six months, so I took a job in Cardiff packing food parcels, still with St John's.

'It was horrible there. All during that bitterly cold winter I was in an icy boarding house. There were eleven of us, with one bathroom between us in which was the only loo. I had a bed with Red Cross blankets and a table with no drawer and one wooden chair. I kept my clothes in my suitcase under the bed.'

For the married, and especially those with children, wartime cold became a fact of life and eking out precious fuel was a constant preoccupation. 'We made one mistake (operational),' wrote a father (in March 1943) to his soldier son, Lieut. Peter Macnair. 'In an excess of zeal for fuel economy we bought a large fire-brick and put it at the back of the fireplace. The result was that the fire would scarcely burn at all, and after putting in the slack, which of course accumulates with startling rapidity at the bottom of the coal bucket, we practically had to start lighting it all over again with two or three precious firelighters. In a very short time the fire-brick was removed and banished for ever to the cellar.'

As the war continued, marriage often became less of an option. 'I met my husband in Saint-Germain and we did our courting in Paris,' said Fanny Gore Browne. 'He'd come for a fortnight's rest and stayed for three months, and that did it! We were unofficially engaged but it wasn't smiled upon. If we had been officially engaged I would probably have been drafted elsewhere – it could interfere with your work, you see.'

Being posted at the wrong moment happened to Judy Impey, who had only been out with her future husband five or six times when she was suddenly sent to the Far East. 'I went out with a ring on my finger. As the war had just ended the announcement of our engagement was put in the *Telegraph* but there we were, me in India and him at home, as he couldn't be sent out because of his leg – he'd lost a leg in Malta at the age of twenty-four.'

※

Often, the war speeded up the process of courtship. 'We only met three times before we got engaged,' said Anne Douglas-Scott-Montagu. 'We knew about each other – I knew a cousin of his who had said that we really ought to meet, as she thought we'd get on well, and I'd seen a photograph of this good-looking young man on her piano. He'd been very badly wounded and was working in the Regimental Headquarters of the Welsh Guards at 18 Wilton Crescent.

'One day he was at a dinner party I'd been invited to and he took me home. He rang up the next day and said: "I've got tickets for a musical – would you like to come?" and I did. Then he took me out to dinner at Quaglino's and we went and danced at the 400 and then we got engaged. Crazy, really, wasn't it?"

Cynthia Denison-Pender got engaged to her husband Roger Mortimer (the racing writer) after meeting only half a dozen times. 'I met Roger in the 400 – I was with another chap, who had been a prisoner with him. Roger began to pursue me but then went to Italy with his regiment and from Italy sent me all sorts of presents. We got engaged after six meetings, which was about as romantic as you can get. We married in 1947 and Roger immediately took up his racing job. At Eton he adored horses and his hobby became his work. He was a regular Coldstreamer but I don't think he was ever a serious soldier.'

Some romances began almost by chance. Mary Toulmin, whose mother was American, had spent the first eighteen months of the war after her London Season in 1939 working for the Mission for Seamen in New York. 'I came back to England in the winter of 1941 because I didn't want to stay in America doing what I felt was practically nothing – all my friends in England were doing something. My parents thoroughly disapproved of my going but they didn't stop me, which they could have done. I went up to Halifax, Nova Scotia, in an old cargo boat, and in Halifax I was able to get on an English boat which was taking a whole lot of Dutch naval officers who had trained in Java to the UK.

'I really liked one of them, Evert von Teyn, who had trained as a naval bomber pilot. When we landed in England it was very sad – he didn't know where he would be posted and I didn't know where I was going to live, so we couldn't exchange addresses. I thought I'd never see him again.

'I went straight to London with an American friend who'd also come over because her husband was in the Royal Navy. She had a job to go to, working on dossiers of prisoners of war in St James's Palace, and they took me on too. We kept track of where our prisoners were and when they were moved and liaised with their families. The Palace was freezing cold but Dolphin Square, where we managed to find a flat, was wonderfully warm – it had central heating provided by the heat from Battersea Power Station that would otherwise have escaped uselessly into the air. My old nanny, Lily, who being English couldn't go with the family to America, also lived with us.

'A fortnight after I arrived I ran into Evert outside the Ritz. It was like a miracle. From then on I saw him constantly. After a while my friend left, when her husband was stationed elsewhere. Evert and I married in 1942, in a church in Pimlico. I was 21 and he was 23. Being a pilot he got quite a lot of leave and was able to come to Dolphin Square. By this time I was working for the Free French [Mary was virtually bilingual: she had been brought up in Switzerland and the family also had a house in France].'

Evert von Teyn was killed in the summer of 1943, flying too low over the sea while searching for survivors from a ship that had been sunk. Months later, on 28 January 1944, their daughter was born. Mary continued with her work and the baby was looked after by Lily 'but it was a very low patch.'

Esme Harmsworth, whose love affair with the young Duke of Rutland had broken up unhappily – in part due to his mother Kakoo, Duchess of Rutland, who thought him too young for marriage at twenty-two – soon afterwards met her future husband Rowley Errington (later Lord Cromer and Governor of the Bank of England and Ambassador to Washington). He showed no such hesitation.

Their daughter was born in 1943 and Esme was fortunate enough to have one of the old-school nannies, the centre of whose world was 'her' baby and for whom a world war figured largely as a tiresome interference to baby's routine. 'The only time I was really frightened was while my husband was soldiering hard, getting ready for D-Day. When the air-raid sirens sounded I told Nanny we had to go down to the coal hole.

'"I'm not taking my baby down any coal hole!" said Nanny. She was a very tough nanny and I was scared stiff of her. But I said that I insisted and at that moment a high-explosive bomb fell near by and flung me to the floor. So we went down and sat in the coal hole and it was quite terrifying – I was nervous because there was nothing to think of but the baby but Nanny was furious because it meant disturbing the baby from her sleep. The next day when we went out there was a gap in the terrace about four or five houses away and that did bring it home to Nanny.'

Cynthia Miller was one of the many whose homes were destroyed in the war, an episode that she too remembers as 'the only time in the war I was really frightened.

'I was living near a small airfield at Long Newnton, near Tetbury, where they had training aircraft. My job then was seeing to the welfare of land girls, sorting out problems such as when they were made to do domestic work or the farmer or husband wanted to get into bed with them, and I'd got back late. It was about ten o'clock on a bitterly cold January night in 1945, with snow on the ground, and I was sitting in the drawing room, still in my outdoor clothes, when I heard one of these planes come over.

'I just had time to think, It seems *terribly* low, when it crashed into the roof, exploded and the whole thing caught fire. There were three or four people in it and they were all killed, which was too awful.

'I got Nanny and my daughter Celia – asleep upstairs – and our four dogs out, but nothing else. By this time the fire had really taken hold. The building where we kept the car was attached to the house but the wonderful old groom who came with me when I married said: "Madam, go and get the car quick, before it goes up." So I got the car and took it halfway down the drive.

'The Tetbury fire brigade, which was much the closest, wouldn't come to us because they said we were not in their zone but in Stroud's. The fire engine from Stroud, which was much farther off, never got to us because there was so much snow it got stuck on a hill. The Long Newnton airfield people came and they'd just begun to get the fire under control when they ran out of foam. So we had to stand and watch everything go up in flames.

'After it was all over and the house burnt down to its foundations, at about four in the morning I piled us all into the car and drove to my father-in-law's in Bath, where we arrived about 6.00 a.m. There was so little petrol left in the car that it couldn't even be moved away from the front door the following morning.

'We lost everything. There wasn't insurance and you couldn't replace things because everything was rationed. But friends were very kind – somebody gave me a lipstick, someone else a pair of stockings and so on. Worst of all was when I had to ring my husband up – he'd just come back from abroad – and say: "We've got no house – it's all gone." "What *are* you talking about?" he said.'

Penny Woosnam had a number of serious American suitors before her marriage and numerous proposals. 'One man sent me orchids every week until after the end of the war and I never knew who it was. I went to the shop and said "I must know – I need to thank him." "No," they said. "He's left the country but he's left money to send you orchids every week."

'My chief American boyfriend wanted to marry me but not until after the war. I felt I couldn't wait that long – and then I met Mont Montague and six weeks later we were engaged. As soon as he heard, my American borrowed money and gave me a huge diamond. I had to put the notice in *The Times* myself as Mont was away on exercises. To my fury it never appeared and when I went round to find out why, they told me: "The gentleman came here and said it wasn't to go in." It was my American and I was so cross I threw his diamond back to him and said: "You could have done this before – but it's too late now."'

Penny and her Mont were married a month before D-Day, on 6 May 1944. 'We had a week's honeymoon in a cottage lent to us by a friend. Mont's regiment moved to the village for exercises so we couldn't go out or they would have seen us and all wanted to come in. He went overseas in June right after the first landings in Normandy. I'd just realised I was pregnant when the doodlebugs started [the first were launched on 13 June]. I'd never been frightened before but when I knew I was having a baby I became terrified.

'So, on August the 16th I went to Mont's family in Ireland. I'd never been before and because I'd always been in uniform I had no clothes – just a coat made in Paris before the war and a beret and skirt made by the local tailor.'

~

Food was a major preoccupation during the war and a good meal with an unexpected delicacy such as fresh eggs loomed high on everybody's wish-list. Those in the services did not have to worry about obtaining food but, for married women, trying to bring up a family, eking out the rations and trying to fill hungry stomachs was a major preoccupation. Happy were those who could establish a relationship with the local butcher who might occasionally slip them a pound of sausages or offal (both not rationed).

Those who lived in the country were luckier. 'We had some rabbits about the place that were shot or trapped and they were an enormous help,' said Cynthia Miller. 'The garden was dug up for vegetables and I had a pony and trap that I used to drive into Tetbury to see what I could collect in the way of food.'

Women who were married and those with children under fourteen were exempt from war work, although plenty did it. Lorna Harmsworth, who married in 1941, worked in a crèche while her husband was stationed at Camberley. 'We had our first child quite quickly. At that time you were allowed one person to work for you, a cook or a nanny, and as I didn't know anything about children I chose a nanny.'

When Lorna's husband was sent to Algiers in 1942, by which time they had moved to Northwood in Middlesex, she and a girl friend worked for an armaments manufacturer in Wardour Street. 'They were making parts for aeroplanes. The employees were mostly girls from the East End who spent their time trying to shock us. We didn't react except to giggle like mad. After work Sybil and I would go round the corner to where they couldn't see us and take a taxi to the station – we didn't want to look as though we were living it up. Then I'd catch the train back to Northwood. I was pregnant but no one ever offered me a seat.

'When my nanny left in 1943, by which time my second child was born, I stayed at home in Northwood looking after them both. It was quite lonely as of course I wasn't able to go out at all. Then when the buzz bombs came [in June 1944], which terrified me with children, I moved down to my mother's house in Dorset, where things were easier as my mother had a kitchen garden.'

Not all married women worked – or were able to. 'On Portland, where my husband was stationed, we were completely insulated,' recalled Mary Armitage, 'and it simply didn't occur to me to do anything to help with the war. Nobody round me was doing anything, we just hung around doing nothing more than our husbands' washing. I used to sit up in bed while Ian was shaving, polishing his buttons, and I ironed his battledress trousers with a good crease. The moment he left I'd start playing patience on the floor.

'Then he was moved to Monty's staff and Monty wouldn't have wives within thirty miles and only allowed husbands twenty-four hours with their wives once a week. So I went to live as a PG with friends near by. It was the only time we were really hungry. Ian would come home once a week and shoot pigeons, I would pick wild strawberries in the woods and my friends would pick nettles and cook them.'

Celebrations often required ingenuity. 'When my little boy was about two I took him to the birthday party of another little boy,' remembered Ann Darlington. 'All of us mothers were amazed because the child's cake had his name written on it in white. We fell on our hostess and said: "*Where* did you get icing sugar? We haven't seen it for five years."

'"Oh, it's peppermint toothpaste – the children love it," she replied.'

For the married, this kind of ingenious substitute and 'making do' became a way of life that was to persist for many years. Though the coming of peace saw the disappearance of sudden death through enemy action, the privations of war largely continued. Not until midnight on 3 July 1954 did all food rationing finally end.

Chapter 12

Bletchley

'How much German do you speak?'

Since the education of most debutantes included two or three terms at a Continental finishing school, they were often proficient in one or more foreign languages. Usually these were French and German, taught along with courses on the culture of the two countries and expanded by sightseeing and exhibitions.

One unexpected result of this accomplishment-based education was that the Government was able to make use of a number of young women of call-up age for services ranging from translation or typing in a foreign language to action behind enemy lines. Bletchley Park, in Buckinghamshire, the centre for decoding instructions from Nazi headquarters to its personnel, was where a number of them worked. Secrecy of such a high order surrounded Bletchley that one girl, Diana Giffard, who later married her boyfriend Airey Neave, did not know that he too worked in Bletchley until they ran into each other in a corridor.

Bletchley Park was the organisation that controlled all cryptanalysis, carrying out most of the work itself in the main house and its surrounding huts and transmitting the results, under the code-name 'Ultra', to Allied operational headquarters in the United Kingdom, and Mediterranean and European theatres of war. The German High Command naturally sent its signals out in code; cracking these codes was of course vital to the Allies.

This mysterious establishment, fifty miles north of London, consisted of a Victorian house and 53-acre estate that had been the home of Sir Herbert Leon and his family from 1883 until his widow died in 1937. It was then split into various lots and bought by a consortium which intended it for residential development. But before this could happen it was taken over (in 1938) as the wartime headquarters of the Government Code and Cypher School, now known as the Government Communications Headquarters.

There was little organised recruitment for this most secret of jobs. At least some of the cryptographers were recruited because of their extreme skill at solving crossword puzzles (discovered by holding open contests). But more usually, it was by word of mouth. A senior officer in one of the services might have a friend or relation with a 'suitable' daughter. Often, the knowledge that a girl was intelligent and came from a family with an impeccable background was enough to convince the authorities that she could be trusted.

'I got to Bletchley in the most casual way,' said Jean Campbell-Harris. 'They were really frightfully snobbish about the girls who worked there. A friend of my father's said: "Maybe when Jean's finished her secretarial course she would like to go to a place called Bletchley, which is to do with the Foreign Office."

'So in the summer of 1941 I had an interview with a funny little man in Lyons Corner House at the top of Whitehall and he said: "How much German do you speak?" and "Do you mind typing things you don't understand? And now I must go back to the Admiralty – go to Bletchley tomorrow." And off I went.'

Joan Stafford King-Harman, who had begun her war work by joining the ARP car service, soon realised that her friends were getting more serious jobs or going into the women's services. Through Admiral Godfrey, the Director of Naval

Intelligence, who knew her family, Joan was head-hunted in October 1939 to go into one of the Intelligence services. 'When I was interviewed I was just told it was to do with the Foreign Office and would be in the country – they wouldn't tell me where. All they said was that I was to report in the morning to Broadway Buildings* and would be driven to the country. I was to use Broadway Buildings as my address for anyone to write to, I would be a confidential secretary paid £3 10s a week in cash, and I would be billeted.

'So I turned up next morning with my suitcase and we were driven straight to Wormwood Scrubs. My heart sank but it was only to collect various papers before we were driven off to Buckinghamshire. I was billeted with a dear old boy called Sir Walter Carlisle in a lovely house near Newport Pagnell [a few miles north of Bletchley] where the Guy Fawkes plot had been hatched. There were six of us girls there and we all got bed, breakfast and supper.'

Joan was there until Dunkirk, when her department was moved to St Albans. 'Because it was quite a fun office to be in, quite a lot of nice people wanted to join. My section dealt with German activities in Turkey.'

Sarah Norton, working in a factory with her friend Osla Benning, was recruited in the best traditions of the secret service 'out of the blue', in the spring of 1941. Her connections were impeccable – her father was Lord Grantley, her godfather was Lord Louis Mountbatten and her mother's lover was Lord Beaverbrook, a man who had the ear of the Prime Minister, Winston Churchill. 'One day a brown envelope arrived stamped OHMS. Inside was a letter saying: "You will leave the factory and report to the Labour Exchange in Sardinia Street for work in a language section as Translator, Assessor and Analyst on German Naval Shipping U-Crypts."'

---

* The London headquarters of the Intelligence services, No. 54 Broadway, backing on to Queen Anne's Gate.

The two girls moved into a small, cold, borrowed flat in Victoria and made an appointment at the Labour Exchange, wondering where they would be directed. Special Intelligence, they heard through a distant relative of Osla's, was recruiting German-speaking staff. Sarah, thanks to her months at finishing school in Munich before the war, had been virtually bilingual in German, as she was in French, having been brought up by a French governess, but it had been two or three years since either she or Osla had spoken these languages on a daily basis.

In February 1941 they were given various written and oral tests, one or two of which they bluffed their way through, determined to do something as valuable as possible for the war effort. Then came silence. Hoping that they had passed, they sat waiting, bored and fearful, in the gloomy London flat.

A fortnight later another brown envelope arrived. In it was a brief letter. 'You are to report to Station X at Bletchley Park in four days' time. Your postal address is Box III, c/o The Foreign Office. That is all you need to know.' It was signed 'Commander Travis'. Osla received the same communication. Both girls had been classified as 'multi-linguists'.

Bletchley Park was a blend of country house and internment camp. It was reached from the station by a rough cinder path up which its recruits staggered with their suitcases. The first thing they saw was an eight-foot-high chain fence topped by rolls of barbed wire, at which point the track became a concrete drive leading to iron gates guarded by sentries. Only those with passes were allowed through.

At the centre of the complex was the original red-brick late-Victorian house, overlooking lawns leading down to an ornamental lake, and flanked on both sides by a collection of prefabricated huts. The first step for everyone was a brief talk, short on detail, explaining only that the purpose of their work was to break the German codes. The need for secrecy was emphasised and recruits were asked to sign the Official Secrets

One of the prime duties of the WVS was serving tea from their mobile canteens. It was very welcome, as here, in the aftermath of a raid.

LEFT: A number of debs opted for factory work, often helping to make aircraft, explosives and naval equipment, to the invariable background of *Music While You Work*. These five girls are riveting the fuselage of a Short Stirling aircraft.

ABOVE: ATS drivers rode motorcycles and drove staff cars, ambulances and lorries up to three tons in weight. BELOW: After the fall of France in 1940, there was a very real fear of a Nazi invasion. These signposts were removed from north Kent and Surrey in case they helped the enemy. This did not make the job of FANY and ATS drivers and messengers any easier.

A FANY motorcycle messenger. Women motorcycle riders were an essential part of wartime communications.

ATS girl Mary Churchill walking with her father the Prime Minister on the deck of H.M.S. *Duke of York*, the battleship which took him to America in January 1942. Beside them is the ship's commanding officer.

Land girls, clad in their uniform of khaki dungarees and dark green sweater, fork manure on to fields.

The Map Room of the underground Cabinet War Rooms, to which Diana Lyttleton was suddenly transferred in 1942.

ATS girls destined for mixed batteries of anti-aircraft guns learn the essentials of aircraft recognition.

A FANY lance-corporal instructs recruits on vehicle maintenance at a training centre in Southern Command.

ABOVE: The Duchess of Kent, watched by the First Lord of the Admiralty and the Director of the WRNS, Vera Laughton Matthews, talks in May 1941 to Wrens who have been selected for service abroad and are wearing the new tropical uniform. BELOW: Wren wireless telegraphists learning to take down morse code messages and transcribe them – as Lady Elizabeth Scott did on troopships, back and forth across the Atlantic, in 1943.

WAAF drivers took pilots and ground crew to their dispersal points when they set out for operations.

Some of the 'Attagirls' (women of the Air Transport Auxiliary) in the flying kit they wore to ferry planes from factory to airfield. Diana Barnato Walker remembers both the joys and terrors of this work.

Cynthia Denison-Pender was one among many who found the V2
rockets more terrifying than conventional bombs: they gave no
warning and their effect was devastating. This was London's
Farringdon Road in March 1945 after a V2 fell in daylight on the
Central Markets.

VE Day – and rejoicing girls in khaki drive their service vehicle
through London's Trafalgar Square.

Act. The penalty for contravening it, they were informed, was imprisonment for thirty years.

Bletchley's beginnings were small: in 1939 it employed fewer than two hundred staff – not nearly enough for the amount of work to be done. When a plea for more help was made by four of the senior cryptographers on 21 October 1941, Churchill minuted the following day: 'Make sure they have what they want – extreme priority – and report to me that this has been done.' Bletchley was granted all the staff it needed and by 1944 almost seven thousand people were working there round the clock, in three shifts, fetched and returned by bus or car from billets up to twenty miles away.

Just before the two girls' arrival came the brilliant naval coup that was to transform intelligence work and, after tremendous losses, win the vital Battle of the Atlantic.

The most difficult of the German codes, hitherto unbreakable, was Enigma. With its double and triple scrambling of messages, unscrambled at the other end by a machine resembling an ancient typewriter, according to a protocol changed daily, it was the despair of even the best mathematical and crypto-analytic brains in Britain. Meanwhile the losses inflicted by German U-boats on the convoys of merchant shipping crossing the Atlantic were terrible.

Then came the lucky break that led to the cracking of Enigma. On 9 May 1941, the German U-boat U-110, chasing a convoy off the coast of Greenland, was picked up on Asdic contact and forced to the surface by depth charges. After gunfire, which killed the U-boat captain, the survivors were captured, the U-boat taken in tow and its precious contents – an Enigma machine, codebook and operation manual – taken aboard the British destroyer HMS *Bulldog*. As there had been no time for the German crew to send a signal, and as U-110 subsequently sank, the German High Command had no idea that Britain could now break the German naval code – and the movements of U-boats could be tracked.

It was vital that no hint of Enigma's capture and the work of decoding Germany's most secret signals escaped to the outside world, either by deliberate leakage or through chance, careless remarks. Thus security was intense. Internally, Bletchley Park worked on a 'need to know' basis: if you didn't need to know something, you weren't told about it. There was no talking to anyone 'outside' and Bletchley workers were not allowed to frequent the local pubs. Many of those who worked there did not even tell their husbands what they had been doing until many years after the end of the war.

'We were nineteen and twenty and it never occurred to us to open our mouths,' said Sarah Norton. 'If anyone asked me what I did, my all-purpose response was: "I'm a clerk in the Foreign Office." I said the same to my family when they asked. We talked to each other but not to anybody in other huts. Whoever on the staff had a boyfriend in the Navy would make friends with me as I could probably tell her where he was, especially if he hadn't written.'

Sarah and Osla were told they were joining the Naval Section, working in Hut 4. The naval scientific cryptographers worked in Hut 8; from them came the intelligence analysed and processed in Hut 4. This, one of the wooden huts built in 1939, was painted green; it measured approximately 145 feet by 30 feet and was used mainly for naval code-breaking – not that either girl realised this at first. 'Nobody explained anything. We were merely told that pieces of paper in German would come through, from which we had to take all salient information and put this on filing cards along with the date, number on the paper and so forth, and index it. Within a couple of days we realised that this information had been obtained by code-breaking but even then we had no idea of the whole picture.'

For Sarah and Osla, their new assignment meant adopting naval routine immediately, with 'watches' changing weekly, first from 9.00 a.m. to 4.00 p.m., then from 4.00 p.m. to midnight, and in the third week from midnight to 9.00 a.m. They were billeted in an hotel and driven to work and back by uniformed FANYs. Almost at once they realised that the work they were doing – cross-referencing and card-indexing – was the top-secret Ultra material involved in breaking the Enigma code.

Based first at a hotel in the centre of Buckingham – which meant sleepless days when they were on night watch – the two girls were soon found a permanent billet with an elderly couple who lived in an exquisite Queen Anne house in a nearby village. The garden was so overgrown that in summer the two could sunbathe topless (then unknown on any beach) but they had to make do with only a small one-bar electric fire as bedroom heating in the winter.

A fellow lodger was the Professor of Philosophy from King's College, Cambridge. For the young and lively Sarah and Osla he was a natural subject for teasing. 'We hid our wind-up gramophone under his bed one evening with the starter handle attached to a long piece of string snaking through the passage to our bedroom,' wrote Sarah in her memoir of that time, *The Road to Station X*. 'At midnight we pulled it and the poor man was violently awoken by the strains of Beethoven's Ninth Symphony. As a result he begged to change billets and was kind enough not to blame us. We truly missed him and were temporarily conscience-stricken.'

Only once did Sarah trip up. Her godfather Lord Louis Mountbatten, then Chief of Combined Operations, was naturally privy to Ultra. One day in 1943 he arrived on a visit, accompanied by a troop of senior officers. 'Uncle Dickie, what are you doing here?' asked the embarrassed Sarah. 'Oh,' he replied, 'I knew you were here and thought I would see how you are getting on. Show me the system of your cross-reference index.' The visit to the index played havoc with the careful timing of his visit and next morning Sarah was summoned by an irate Commander Travis. Only when she explained that she had known nothing about the visit and that Lord Louis was her godfather did the Commander simmer down, even lending the tearful Sarah a handkerchief to blow her nose.

Her time at Bletchley Park was enlivened by encounters with some of its more brilliant and eccentric inmates. One of these was the great mathematician Alan Turing, who was a pioneering figure in the invention of the modern computer. The Colossus machine with which he was involved was capable of reading and checking some five thousand characters a second and played an essential part in cracking the German Enigma code.

He was greatly admired by Sarah, who wished to be on friendly terms with him. 'I once offered him a cup of tea but he shrank back in fear. He seemed terrified of girls and on the rare occasions when he was spotted, like a protected species, he would be shambling down to the canteen in a curious sideways step, his eyes fixed on the ground. It was explained to me that if you had spent most of your adult life closeted away in a study in Cambridge, you too would be scared of women and not know how to handle them.'

Alan Turing's other notable habits were wearing his gas mask as he cycled to work (he suffered from hay fever but many of the locals who saw him thought at first there must have been a gas attack) and refusing to mend the bicycle chain as it gave him pleasure to count the number of times the pedals went round before he had to dismount to fix it. Another professor of mathematics, Alan Ross, would wear a pale blue pixie hood over his long red beard on cold days, tying it round his chin, while the novelist Angus Wilson once threw himself into the lake in a tantrum and had to be fished out.

For the young, Bletchley's great drawback was its isolation. Circumventing this was a priority. Joan Stafford King-Harman began to save from her salary straight away. 'Pretty quickly, with another girl, I was able to buy a car for £25 from a chap who was going off to France. This meant we got petrol coupons and we'd take it in turns driving up to London. Once we passed a pile of telegraph poles on the road – later we learned there'd been a major air raid and that under the poles were a lot of unexploded bombs.'

Jean Campbell-Harris and her friends would go up to London on their days off. 'I made some really good friends at Bletchley. We used to go out in a group. Then one began to have serious romances – going as far as one could without actual sex. We were pretty virginal – and really the boys were awfully good about it. But there was always that feeling that they were on leave, and you mightn't see them again, which made it awfully difficult.

'At Bletchley there were very few men – at least very few of the kind of young men who interested us. Some of the women who worked there got so desperate that they would pull open a roll of loo paper, scribble a note saying "Please write to me ... Joan X", roll the paper up again, and hope it ended up in the gents' lavatory – rather like putting a note in a bottle and chucking it into the sea.'

As the number of staff at Bletchley increased, so did the buildings. Sarah Norton had to leave her beloved Hut 4 for a 'horrible concrete building with a long wide corridor'. One day she and Osla decided to liven up their morning by giving their friend Jean Campbell-Harris a ride in a large wheeled laundry basket used for moving secret files around. As they pushed it rapidly down the corridor it gathered momentum and to their horror the two girls saw the basket, with Jean inside, crash first through double swing doors and then straight into the men's toilets. 'A serious reprimand was administered and our watches were changed so that we were distributed among a more sober group.'

Another reason they disliked the new Hut 4 was that it was even colder than the earlier one. Freezing air seemed to rise from the concrete floors with their scant coating of red tile paint, the unshaded light bulbs added to the atmosphere of discomfort, and the 'heating' system was inadequate: the odd inefficient electric fire or coke stoves with metal chimneys that went up through the asbestos ceilings. Many of those who worked around its wooden trestle tables wore overcoats and mittens.

Occasionally signals would come through from the Admiralty, usually about floating or acoustic mines on which Naval Intelligence might be able to shed some light. 'Gracie Fields making water,' read one, regarding a convoy, and referring to a merchant ship that had been torpedoed. 'I am ashamed to say', wrote Sarah in her memoir, 'it had us all rolling on the floor with laughter while at the same time wishing her crew a safe rescue.'

'There was plenty of fun at Bletchley,' recalled Joan Stafford King-Harman, working there with Naval Intelligence. 'There were parties – at one fancy-dress party people dressed up as nuns with huge boots, apropos those stories of German parachutists landing disguised like that.'

There was also a certain formality. 'I worked with lovely, rather elderly naval officers, most about to retire. We were never referred to by our Christian names – it was always "Miss King-Harman". I wasn't really officer status; I was first a confidential secretary and then head secretary. When my chief got ill, I was sent for and asked if I was prepared to do his work for a few months. You were training people and sending them abroad.'

Apart from the mines, Naval Intelligence at the Admiralty had a tendency to ignore information that came from Bletchley. This disbelief in its accuracy reached right to the top: unlike the Army and the Royal Air Force, where most orders came from commanders in the field, all commands to ships, plus tactics and strategy, came from the Admiralty.

Before Sarah's arrival, warnings that German warships were about to break out of the Baltic were ignored, leading to the sinking of the aircraft carrier HMS *Glorious* and her two escort destroyers, with the loss of 1,500 men on 8 June 1940.* The

---

* Chronicled in the official history of British Intelligence in the Second World War.

Admiralty's determination to rely only on its own intelligence surfaced again during the pursuit of Germany's most powerful battleship, the *Bismarck*, during May 1941.

She was sighted on the evening of 23 May, engaged the following morning by the *Prince of Wales* and the *Hood* – which was sunk – then disappeared. Bletchley's repeated insistence that she was heading for the safety of a French port (having learned that radio control of the *Bismarck* had switched from Wilmhelmshaven to Paris, a clear signal that she was sailing south to France) was ignored for two days and it was not until the evening of 25 May, following yet another heated telephone call from Bletchley, that the Admiralty accepted this reasoning. Dramatically, a few minutes later, Hut 6 deciphered a Luftwaffe Enigma signal from the Chief of Staff over the fate of a relative who was a *Bismarck* crew member; the return signal told him that the battleship was making for the safety of Brest. The next day she was sunk.

The Prime Minister, Winston Churchill, recognised not only the contribution those at Bletchley were making to the war effort but also their extraordinary success in keeping this work secret – not even the youngest employee, like Sarah Norton, had so much as breathed a word of their code-breaking activities to family or friends.*

The hard slog of decoding continued. On 1 January 1944 Sarah and Osla were delighted to learn that they had been promoted to Technical Assistants ('we were instantly known as Tech Asses') and would earn the dizzying salary of £3 5s a week.

A few days later, most of the Naval Section were summoned by their boss. Sarah, wondering if she had inadvertently done something wrong but aware that sacking was out of the question

---

* Although by the end of the war over 10,000 people worked at Bletchley Park, no information about the work carried out there emerged until the mid-1970s. Only when word began to trickle out then did Sarah Norton, Jean Campbell-Harris and Joan Stafford King-Harman tell their husbands what they did in the war.

(all of them knew too much), feared a return to the duller task of indexing. She was as surprised as the others to be told that in six months time the Allies were planning to invade France.

From that moment, the deception and destruction of the Luftwaffe was top priority and the excited staff flung themselves into analysing the decrypts pouring in – the Luftwaffe had always relied on Enigma to transmit all orders and information. 'We learned of the damage done by our planes,' she said, 'the holes on runways which put the airfields on the other side of the Channel out of action for several days, the progress reports on repairs and the crippling harm done to the German synthetic oil refineries.'

On 5 April Sarah's long overdue week's leave was cancelled with no reason given and a travel ban imposed on all at Bletchley. It was then that they learned the date for Operation Overlord, as D-Day was codenamed (originally May 1 but finally, owing to bad weather, postponed to June 6).

There was one terrible moment when it seemed as if a leak might have occurred. The codenames for the assault beaches in Normandy had already been chosen: Omaha, Utah, Juno, Sword and Gold. At the beginning of May, one of the crossword fanatics who used to compete against each other in the tea break to see who could finish the *Daily Telegraph* puzzle fastest, noticed that two of the answers were Utah and Omaha. The worry was intense until it was discovered that the crossword setter had used these words in all innocence.

Most of May was spent translating urgent intercepts regarding the positions of mines in the English Channel and following the movements of mine-laying ships – vital for the safety of the armada that would later land in Normandy.

Sarah, on leave at last, was having dinner in London with a boyfriend on 5 June 1944, the evening before D-Day. As they stood under an umbrella at about 11.30 p.m., waiting hopefully for a taxi, she heard a sound that she had been expecting. It was the monotonous drone of a flying armada – 1,136 RAF bombers towing gliders, bound for the shores of Normandy. Sarah's boyfriend, speechless at the sight, asked her if she had any idea what was going on. 'I haven't the faintest idea,' she replied in a voice she hoped was steady. Next morning the British public knew that the invasion had begun; Sarah, longing to know the inside story and thinking she might be needed, had abandoned her leave and already caught the milk train back to Bletchley.

In November 1944 she was sent for by the head of the Naval Section, Frank Birch, a charming and popular Old Etonian and a brilliant comic (who later appeared as Widow Twankey in pantomime at the London Palladium). 'Don't look so worried,' he said. 'You've got a new job. You know we have difficulty with the Admirals accepting Ultra?'

'Yes,' she replied.

'I'm sending you up to the Admiralty to join three other girls from this section,' said Birch, and went on to explain that she was to be Liaison Officer for Bletchley Park. 'Your office will be called NID 12A and you must man it twenty-four hours a day – and try to be nice to the Admirals.' 'Are you sending me to the Admiralty for my brains or for my exceptionally good legs?' asked Sarah. 'A bit of both,' replied Birch, smiling.

Sarah's aunt lent her a flat at the bottom of St James's, within easy walking distance of the Admiralty in Whitehall. On arrival, she knocked at the door of room NID (which stood for Naval Intelligence Division) 12A but there was no reply. 'I was soon to learn that you never said "Come in," in NID 12A for the simple reason that nobody was allowed in, whatever their rank.' Fortunately, the door was soon opened to Sarah by someone who turned out to be a friend from Bletchley.

Alternating with each other, the three girls did three day watches and two night watches and got one day off a week; daytime working hours were from 10.00 a.m. to 6.00 p.m. and nights from 6.00 p.m. to 10.00 a.m. Sarah did night watch as often as she could. 'It was horrible sitting alone in my fifth floor flat with the V-2s crashing down.

'The Admiralty was about the best job any girl could have. The responsibility was awesome – you were alone in this room, completely responsible for every decrypt that came from Bletchley and you had to decide who saw it. No one was allowed into our room, not even an admiral. All the telephones were scramblers and I also had a direct line to the Prime Minister. I still sometimes now wake up having a nightmare about it – how could I have managed it?'

Winding down, as the war neared its end, was – as could be expected – different at Bletchley from anywhere else. 'After V-E Day we were doing Japanese naval stuff, which was very boring,' said Jean Campbell-Harris. 'Because Bletchley was so secret it was very difficult to get away. I only managed it because my mother had broken her arm and I said I had to be near her. I got a job in London, which then moved to Paris.'

Sarah Norton, relieved and happy though she was on V-E and V-J days, was also conscious of 'a feeling of being forgotten. No campaign ribbons – not that we deserved any – no Certificate such as our colleagues in the Red Cross received. Just . . . nothing.'

Perhaps Bletchley's best accolade was that given by Winston Churchill during a secret visit on 6 September 1941, when he stood on a soapbox outside the main house and addressed all the staff able to leave their work. 'To look at you,' said the Prime Minister, 'one would not think you held so many secrets, but I know better and I am proud of you.'

Chapter 13

On the Land

'We don't want any bloody land girls here'

Before the war, Britain imported well over half of her food. When war began in 1939, with Hitler's U-boats attacking the merchant shipping that imported foodstuffs, she had to grow as much as she could, especially the staples of wheat and potatoes, the most efficient use of land. Every square inch of soil was pressed into service. Crop-growing land was increased by a good 50 per cent, mainly by ploughing up pastureland, draining marshes and, to a lesser extent, utilising every square foot that had hitherto been untouched or used for more decorative purposes. Flower beds were turned into vegetable patches, lawns and tennis courts dug up and planted, golf clubs and parks ploughed up – even Kensington Gardens and the moat round the Tower of London were given over to vegetables. Within months, almost 1.5 million people had allotments and by 1943, over a million tons of vegetables were being grown. In the country, rabbit pie became even more of a staple dish, and from banks and hedgerows came nettles for soup, dandelion leaves for salad and blackberries for fruit.

Farming was then labour-intensive, with men and horses doing the work now done by machines. In any case, there was no incentive for mechanisation in wartime as horse-power saved the petrol that had to be brought from overseas and for which merchant seamen were risking their lives.

A farm worker's life was one of hard physical labour, working from dawn to dusk at harvest time and in winter often in freezing conditions. When the Women's Land Army was formed during the 1914–18 war it was in the teeth of doubts that a fragile female could fill the heavy boots of a husky male labourer; and after the war ended the organisation was quickly allowed to lapse. It was hastily brought back into being at the outbreak of the Second World War to replace the male farm labourers who had gone off to fight: by March 1940 over 30,000 agricultural workers had joined the British Army.

By 1943 there were some 90,000 'land girls' lifting potatoes, handling the heavy horses and milking cattle. Some even trained as rat-catchers – a rat could eat about 50 kilograms of food a year. In theory, land girls were supposed to be given training in basic tasks like milking, mucking out and harvesting, with an agreed working week of fifty hours in summer and forty-eight in winter. In practice, most learned on the job and did what was needed, especially at harvest time.

'I was very taken aback by how hard the work was when I first started as a land girl,' said Rosemary Wynn. 'I'd wanted to be a nurse but was prevented by a medical problem. So I joined the Land Army and worked on a farm quite close to my home in Cannock Chase [in Staffordshire].

'At first the farmer's two sons bitterly resented me. "We don't want any bloody land girls here!" was their cry. So I was determined to show I could do it.

'I lived at the farm. We started about 7.30, when I put on my Land Army uniform of breeches, boots, green V-necked jumper, khaki shirt and a felt hat and went out and milked the cows. The two sons would laugh at me if I got kicked over when milking or the cow put its foot in the bucket – though I got told off for that, for wasting milk.

'I fed the calves and cleaned out their stalls – there was quite a big herd of shorthorns – and I did a lot of work with the big horses. I'd been brought up with horses so I liked that. These ones were too big for me to reach to put the harness on, so I had to climb up into the manger, put the collar over the horse's head, turn it round, then climb down and do the rest of the harness. They had a pony for the milk float so I used to ride over on it every Saturday evening to do a Red Cross course at Shugborough Hall.'

Farm work had many hazards, from being crushed by machinery to being attacked by some angry animal. One morning Rosemary, though slender and petite, was asked by one of the farm workers if she would feed the bull.

'He said: "Will you go in there and feed that bull?" as they knew I had no fear of animals. Next thing I knew I was flat on my back on the muck heap. The bull had simply tossed me over the post and rail fence. Luckily only my dignity was hurt.'

There were other risks. 'In the first winter of the war we'd be working in the sugar beet fields and we'd hear a low-flying plane come over one of the woods that dotted the farm. They used to bomb Stafford, to try and get the English Electric factory there which was making aeroplane parts, and on the way back would jettison their bombs and strafe anything that moved.

'Suddenly one of the men would shout "Lie down!" and we'd fling ourselves face down in the mud, as the German gunners would machine-gun us as they went over. I was lucky, I never got hit but one of the men got a bullet in his leg.'

Rosemary faced one of the commonest problems suffered by land girls who 'lived in' at the farm where they were working. Because they were female, they were often loaded with domestic work as well, which was strictly against the rules. 'We were working very hard from dawn onwards but when I came back with the men for a meal at midday or in the evening their stepmother always made me help with the washing-up while the men just sat and rested. In the end I struck. I said: "I'm not going to do this. I want to sit down and have a bit of rest too, the same as the others." She wasn't best pleased but I stuck to my guns.'

Farming was not the only kind of work women did on the land. Susan Meyrick worked on a market garden near Ringwood, close to her home at Beaulieu on the South Coast. 'There was a lot of discussion as to whether I should go into the Wrens or the WAAFS. But I had a friend who was going to work at a market garden fairly near, and I thought it would be very nice to be able to live at home.

'We worked from 8.30 to 5.30 which was quite a long day when you were doing physical work the whole time. First you had to get there – the garden was about ten miles away but I could only go part of the way by car because of petrol rationing, so I kept my bike at a farm and pedalled the last five miles. Later in the war there were a lot of Americans about and you invariably got whistled at as you pedalled along.

'Very often you were hoeing all day. I hoed lettuces for hours and hours, as well as cabbages and carrots. What made it exhausting was being bent double all day. If you were tall, like me, it gave you an awful backache. One got very tough.

'It wasn't a very social time as it was such hard work but we met a lot of the Americans and used to go to dances at the US air base.

'In the winter it was awful driving back with only those little slits of light. The blackout made everything very difficult – once I actually fell out of a train. I was travelling to our little station, Hinton, and when we got there I thought the train had stopped – it was so dark I couldn't see that it was actually moving, so I got out and fell straight on to my face.

'Then there were the air raids. You could watch Southampton being bombed and when they blitzed Coventry in November 1940 the German planes went over us all night long. At home, when the siren went off, we would go down into the basement and sit there half the night listening to that awful droning as they went over.'

Lady Barbara Stuart-Wortley began the war by working on a farm near her home, Wortley Hall in Yorkshire, for two months. She had become unofficially engaged to her future husband, David Ricardo, during her debutante Season in 1939. 'We'd come back to Wortley at the end of the Season, and I asked Mummy if David could come and stay, and he did. His birthday was on 3 September and he asked me to go and stay with his parents at Lingfield for it. I was longing for it. Then of course we heard Chamberlain and I had a telegram from Mrs Ricardo saying "Please don't come, we have had people round and they're taking the house over for evacuees." Later they had a whole lot of soldiers planted on them.

'I was longing to do something in the war but I had the most frightful phobia about myself. We'd had the most appallingly bad governess and I felt uneducated and stupid and didn't think I'd be able to cope with anything – I didn't think I could manage in an office or anything like that because my spelling wasn't good. In fact I totally lacked confidence. I couldn't even cook as we weren't allowed to do anything at home. I wanted to go into the kitchen and learn but that was forbidden.

'Soon after the outbreak of war I was keeping pigs – about all I felt myself fit for! David had joined the Army and was made an officer. He came to stay again and then was sent up to Catterick. He asked me to come and stay up there but my mother got very tedious about it and said I couldn't possibly go unless I stayed with somebody she knew. Luckily she had a cousin who lived near Richmond and David met me at the station. We went and had tea at a café and when we got to the house we found an enormous tea waiting for us, so embarrassing.

'Then I joined the Land Army. A great friend and I got a job with a farmer three miles away. We used to ride there and back on our horses. We got the sack in the end because we didn't realise that one of the stalls, which was deep in straw, was for pigs and cows giving birth – we just thought that it was filthy, and cleaned it out. Apparently this was dreadful – you just add more and more straw, and it gives warmth. We couldn't get a job for a bit after that.'

As the WLA was a civilian organisation rather than a military one (although it came under the control of the Ministry of Agriculture, Fisheries and Food), its members were recruited by the farmers themselves – and could also, as happened to Lady Barbara, be dismissed by them. Her next job was much more successful, especially for someone who had ridden all her life.

'A friend told me about a Remount Depot at Melton Mowbray.* So I wrote and applied and got a job there. I lodged with three brothers – one was queer and one was strange. I took along a dictionary, an atlas and a volume of Shakespeare's plays to try and educate myself.

'Work began at 8.00 a.m. I was one of three girls among a number of men, some elderly and some who hadn't been called up because they weren't physically up to it. We girls had five horses apiece to feed, muck out and groom.'

As the stables expanded Barbara found herself working alongside several girls of her own sort. Soon her experience with horses and riding all through childhood and adolescence was standing her in good stead. 'I became a rider, which was much more fun. The horses were mostly hunters, which we were schooling to pull wagons. The Colonel of the Depot would go off to Ireland to get heavy animals, and we had quite a lot of horses from the regiments. Some came from cavalry regiments that had been stationed in India and quite a lot of these had obviously been badly treated, hit over the head, often with the loss of an eye.

'When they were schooled, the ones that were chestnut and

---

* Horses that had been requisitioned during the war were taken to Remount Depots, where they were reschooled either as officers' chargers or as draught horses. Strings of hunters being led away for this purpose were a common and melancholy sight for their owners.

grey were sent off to Egypt and Palestine because they didn't show up so much against the sand.

'We had to take them out in all weathers, pouring rain as well, though in really hard weather we exercised them in a riding school. What made us cross was that we didn't have a uniform and had to wear our own clothes. Eventually, after making a fuss, we were given short mackintoshes to wear.'

Schooling the horses could be hazardous. The wagons these horses had to draw had a central pole on the front, with a horse harnessed on each side. Sometimes a young hunter, unused to this, would rear up and the whole thing would come crashing over on to the driver. 'The important thing was to avoid the pole,' said Lady Barbara. 'Once I was run over by a wagon – luckily it was very wet and I was just pushed into the ground and didn't break anything.

'Another bit of damage happened when I was putting a hay net up in a stall. I had to climb on the manger to do it and this ruddy horse bit me in the leg and getting down I cut my finger badly. It had to have stitches and I was told not to use that hand.

'One day I was riding a quiet horse round a field at the back, and suddenly out of the sky came masses and masses of long thin ribbons of silver stuff. I went back to the stables and reported it to the Colonel. He told me it was being dropped by the Germans to confuse our radar.

'There was quite a lot of bombing. On the moors they'd lit false fires, to make it look like a factory from the air. It must have looked very realistic as it got bombed regularly. Sheffield was bombed quite badly, and we used to take food to collecting places for people who had been bombed out.'

Accidents in daily life were more likely on farms than in most other places. Rosemary Wynn could easily have been killed in one. 'We were carting hay – it was all loose then, of course – and I was right on top of this big wagon, loaded high with hay. The old Irish labourer holding the horse hit it with his hat because he saw a horsefly on it. The horse, Captain, went off at a flat-out gallop straight for the farmyard. Most fortunately he didn't hit the sides of the gate at its entrance, or the whole thing would have turned over – with me crushed underneath that enormous weight.'

On one occasion Barbara's prompt action probably saved a friend from more serious injury. 'My friend was kicked on the head and they were determined to move her. I became furious and made them send for an ambulance as I knew moving her could be dangerous. I was quite diffident when I was growing up, as I was so squashed as a child, but when a situation like that arises I do become a leader.'

Barbara, who had got engaged to David Ricardo before he was sent abroad, married him in 1943, when he was sent back after being wounded. 'He got chickenpox on our honeymoon and wanted to go back to his mother, as we hadn't got a home then, so I had to go back to the Remount Depot a fortnight early. We used to meet for dinner, but his parents never had me to stay. When I went home my father said, "David should be providing a home for you" and implied that they didn't want me there. I felt dreadful, homeless. The Millbank doctors had told him that he couldn't live in England, it had to be in a warm country, so he went back to Kenya where his sister lived. I was to follow him when I could – but I couldn't go until the war was over.'

Rosemary Wynn also married during the war but her work on the land continued. It was a hard life and a constant financial struggle – for Rosemary, her debutante days were just a distant dream. 'I married John Boydell, the second son of the farmer for whom I worked – who had earlier been a naval officer. John and I had our own farm in Gloucestershire, with a herd of Ayrshire cows and our own chickens. We only got eight pence a gallon for milk during the war so money was terribly tight. One winter John got a job driving a lorry to earn more. He would milk the cows before he went – we had a milking machine then – and I would turn the cattle out, clean the stalls, feed the calves, get the milk ready in the churns for the milk lorry and put the straw down for the afternoon. I did my housework and washing at weekends. It was just an incessant battle to keep our end up.'

Even the pay of agricultural workers – at 38 shillings (£1.90) a week in 1940 this was half the national average weekly wage – reflected the difficulties of earning a living from the land. Land girls received a weekly minimum of 28s (£1.40), with half of that deducted for board and lodging. Only after 1943 were they granted the right to a week's annual holiday and a half-day off a week. Yet despite the long hours, the hard physical work that ranged from shovelling pig manure or clearing land for the plough to acting as midwife to cows and, often, the isolation, the Land Army proved so popular that in August 1943 the Government had to ban further recruitment. Too many women seemed to prefer life on the land to the women's services or the factory floor.

Chapter 14

The Class Barrier

'We'd never met girls like these before ...'

What seems extraordinary in the experiences of the forty-seven pre-war debutantes I interviewed is how little the bringing-together of all classes of society affected the customs and attitudes with which they had been brought up. Where men were concerned, 'suitability', though seldom consciously formulated, was an underlying stratum on which many of their judgments were based. This was helped, of course, by the fact that many of the young men with whom they had danced their way through those last Seasons were still their friends and therefore the ones who sought them out when home on leave.

'I suppose we did stick rigidly to our own class,' said Cynthia Denison-Pender. 'I didn't really meet anyone who wasn't. Even then it was a closed shop – the thing is, you went out with the people you knew. They were all around. To this day I've got men friends who are around because they were friends, and just that.'

'I was very choosy,' said Diana Barnato, now flying for the ATA (in which pilots were given officer rank). 'I went out with people I already knew and a lot of fighter pilots. And Guards officers – you didn't look at other regiments. In general, the RAF was a lower echelon socially. I would say, in the nicest possible way: "Sorry, I can't – I've got to fly tomorrow."

'Of course, the ground crew always flirted with you. One

Christmas I'd put my name down for a turkey and I picked it up on Christmas Eve, in a Spitfire, in transit to Smith's Lawn, which was an airfield. I got down to Eastleigh, dragging this turkey, on one side of my seat in the cockpit, with my overnight bag onto the other side and when I landed one of the ground crew sprang on to the wing and produced a little sprig of mistletoe. "Aha, two birds in one cockpit!" he said. "Now chaps, it's your turn."

'But another one said reprovingly: "Airmen don't kiss officers."'

When love did cross the class divide it could cause difficulties at home. 'I had a tremendous walk-out with the staff sergeant who was the physical training expert,' said Virginia Forbes Adam. 'This shocked my parents into the ground. I was eighteen and Staff Sergeant Bill must have been twenty-five or so and very good-looking.

'We were living at Escrick Park then. It had originally been a Forbes Adam place but my parents had turned it into residential flats with a communal dining room where we used to go on Boxing Day for a cold lunch so that the servants could have Christmas lunch unfettered. As our own house, Skipwith Hall, had been requisitioned for use by the Army when the war started we'd moved into one of the flats there.

'I took my sergeant home and dinner was rather agonising. No one seemed able to speak. Afterwards we retired to our own sitting room and sitting there with my father was absolutely ghastly. My parents behaved terribly badly, I thought. As soon as I was in the car with my sergeant we had a good smooch. Later, I talked to a friend of mine and my mother's, who had seen us there and who always asked me questions. "Oh, that's Sergeant Bill, the man I love at the moment," I said. "He's madly attractive," she said to me and oh! what a relief it was to hear that!

'Of course I went on seeing him. My parents had a little car, which they would occasionally lend me and I would meet my sergeant in York. He was a beautiful dancer and there was a dinner-dance place near by where he'd give me dinner and then we'd dance and smooch in the car on the way back.

'But it never occurred to me that I would marry him. At the back of my mind I suppose I felt that the classes couldn't mix, also that I didn't quite love him in the way I should love the man I would marry. But it was all incredibly romantic – although it was cold it was wonderful weather, with moonlit nights, and I was thrilled that he had chosen me above all the others.'

Lavinia Holland-Hibbert was another who fell in love with someone from a different background: in Italy she met the soldier who would later become Labour's Foreign Secretary, Denis Healey. 'I never brought him home, although they teased me about him. It would have been so embarrassing for my parents, who wouldn't have been able to relate to him. They would have been very suspicious of him being a socialist and I wouldn't have liked to put them through it.

'I fell in love with him but I wouldn't have dared marry him, it was too much of a challenge. When the war was over I hankered for people like my father. Denis regarded me as different – his final remark when he'd seen the last of me was "You never made a fuss." He expected histrionics. He said he was finally converted to aristocratic values through me. We taught each other.' Or, as Healey put it in his autobiography, *The Time of My Life*: 'It was the combination of Yeats with Lavinia that finally convinced me that Lindsay's support for aristocratic values was acceptable.'*

Getting on with people was another matter. For Lady Barbara Stuart-Wortley, this was never a problem when she joined the Remount Depot, reschooling horses for war work. 'They were all a different class but I got on with most of them straight away. I made it my business to get on with them and make friends.

---

* Alexander Dunlop Lindsay was Master of Balliol College, Oxford, while Healey was a student there in the late 1930s, and a noted political philosopher.

One or two were horrid to me because of my voice. I tackled one girl about it just as I was going to bicycle home. I said to her: "Why are you so beastly to me? What have I ever done to you? I've never done anything to hurt or upset you, so why are you being horrid to me?"

'This completely changed her and she became very nice and we became friends. In fact, she was a bigger help to me over my marriage than my mother was – I wish I'd asked her more, I'm sure she'd have told me. She wasn't married but she certainly wasn't ignorant.'

When Ann Reid, newly married, combined her work with rescue units based in the garages of London's Savoy Hotel with nursing in the Charing Cross Hospital, it was, she said, 'the first time I'd come across people of a different class. We worked day shifts in the hospital and at night we slept on stretchers in the garages. When the Blitz started we were really busy. I learned very quickly – I didn't know how to wash up a spoon but I didn't admit to it. I just watched how the others did it and then did it myself. They never teased me because of my voice, they were absolutely sweet. I had such admiration for all my workmates.'

Voices often caused problems for former debutantes who trained as nurses. 'I'd signed on to do my training at the Radcliffe Hospital in Oxford,' said Jean Falkner. 'There I jolly well realised the difference between "us" and "them". I had a great friend there who was a prostitute and she wised me up – she told me not to bring my silver powder compact in my handbag because it would be pinched, and not to take money with me or put my watch in my bag, for the same reason. I'd never thought of such a thing before.

'I was punished for my accent – I don't mean by my fellow nurses, among whom I had some very good friends, but by the Sisters. They always had a go at me. Quite a lot of the doctors rather fancied me, I suppose because I was a novelty, and that made the Sisters jealous.'

Voices were also what identified Sarah Norton and her friend Osla Benning. 'We were sent to a small parts factory, in Slough Trading Estate. We filed metal called Durol – we filed, we riveted, we worked eight solid hours non-stop. We made great friends with the people there. We got on because we did our best to make them feel they were cleverer than us. The only thing that worried Osla and me was that they thought our voices were odd.'

Yet, as Lavinia Holland-Hibbert remarked: 'It's funny the way one automatically finds and makes friends with one's own sort. Voices were the great marker. But I don't think the others noticed them as much as we did. The other thing we noticed most was that if baths weren't available we never washed but the lower classes stripped before the basin every day because as they had never had baths that was what they normally did. We admired them greatly for that.'

The services were more democratic, with the demarcation line being rank rather than class (though of course, at that time, most of the higher ranks came from the upper or upper-middle classes). When Lady Anne Spencer, who had done her nursing training at two Northampton hospitals, worked during 1940 at Middleton Park, then a hospital and convalescent home for those in the armed forces who had sustained head injuries), this barrier was enforced by a simple rule: 'The "other ranks" never asked us out – they weren't allowed out.'

Daphne Brock, a good mixer like Barbara Stuart-Wortley, had no worries about getting on with anyone, either her fellow Wren ratings or, later, fellow officers. 'I was never laughed at because of my voice. What I did notice was that a lot of the better-educated girls weren't house-trained. My mother's lady's maid was never allowed to touch my clothes but she did teach me how to look after them. When I was a junior officer and had a section of Wrens to look after, communications Wrens, better educated than most – they were mostly ladies – I got a shock.

'Because of trouble with rats I had to inspect every bit of their dormitory, which was a Nissen hut. I had to open their drawers and I can't tell you what I saw inside – food, untidiness, dirty clothes. You wouldn't have found that with the cooks. Girls from poorer homes would have learned all about tidiness.'

Diana Lyttelton's sergeant had a separate room at the end of the hut shared by the rank and file. 'She was quite butch. She said: "One of you has to look after me." I volunteered. Every time she came back I had a jug of hot water for her and her bed ready for the night. I'd never done anything like that before but I'd seen it done. I decided I would be the best personal maid ever – it was like acting a part. Anyway, it was much nicer than doing the ablutions – washing out the loos and so on. When I left she said: "I didn't think you'd be any good but you were the best ever." I was really pleased.'

For Ursie Barclay, the first encounter with people from a different walk of life came in Norwich. 'When I'd suggested going to work in Harrods to earn myself some pocket money my father had said: "You are not going to work at Harrods. You will be taking money from people who really need it."'

Instead, she had joined her mother's company of ATS and was attached to the fourth battalion of the Royal Norfolk Regiment. 'I was never asked out by the sergeants because they knew where I came from and never later because by then, being an officer, I never came in contact with them.'

When she became an officer, Ursie was struck forcibly by one point. 'If they were close, their families were much closer than ours. But if a girl's mother was a prostitute, she would be out on a limb. Some were enormously close-knit, others had horrible parents. A lot of my ATS girls didn't hear from their parents at all.

'I found I was much better at getting on with the really scruffy ones than the half-and-halfs, who resented you more. I was twenty-one and bossing them about, and they were often thirty-something.'

The first thing Christian Grant noticed when she went to work in the Handley Page aircraft factory in Cricklewood was a far greater frankness than she had been used to. 'The girls in the factory were pretty lewd, no skating around subjects. I soon began to know what certain words meant that I'd never heard before. I'd never heard a woman swear before, nor a man – unless he hit his thumb or something. It was a tremendous eye-opener.'

She was quickly recognised as 'different' and encountered much active hostility. 'More than anything else there was a turning their backs on me. One of the worst moments was when they noticed a suitcase my mother had lent me. It had a label saying Lady Grant. "So you're into stealing things now," someone said and I had to say: "Well, no, actually that's my mother's."

'Once the girls were friendlier everything was okay and I wasn't left out of the giggles, though when they did call me by my name they called me Chris, which I hated.

'The thing that surprised me most was the snobbishness and social ranking inside the factory. They were snobbish about what someone's husband did – if he was a charge-hand or you were a charge-hand's wife you were a cut above someone working on the benches. The white-collar workers had no contact with the people working on the factory floor. They didn't even eat with us. There was only one person lower than me, a sweeper.'

Val Canning, running a hostel in Shere, Surrey, for thirty boy evacuees – for whom she also did the cooking – with the aid of a conscientious objector (CO) and one elderly woman helper, also had a lot of trouble at first. 'The conchie and some of the mothers objected on a class basis to someone like me doing the job. They said: "You're taking the job away from other people."'

'Apart from their voices, the other great difference was that they all had nits,' said Ursie Barclay. 'They had very greasy horrible hair but if they came from the slums of Liverpool you could understand it. I don't think they cleaned their teeth too much, though their nails had to pass inspection if they were working in the kitchens. It was the first time many of them had seen a bath. They were issued with blue-and-white-striped pyjamas but some of them didn't know what they were for.'

~~⌒~~

Judy Impey, also in the ATS and stationed at York Barracks in the summer of 1942, found that she and her fellow privates were working much too hard to worry about social differences. 'None of the others spoke like me but they didn't tease me about my voice. We were having a tough life. After York Barracks was bombed – glass all over our beds but luckily we were in the shelter – we'd been moved to Queen Ethelburga's College near Harrogate, previously occupied by the Glasgow Pioneers. It had the most horrendous sayings written all over the walls and the floor. I didn't even know what they meant, they were so sordid. For three weeks we did nothing but scrub the floor. That was a great leveller. I remember one officer got down on her hands and knees and scrubbed the floor with us, so she was held in tremendous respect.'

Cynthia Denison-Pender, working in a factory, was another who was never teased because of her voice. 'I looked so scruffy I don't think they thought that I was any different from them. I made a great friend of a Welsh girl called Gwyneth. We used to go to the cinema together and have tea in the Cadena Café. Then I asked her home, taking her on the back of my autobike, but she never felt the same after she was waited on by a parlour maid and our relationship changed completely – on her side. I suppose she thought I was posing. She was the one who felt it, not me.'

In many places, speaking with a posh voice appeared to send out a signal that you believed yourself superior. Tact, and an obvious willingness to take on any job, usually countered such suspicion but often meant that girls from grander backgrounds were given the worst jobs – especially those with titles. This was particularly true in nursing.

'The first time I'd worked with people from a different background was when I went on a concentrated fortnight's living-in course at the St John's Ambulance headquarters in Oxford,' said Esme Harmsworth. 'That was a slight revelation to me. They were uneasy with me – or I was with them, I'm not quite sure which. It was difficult. You had to be very careful with things like not having too much marmalade on your bread at breakfast or a quarrel would break out.

'I think I was avoided, thought of as a toff – anyway I was immediately given the worst jobs. I had to go round and collect all the sanitary towels and dispose of them by putting them in the furnace. I thought: Well, I can't complain. I've chosen to go into nursing and I expect it'll get a lot worse than this. At first I thought it a bit unfair, this attitude: "We'll give them to her because she's a toff" but then I thought: Well, someone has to do it.

'When I went to work in a hospital there was no problem. They'd evacuated the first-year nurses so we VADs were doing the first-year jobs, which mainly involved bedpans. They were very old-fashioned hospitals. The patients weren't aware that I came from a different background, one was just Nurse, and they were very sweet to one. The other nurses were very nice – but again one had to do the worst jobs.'

In general, the most unpleasant tasks were routine for the posh VAD. 'One was treated pretty roughly,' said Fiona Colquhoun. 'You were yelled at and told what to do every minute of the day. It went against me that I came from a different background. They took it out on me because of that – sarky remarks and so on. They were a bit suspicious of me – I felt they were thinking that I thought myself too grand to do a lot of the jobs. But when they saw one was as pleasant as they were, it was all right.'

Similarly, Lady Moyra Ponsonby's title earned her extra-strict treatment from Matron to avoid any appearance of favouritism, as did that of Betty Shaughnessy, who had married Lord Grenfell before the war. She had joined the Red Cross and lived in a rented house in Northamptonshire. 'I worked in the Northampton hospital for a year, looking after wounded soldiers. The Matron had it in for me because of my title. I remember nearly fainting when I passed an open door and there was a severed leg in a bucket. All she said was: "Pull yourself together, Grenfell."'

Fanny Gore Browne was another for whom being plunged among those from a different background was a rude shock, and whose voice got her into trouble at first.

'The Wrennery at Dover was in Dover College boys' school, and I'd joined it as a plotting Wren. The accommodation was ghastly. I was put in a villa alongside the main building. In the front room, where I was put to sleep, there were double-decker bunks, six in all, close to the bay window, with the blackout permanently in place and the window kept closed. The smell of BO was appalling. I found an empty drawer and unpacked. I was slightly shaken.

'Then I went over to have lunch and was immediately welcomed by the other Wrens, who were wonderful. But I'd been put in with the roughest of the rough – they were all stores assistants and canteen workers at Dover Docks, who worked different hours. Everyone smoked except me. They were very poor and their conversation was very coarse. They stole from me – my make-up, for instance. I was fair game because I talked different, didn't I? Another great difference was that they slept in their underclothes while I slept in pyjamas. There was hostility on both sides, though there was one girl I liked, from a London slum.

'Then there was an incident that I will never forget. I was woken up in the middle of the night by a tremendous fracas going on in the room. A girl in one of the top bunks was being removed by ambulancemen – I learned later that she'd taken an overdose, thinking she was pregnant.

'So I went to see the Quarters Officer and said: "Ma'am, can you move me to another cabin?" She looked me up and down and said: "I wondered how long you'd last." I thought: You bitch! But she moved me.' The new quarters, this time with other plotting Wrens, were a great success.

'My other life was always nearly spoiling things,' said Frances Grenfell, a Wren rating stationed in Oban on the west coast of Scotland, where naval ships would come in to refit. 'My parents had a friend called Arka Strutt, the son of Lord Rayleigh, who'd gone back to sea in the war. One day somebody said to me: "D'you know, we've got an Honourable coming in today? He's in command of the convoy." They pointed him out and I saw him through a telescope coming in in his pinnace. No time to escape – he was brought into the Operations Room where I was working. "Good God, Frances, what on earth are you doing here, dressed like that?" he said. The Captain had laid on lunch for him but he said: "No, no, I'll take Frances out to lunch." I was scarlet – I knew what a breach of protocol this was. It got worse. I, a rating, was swept into the Station Hotel – where other ranks were not allowed.

'That wasn't the end of it. Arka ran into an old friend who was also lunching at the hotel. They shouted at each other across the room – that generation were capable of simply ignoring what was going on around them: "When did we meet last – was it in Downing Street?" "No, it was Buckingham Palace." I wanted to sink through the floor.

'Everyone was rather suspicious of me after that. The Wrens didn't mind – they didn't know what an Honourable was and didn't care either – but the RNVR officers did. They were a bit miffed as I was just a rating.'

The Legge sisters, as young and pretty FANYs, aroused the protective instincts of an elderly general near their first billet. 'My sister Josceline and I got our calling-up papers as soon as war broke out, as we were already FANYs,' recalled Lady Barbara Legge. 'We were sent to Shrewsbury, where we were handed over to a very nice police sergeant who found us billets in the Britannia pub, along with twenty Tommies of the Shropshire Yeomanry. They were very nice but we used to push our chest of drawers against our door every night.

'We were there for three months, until an old man called General Lloyd heard about us and was absolutely horrified that two "nice" girls should be in a pub – needless to say, we'd never been in one before* – *and* with a lot of private soldiers. He had control of the Judge's Lodgings in Shrewsbury so he moved us there, where we froze – it wasn't nearly as warm as the pub – although the food was very good.'

As ambulance drivers, the Legge sisters were commandeered by the short-handed medical staff in Chester, their next posting. 'There was an enormous intake of ATS from Liverpool and one of our jobs was to delouse them – they were crawling. Our other responsibility was to make sure they put on their army-issue pyjamas and didn't go to bed in their clothes, which they always tried to do – we had to report them if they did.

'We'd never met girls like these before and we were sorry for them. I suppose what we noticed most of all was their dirt. And it was quite difficult to understand what they said. But they were all right.'

Dealings with men often produced the greatest culture shock. Cynthia Denison-Pender was appalled to be subjected to a physical assault, which she could never have imagined from someone of her own background. 'My second year in the factory we weren't allowed off until late on Christmas Eve. The draughtsmen had all been out for drinks at lunch-time and when they came back they tried to push us on the floor and have their wicked way with us. We had to hit them with the

---

* Before the war, women almost never entered pubs and then only under male escort, a custom that changed during the war.

steel rulers on our desks – thank goodness for those rulers, otherwise we could have done nothing. We got a pass out and I shot off on my bike home. I was terribly upset by that. It was my first encounter with sexual mores different from our own.'

~~~

Few girls crossed the class barrier when it came to the serious business of finding a mate, often because of expressed or implied parental disapproval.

'My parents' word was absolute law,' said Pamela Joyce. 'I can remember taking endless boyfriends home and being told: "Darling, I don't think you ought to go out with him." And there was no question of me saying: "Oh gosh," and pushing off with them. One stopped seeing them. Thank God my parents did say so or I would never have married Graham – I should probably have married the garage hand because he was so good-looking.'

'By instinctive choice one did seem to have boyfriends from the same background,' said Jean Falkner, who spent the war years nursing. 'From time to time I did have one who was disapproved of [on class grounds] at home.

'My parents were very clever. They didn't actually freeze him out, in fact they were rather too nice to him so that I realised how different he was, what awful clothes he wore or what extraordinary manners he had. And then I didn't want to see him again.

'That happened over and over again. Doctors who were passionately interesting in the hospital seemed too ghastly when they came home for the weekend and I couldn't wait to get rid of them. My parents would never have disapproved verbally – although my mother might have said: "Oh, he's rather common."

'But they arranged it so that I could see what they saw. In the end, on the whole I found I didn't really like the way they lived.

And anyway, when I was at the Radcliffe there were nice cavalry regiments within range so I used to go out with them.

'In fact, that was really why I left the Radcliffe. Even when I'd got rather senior I still wasn't allowed to stay out beyond half past ten on an evening off. So I crossed swords with the Matron. I said to her: "This is quite ridiculous. You leave us on a ward of twenty people, all of whom are on intensive care, and expect us to be totally responsible for them, and then you tell us we have to be in bed by half past ten if we go out dancing." So I went off to a job with Sir Harold Gillies – and Matron was sacked.'

Chapter 15

Wrens

'We began to learn to do without sleep'

As a service, the Wrens had glamour. While girls with an army connection or – more rarely – a passion for flying went into the ATS and WAAF respectively, next to the FANYs the Wrens emerged as the service of choice for the upper-class girl.

Woman after woman, terrified of appearing frivolous, shyly confessed to me that the uniform had a lot to do with it. For style and elegance, it left the other services far behind. Its near-black blue had all the chic and slimming qualities of black but was softer for English faces – to this day, navy blue and white is a perennial female favourite – making the most of the youthful good looks so many possessed. The colour itself, with its sub-liminal references to other reassuring figures such as policemen, exuded a sophisticated authority. To see a Wren officer in full fig was to view an attractive woman with just that hint of the dominatrix that seems to appeal to so many Englishmen, especially those from a public-school background.

The Wrens had, in fact, a strong claim to be the senior women's service since the Royal Navy was the first of the armed forces to recruit women. Heavy losses during the first three years of the 1914–18 war meant that there was a serious shortage of sailors to man ships. There were, however, hundreds of sailors working ashore and to replace them the Women's Royal Naval

Service was founded in November 1917 with the rallying cry: 'Free a Man for Sea Service'.

With the strong contemporary prejudice against women doing any kind of work that could be perceived as masculine territory, the Admiralty decreed that recruits to this new service could only do domestic, or 'female' work – cleaning, cooking, waiting at tables and so forth. The initial intake was three thousand and these early Wrens were so successful at what they did that they quickly took on other jobs – many of which had previously been considered too difficult for women – working as wireless telegraphists, code experts and electricians; and their numbers grew to over six thousand. They were disbanded on 1 October 1919.

With the near-certainty of war after the invasion of Czechoslovakia in mid-March 1939, the Wrens were quickly re-formed. This time, they were greatly expanded – at their peak in 1944 they numbered over 74,000 – while the scope of the jobs they did also greatly increased. Wrens played an important role in the planning and organisation of many major naval operations. Wrens served overseas and thousands worked with the Fleet Air Arm, Coastal Forces, Combined Operations and the Royal Marines.

After the war, their numbers were reduced to an average of three thousand. In 1977, along with the other two women's services, they were brought under the Naval Discipline Act. In the case of the Wrens this had little to do with discipline but had the merit of opening up many trades that had hitherto been male-only, thus paving the way for their total integration into the Royal Navy. They were again disbanded in 1993 and the final integration – when the first women served on ships – came in 1994. Women now serve on at least one-third of all naval ships.

Back in 1939, the pulling power of the uniform was immense – not that many of the girls who managed to join the Wrens put it quite like that. 'I chose the Wrens because a lot of my friends had joined them,' said Lady Anne Spencer, before adding: 'and I liked the uniform – the tricorn hat [worn by officers] was extremely becoming.' Another perk of being an officer was being allowed to wear stockings of black silk rather than cotton, although usually only those with an American boyfriend managed to obtain these.

Unlike some, Lady Anne found becoming a Wren (in 1942) quite easy – by then the real expansion of the service had started. The initial recruitment, in April 1939, saw a mere 1,500 women approved, whose uniforms did not arrive until the beginning of the following year. By the end of 1940 there was a total of 10,000 officers and ratings, and from then on the service expanded enormously.

When asked about her qualifications, Anne Spencer told the interviewing board that she could drive a car but that was all. 'I hadn't got School Certificate or Matriculation. I was put as a trainee for radar plotting in the tunnel at Chatham and started off at Rochester in Kent in a double-decker bunk in a very large dormitory.'

For the governess-educated Lady Anne it was the first time she had shared a room with anyone. 'I hadn't been used to rules and regulations and at first I hated things like undressing in front of the others – not that there was anywhere much to put clothes, we had half a drawer each, really just enough for a change of underwear and another jersey. The other girls said it was just like being back at boarding school. Some of them used to climb out of the bedroom window, leaving bolsters in their beds to deceive the duty officer, and go up to the 400 and be back in time for morning watch.

'It was a bit of a shock when I found that by the head of my bunk was a big wooden square holding rat poison – it had food in the middle and sticky stuff round the edges to catch rats.

'I was then moved to Gillingham, where we were twenty-six in a cabin with double-decker bunks. You tried to get the top one which was much nicer as you got more air – we were allowed the windows open. We were all ratings but there were lots of people one would know anyway and we had a good time – one used occasionally to go on board ships for drinks with people one knew and we went to parties at the C-in-C's house when they asked for Wrens.

'The work was jolly hard. We plotted the convoys going north and south. The plots came in by telephone and there were e-boat battles at night.* Everything was very secret. I'd signed the Official Secrets Act when I joined the Wrens. We didn't even talk to each other about ships' movements. One just talked of other things.

'We did 2.00 a.m. to 8.00 a.m. one day, 8.00 a.m. to 2.00 p.m. the next day and the third day from 8.00 p.m. to 8.00 a.m. – that one was the killer. We had a meal before we went into the Wrennery and then nothing for twelve hours except cocoa and biscuits – you couldn't eat while on duty. We got breakfast when we came off at 8.00 a.m. and then we would either go to London or to bed – it was difficult sleeping as other Wrens in the dormitory were doing ordinary nine-to-five jobs and walking around, dressing and so forth, so most of us went off to meet someone.

'You could always rely on the trains – they invariably ran on time unless there were bombs. We always had to be in uniform but in the tunnel between Gillingham and Chatham we would change from our thick black uniform cotton stockings into black silk stockings we'd been given by some boyfriend. We were allowed to wear make-up but not nail polish, we had to have short hair and even our shoelaces had to be done up in a certain way – not criss-cross but straight across.'

Social connections were as useful in the Navy as elsewhere. Fanny Gore Browne, called up in January 1942 to work as a

---

* German high-speed torpedo boats, capable of operating at speeds of 34–36 knots, were known as e (for enemy)-boats. They often patrolled the Channel at night.

typist in the Wren headquarters in Great Smith Street for the Director of Clothing, disliked both her job and her boss.

'She used to enjoy making me blush with risqué comments and the work was tedious in the extreme – endless letters to clothing manufacturers complaining about late deliveries. I was never backward in coming forward so I went to see the Drafting Officer and asked for a transfer to a port.

'Then Fate stepped in. My father, who was Chairman of Southern Railways, was sitting in his first-class carriage when an admiral came in. They got chatting and my father said: "My daughter's in your service and she's bored out of her mind." "Oh?" said the Admiral. "I'm terribly short of Wrens – what's her name?" A week later the Drafting Officer called me in and said: "What have you been up to? I've got a letter here from Admiral Ramsay asking for you to go to Dover."'

Three months after joining up, Fanny was in Dover. 'It was wonderful. I arrived there, fresh, green and with no idea what I was to do. Thank God I'd been to boarding school or I couldn't have coped. I didn't know a soul – I didn't know about anything.

'I found I was to be a plotter. There was a team of three each watch, a Petty Officer, a Leading Wren – which I became after a year – and a Wren rating. We were on duty either every third or every fourth night, so we began to learn to do without sleep. If there was thick fog in the Channel or if there was a real gale, we had a nap. And if it was a clear moonlit night probably very little happened – on bright moonlit nights you could see the coastal force boats coming in, whereas on a cloudy night they could creep up. There was most action on a cloudy moonlit night.

'Dover was very much the front line. The town was being bombed and shelled and I was often terrified. I was much more frightened in Dover than when I went to London because it was so concentrated. On a clear day at the Castle you could see the Germans calibrating their guns across the Channel, which was very frightening.

'We were in contact with the naval officers all the time, which was a great plus. We worked at incredibly close quarters. There were a lot of romances, not between the staff officers and Wrens as they – the staff officers – were so much older but among coastal force officers. But it was on a wartime footing as they were being killed all the time.

'Most people behaved amazingly well. We had a very good Chief Officer Wren, a sister of Leslie Henson,* who was very tough but very fair and nice. She'd been a games mistress at St Paul's.† One evening she got us together in the big hall for a talk. She turned the lights low and told us to sit on the floor, then gave us a talk about sex and boys. A lot of the girls were very inexperienced and her point was, "Don't lead the boys on. You can stop, they can't." She did it beautifully and it made a great impression.

'I was at Dover for almost two blissful years. It was a very good job and I made wonderful friends who are my friends to this day. We worked and played incredibly hard. Best of all was being absolutely at the heart of things. Anybody who was anybody visited the Ops room and we Wrens saw and heard everything – Churchill, Mrs Roosevelt, various admirals, General Smuts.'

Fanny was then put forward for a commission. Selection for officers was rigorous: potential officers were supposed to be at least twenty-three but youth did not always stand in the way of those considered 'officer material'. Fanny was accepted for the three-week training course at Greenwich in January 1944, when she was a week short of her twenty-first birthday.

Gieves, the naval tailors, measured the new arrivals on the course for their officers' uniforms straight away but, ominously, did not complete them until after the verdict of the Board. 'I went in for my own final Board not at all confident that I'd passed,' said Fanny. 'The girl before me came out in floods.

* Well-known actor and comedian.
† The girls' school in Hammersmith, London.

She'd been failed because she'd left her notes in a telephone box in Trafalgar Square when she went up to London.

'"You're very young," said Lady Cholmondeley,* when I appeared in front of the Board. Not only that but we'd been warned that the slightest blot meant failure and I'd had two. When the air-raid warning went at night we had to get up in full uniform – boarding school again – and muster in the hall. The Wren officer pointed at my feet and I realised I was wearing my bedroom slippers. "Well, what use would you be, Gore Browne, if there was glass all over the road?" she said. I turned to go back upstairs to get them and she screamed at me: "You must *never* go back upstairs!" Which of course I knew but had forgotten because I was sleepy.

'My second blot was when I was sent off parade. We were taught by a colour sergeant of the Royal Marines. When we were inspected by the Commandant, she stopped in front of me and said: "Take this cadet's name – she's got too much make-up on." And to me she said: "Moderation in all things. Leave the parade." I thought: That's torn it – two mistakes. But somehow I passed, which made it worth having my twenty-first birthday at Greenwich.

'Then – luck again – Dame Vera Laughton Mathews,† sitting at the centre of the panel, said: "I've got a letter here from Admiral Ramsay asking for you. Get your uniform together as quickly as you can – you are to go on Monday to Norfolk House, St James's Square, as PA to Admiral Tennant." He was in

* When she was Lady Rocksavage (her husband succeeded his father as Fifth Marquess of Cholmondeley in 1923), Sybil Cholmondeley is said to have put the idea of the Wrens into the head of Sir Eric Geddes in 1917 – soon after he had become First Lord of the Admiralty – when she invited him to drinks and, upon hearing what heavy losses the Royal Navy had suffered in the first three years of the war, had said to him: 'The Army uses women for shore jobs – why not the Navy?' During the war she was Staff Officer to Dame Vera Laughton Mathews.
† Mrs (later Dame) Vera Laughton Mathews was appointed Director of the WRNS early in 1939.

charge of the Mulberry Harbours for the invasion – Norfolk House was where it was planned. This was in January 1944.

'It was a wonderful posting. My admiral was very nice, but not used to Wrens. I liked them all there. I was the only Wren on his immediate staff. We were there until late April 1944, when we moved to Southwick House, HMS *Dryad*,* where we put the finishing touches to the invasion plan – I was there the other day for the 6 June reunion.

'Then came the invasion. I had been working myself out of a job with Admiral Tennant as I knew that once the artificial harbours were towed across and the pipeline laid under the sea, his job would be over. So I said to him: 'They are recruiting plotting officers downstairs for the Ops room. Do you think I might be considered?" He went in to lunch and said: "My PA has given me notice, just like the parlour maid!" So he got a little Wren officer out of training and I walked down to the Ops room in triumph and I was in it all over D-Day.'

~

Many Wrens served overseas. The first draft, for Singapore, all volunteers – twelve cipher officers, ten Chief Wren special operators and a naval nursing sister – lost their lives, killed instantly when their ship, the SS *Aguila*, was torpedoed on 19 August 1941 *en route* from Liverpool to Gibraltar. The *Aguila*, a slow ship, had been travelling in convoy and was the first to be attacked by a U-boat pack; when hit amidships by a torpedo from U-201 she went to the bottom in ninety seconds. But by the end of 1942 there were 211 Wren officers and 741 ratings serving overseas at eleven establishments.

---

* Following heavy bombing raids in 1941 the Royal Naval School of Navigation was moved from Portsmouth to the recently requisitioned Southwick House (the ancestral home of the Thistlethwaite family). It served as the forward headquarters of SHAEF (Supreme Headquarters, Allied Expeditionary Forces). Today it is the Maritime Warfare School.

Another draft suffered massive fatalities when all but two of forty Wrens, who had sailed in SS *Orbeter*, in the first convoy through the Mediterranean and the Suez Canal to South Africa in December 1943, were torpedoed on the way to Colombo. Still others lost their lives when the ships they were on were torpedoed in the Mediterranean.

'The first lot of Wrens sent out to Malta were torpedoed, rescued, torpedoed again and all went down,' said Daphne Brock. 'I was scheduled for the next lot and our departure was put off for three months until they thought it was safer.

'Everything to do with convoys was very tight security. The sailing orders would be delivered by an officer only after the convoy had started so that no one could know where they were going. I did this delivery for a couple of months because I could climb rope ladders.

'Going to Malta I was entirely fatalistic. There were thirty of us in a large cabin with only one exit so if we'd been torpedoed there would have been no chance of getting out.

'On board we used to spend hours playing bingo – the only thing to do. It was a French ship, and as I spoke French because of being "finished" I used to eat with the officers and their food was delicious – they went on to Oran, in Morocco.'

No thought of danger stopped girls who were anxious to go to sea. In 1943, the year after she became a Wren, decoder rating Lady Elizabeth Montagu Douglas Scott was delighted to be offered a commission, which meant imminent despatch to the Officers' Training Corps.

'A week later I heard they were taking Wrens to sea because they were running short of men decoders. I went to see the Signals Officer and, standing very erect, said: "Please, sir, can you delay my OTC because I would very much like to go to sea. Sir." He said: "Well, Scott, I'm afraid you're down for OTC and that's that." "Please, sir, couldn't you delay it just a little bit?" "Well, I'll see about that."'

Lady Elizabeth was successful in her plea and allowed to go

with two other Wren ratings to join the liner *Mauretania* in August 1943. 'We were sent to Liverpool and spent a couple of days learning about what we'd be doing. A big thrill was to see my brother, then serving on a little frigate which came into Liverpool. From his frigate, you could see this great big grey ship, the *Mauretania*.

'Next day we all set off, us three Wrens in one cabin with two Wren officers also on board. I was thrilled to bits. It was terribly rough and one of the girls just collapsed so we had to work watch on, watch off for the first two days. Then we told her she had to pull herself together because we were alternating sleep and waking every two hours and were just exhausted.

'It took ten days to get to New York, zigzagging to avoid U-boats. The excitement of arriving there, seeing the Statue of Liberty floodlit and lights everywhere after wartime blackout! We had a whole week there so the ship's officers took us out, and we danced and saw New York. Then we filled up with eight thousand American troops and brought them back, had a few days in Liverpool to recoup, and set off again for Boston, Massachusetts. It took a week to get there.

'My job was decoding the messages that came in. We had a Petty Officer Telegraphs next door to us who brought the messages in, we decoded them, and then they went up to the bridge, taken by one of the Wren officers; because we were ratings, we weren't allowed on the bridge. But thanks to the *Mauretania*'s Merchant Navy officers, who said we girls could not be allowed to eat below decks with the sailors – we'd be torn to ribbons and must be allowed to eat in the Officers' Saloon – our Wren officers rather crossly allowed us to eat upstairs. Very tiresome girls they were.

'The next two trips were to Halifax and Nova Scotia, with much the same routine – the last one, in November, was very cold. Wrens were only supposed to do three trips, but being the senior rating I'd been allowed a fourth, to initiate the next lot. By which time I just loved that ship, she had become home to me and I knew so many of her officers – I was made godmother to the baby of one of them, born while we were in Boston. When we had a farewell party in Liverpool at the end of November I was in floods of tears at leaving my ship.'

In contrast to the mobility of Wrens who served overseas, there was a smallish group of what were known as Immobiles – in fact, Mobile service was approved only three days before the outbreak of war.

Immobiles harked back historically to the early days of the Women's Royal Naval Service when women's lives traditionally revolved around their homes. In the Second World War most Immobiles came from families that lived near the big naval bases – the Nore (Chatham), Dover, Plymouth, Portsmouth, Rosyth, the Orkneys and Shetlands and Western Approaches. Often, their fathers or brothers were naval personnel and they continued to live at home (known as 'going ashore'). By the end of 1942 there were twenty-six Immobile officers and 9,938 ratings (compared to 1,775 Mobile officers and 26,615 ratings). One of these Immobiles was Frances Grenfell, who had married Patrick Campbell-Preston just before war broke out and was living with her widowed mother-in-law and her own small baby at Ardchattan, on the west coast of Scotland.

'My husband was a regular soldier who was taken prisoner in 1940 and I didn't see him again until 1945. In 1941 I joined the Wrens. Oban had been turned into a naval base, and I was an Immobile Wren there. We Immobiles had signed on on the condition that we weren't sent away from our base.

'In our office we used to keep the signal books corrected up to the latest information, from various texts. There were three or four of us in my office. The whole establishment of Wrens was somewhere between twenty-five and thirty. A lot were local girls.

'It was the first time I'd ever worked in an office – I had to turn up on time and stay until the work was done and have whatever there was for lunch, so all that was new. I'd been vaguely prepared for it by St Paul's, the school I'd been to. I had a baby Ford car and petrol to take me into the office and we had various evacuees who attended high school in Oban so I gave them lifts as well.

'It was interesting and extremely funny. An awful lot of the war in Scotland was funny – it was sort of *Whisky Galore* stuff. For instance, there was the terror of the dentist on the west coast of Scotland. If there was any trouble with your teeth you had them all out and a frequent twenty-first birthday present was some snappers. When I was in the Wrens we were told one day that there would be a dental inspection. The girls were so frightened they went to their dentists the night before. Next morning I was the only one of my team to turn up – the others had had all their teeth out.

'I think that what helped was that unlike many who came out I wasn't used to being in a totally upper-class world. My great friend was Maggie, the daughter of a policeman in Stoke-on-Trent – I don't know if she'd even known about Scotland before. She was marvellous and so funny. She had a boyfriend on the *Ark Royal*, who was going to come on leave and as there were no spare beds in Oban, she asked me if I could find a bed for him. I asked the Provost, who was awfully nice, and he said of course, he can stay with us. He went up there while Maggie was still working and they gave him high tea, and she was most impressed that they'd put the silver out.

'After the boyfriend came to stay there was a bit of a blip. Maggie thought she was pregnant, which for her would have been the end of the world, a terrible disgrace. We all had great consultations and we thought quinine and gin and a lot of jumping up and down might solve the problem. So we administered quinine and gin and she jumped up and down on the esplanade in Oban and mercifully it worked. I never got passes made at me, but then I didn't give anybody half a chance.

'What I remember chiefly was being terribly, terribly cold in the war. My husband's home had no central heating, electric light was from a generator, and there was a fire just in the kitchen, built up so that you were quite hot on one side and icy cold on your back. At the beginning of the war there'd been a fire in one's bedroom but that stopped quite quickly. One winter I had ten blankets on my bed. The extraordinary thing was that people like my mother-in-law never seemed to notice it.'

Immobile Wrens (later the category was abolished) were paid more than their Mobile counterparts, who were of course given their accommodation and food. First Officers, for instance, received £240 p.a. if Immobile, £165 if Mobile. For Immobiles, because they were so few, promotion was difficult. Most, like Frances, seldom achieved more than Leading Wren.

'This upset my father considerably. But the Captain of the station, a terribly nice old boy, was passionate about fishing and of course we owned fishing, so he and I used to go fishing together. Ranks weren't supposed to mingle so I used to have to sneak out and go off with the Captain to fish in the evenings.'

Daphne Brock, with a father who was one of the most famous admirals in the Navy and therefore familiar with naval ethos and tradition, was not only a natural for promotion but also prepared to stand up for herself.* Within the first week of joining the Wrens she was reported by a Petty Officer for insubordination – refusing to eat her breakfast porridge. When asked by the Second Officer 'what she had been up to', she responded: 'That Petty Officer is a sadist. I joined the Wrens to beat the hell out of Germany, not to eat porridge.' The Second Officer laughed.

She was first posted to Chatham as a plotting Wren, which meant fast thinking. 'Learning to plot, you had to have a fairly

---

* Her father was Admiral of the Fleet Sir Osmond de Beauvoir Brock, Chief of Staff Grand Fleet 1916–18 and Commander in Chief, Portsmouth, 1926–9.

quick brain, especially if there was a crisis, such as convoys being attacked by e-boats.' But she was only there three months before being sent to Greenwich for an Officers' Training Course. 'I wasn't particularly ambitious but I'd decided that the sooner I got a room to myself the better.'

Once, when stationed at Immingham on the Humber, this nearly led to tragedy. 'In early 1943 I'd been selected as an officer and went to Greenwich for the course. There were very good lectures but it was quite scaring as all the female officers made you think you were going to fail. When I got my commission I was sent to Immingham, a port near Grimsby, to the staff of Flag Officer Humber. I worked with very nice cipher officers, duty staff officers and plotters – I was in charge of the plotting there, with three or four Wrens under me. We worked very hard and our watches were much closer together than before.

'Immingham had once been a sewage bed on which they'd built huts. We lived in Nissen huts and as an officer I had a bedroom to myself. Our Nissen hut had five or six cabins a side, with bathrooms, loos and washbasins at the end of the hut. The outside door at the end of it was left unlocked because people came and went through the twenty-four hours.

'One night, I was suddenly woken up. I hadn't got my curtains drawn and it was a lovely bright moonlight night, so that I could see someone standing by my bed. It was a sailor, and he started trying to strangle me. Somehow I got him off and as I got rid of him he must have hit me. I opened the door and went into my friend Anne's cabin opposite. She almost had hysterics when she saw me – I was streaming with blood.

'A few days later my father rang and when he heard what had happened all hell broke loose. I found it rather embarrassing. Apparently someone had heard the intruder trying the doors before he got to me but the previous cabins were empty because those Wrens were on duty.'

For Lady Elizabeth Scott, made a Leading Wren and sent to Chatham, decoding on the *Mauretania* was not the only excitement. 'I was there until D-Day and it was terribly exciting getting all the messages.' Shortly afterwards, in midsummer 1944, she was made an officer and then, as she had volunteered to go abroad, was told that she would be posted overseas.

'I was full of excitement, thinking it would be Italy or Greece or anyway somewhere in the Mediterranean. Instead they told me it would be Australia. I'd been getting together with my future husband and I said: "Oh no, not Australia – it's too far away." But they said very firmly that the war in Europe was beginning to close down and the British Navy was going to the Pacific, where everything was happening.

'I got embarkation leave over Christmas, sat up all night in a train for Liverpool, went to New York on the *Aquitania* and then went on a four-day train journey across America. There was a week's wait in San Francisco and then we – twelve Wren officers and a few naval people – were put into the biggest seaplane ever invented. It was a Mars.* They rigged up seats and a temporary loo in the tail. We were in it for fourteen hours so it got a bit grubby at the back.

'We landed at Honolulu, swam on Waikiki beach and caught another seaplane to another island, where we were greeted with terrific enthusiasm by American bomber pilots and Australian and New Zealand fighter pilots who hadn't seen white women for months. We had the same great welcome on the next island, Espiritu Santo in the New Hebrides, and eventually got to Australia.'

❧

Lady Anne Spencer, who married a serving naval officer in February 1944, was put on censorship duties after her wedding.

---

* These gigantic aircraft, designed for transport, were among the largest ever built, with a wingspan of over 200 feet and a crew of eleven. Only five were ever made.

'It was an awful job, reading other people's letters. Normally this was done by a ship's officer but on little ships, where there were only two officers and a few men, it was far too personal, so letters were sent to the Wrens in High Holborn.

'One learned a lot of new expressions like NORWICH – though you had to cut the place names out as they might have been giving information on where they would be sent – and SWALK. But none of us understood what EGYPT meant.'

Perhaps it was not quite what Dame Vera Laughton Mathews had in mind – although all would have agreed with her sentiments – when she addressed Wrens towards the end of the war with the words: 'Our lives are going to be wider and deeper because of all we have learned in the Service. And when peace comes you will take your place in civilian life to such good purpose that people will say: "Well, you see, she *was* a Wren."'

Only a few years later, on 1 February 1949, the Wrens became a permanent part of the Senior Service, so that they are now within, rather than alongside, the Royal Navy.

Chapter 16

The Air

'Why are you bringing us only half an aeroplane?'

The Women's Royal Air Force (WRAF) was the youngest and most exotic of the women's services, its allure harking back to the dashing early days of flying, then well within living memory. The first controlled, powered flight (by the Wright brothers) had taken place only in December 1903.

At the beginning of the 1914–18 war pilots were chiefly used as observers, flying over enemy lines and then returning to report what they had seen. Within a couple of years, fighter pilots had established an image of gallantry and a cool yet reckless bravery in single combat that reminded many of the age of chivalry. So new was this form of warfare that airmen were not yet a separate service but branches of the Army and Navy.

As the role of the embryo air force expanded, so did their needs; women were employed not only in clerical and domestic jobs but also to work on the aircraft themselves. Only towards the end of the war, on 1 April 1918, was the Royal Air Force (RAF) officially created. The Women's Royal Air Force came into being on the same day.

The uniform for both services took almost as long to establish. In its early years the infant air force wore khaki, navy blue and different lighter blues before settling on air force blue (a mid- to light blue-grey) late in 1918. The service that became the

WRAF was dressed in khaki (early airwomen were frequently reproved for being 'improperly dressed' – the commonest offences were pinning on brooches, lowering necklines, or putting on an officer's cap badge when out of sight of the camp). Even when a blue uniform was authorised for female officers in September 1918, most of the rank and file remained in khaki – but, in any case, most of them were demobilised as soon as possible after the war ended.

Between the wars, the popularity of flying leapt ahead. Small flying clubs sprang up all round the country, often with former wartime pilots as instructors, and the first commercial airlines came into being (though regular transatlantic passenger flights did not begin until after the Second World War). But the conditions of those early years still lingered: leather coats and flying helmets were worn to counteract the cold in the upper air and the Imperial Airways services to different European cities (from Croydon Airport) were often so noisy and bumpy that earplugs and the tough paper air-sickness bags provided by the airlines were frequently used.

For the young and the rich, flying was the new thrill, superseding the fast sports car. Although most amateur pilots were men, women, too, were fascinated – like Amy Johnson,* the extraordinary young woman who with virtually no money, learned to fly and became the first woman to make a solo flight from England to Australia.

As the threat of war increased, so did the need for women's services to complement the armed forces. On 9 September 1938, Leslie Hore-Belisha, Minister for War in the Chamberlain Government, signed the Royal Warrant that created the Auxiliary Territorial Service (the ATS). Some of its members were

* Amy Johnson, born in 1903, began to learn to fly in the winter of 1928–29, paying for tuition from her salary as a legal secretary. She also became the first British-trained woman ground engineer. She set off from Croydon in May 1930 in a single-engine Gypsy Moth on her record-breaking 11,000-mile flight to Australia. Other record-breaking flights followed.

attached to the RAF and it was soon obvious that these latter would operate more efficiently as a separate body. Their numbers increased rapidly and by the spring of 1939 there were forty-eight different companies countrywide training to help the RAF. On 28 June 1939, the Women's Auxiliary Air Force (the WAAFs) was formed. Their new uniforms, with badges identical to the RAF, were seen in public for the first time at the Great National Defence Rally in Hyde Park on 2 July 1939.

(Later this uniform – or rather, the lack of it – was to cause a hiccup in the rapidly expanding service. Recruiting had begun as soon as war was declared but many of the women who had volunteered had joined up in summer dresses and sandals, relying on the promised uniform – which did not always materialise. The worst problem was shoes: unlike the sturdy regulation issue, the shoes of the recruits quickly wore out on the hard surfaces needed for drilling.)

When the Manpower Act of December 1941 introduced conscription for women, the WAAF already had a long waiting list. By April 1942 their strength was over 110,000 and by January the following year they formed just under half of the entire personnel of Balloon Command, the barrage of hydrogen-filled balloons, 66 feet long, that surrounded large cities as a deterrent to bombers; their duties included splicing the cables of these monsters and patching them when damaged. As both cities and airfields – where the WAAF of course also worked – were particular targets of the Luftwaffe, airwomen quickly became used to bombs falling around them. 'There is hardly anyone now who has not lost a friend,' wrote one WAAF in October 1940.

One of the most vital jobs done by WAAFs was plotting – tracking the arrival of enemy planes. This was done on a large table, on an enormous map divided into numbered grids, by girls wearing earphones and pushing the markers that represented enemy aircraft with rods, rather as a croupier pushes counters on a roulette table.

Diana Lyttelton, who had learned plotting at Leighton Buzzard, was posted to Fighter Command at Stanmore in Middlesex in the summer of 1941, where she worked in the underground plotting room. 'We'd get the message that enemy planes were coming over and we'd plot their arrival.

'All round me were other WAAFs with rods and earphones. Then one would hear through these earphones the words: "Two up and one along," and you'd move the marker along on your section.

'We did shifts, 8.00 a.m. until noon, noon until four p.m., then four until eight. The night shift was 8.00 p.m. to 8.00 a.m. You did the same shift for a week at a time – the first time any of us went on night duty it was a great excitement. The nicest shift was noon until four because you could get up late.

'I did that for two and a half years, as the lowest form of air force life. Then I thought I'd try and get a commission. I applied and was accepted, and sent to the Officers' Training College at Loughborough in the winter of 1942. There were a lot of American soldiers there who gave us chocolates and chewing gum – we each picked up one, who adopted one as a companion for the week.'

After being commissioned, Diana was posted to the Air Ministry War Room, in the deep basement of the Air Ministry in King Charles Street. 'There were three desks – Fighter, Coastal and Bomber – and a Duty Officer. I was on the Fighter desk. We would track every plane that went out and then track them in again, so you knew if any were missing. This was for a report made by the Duty Officer for the Air Chiefs, who had a meeting first thing in the morning.'

One day in 1942 Diana's life changed abruptly. 'I'd just gone back after a night shift to my aunt and uncle's house in Wilton Street, where I was living on the top floor with a friend, when my boss rang up. "Come back here at once, please," he said. When I got back to the Air Ministry I was told that Winston

Churchill wanted a Map Room, which he'd had in the 1914 war, and I was to work in it.*

'There was an army officer, a naval duty officer and me for the air force, in which the PM was then singularly uninterested – the Battle of Britain was well over and everything was revving up for advances by the Army. Even when we bombed the prison in Amiens and all the political prisoners rushed out he was quite uninterested. But he was very interested in the flying bombs when they started.

'I saw a lot of him. He had the most beautiful manners, always greeted you, although for the first few days he ignored me until I was introduced. He talked exactly the way he made speeches, with wonderful rolling sentences. He used to bring in guests who had lunched at the annexe and point out features on the maps of Europe or the Far East. On one of those occasions Mrs Churchill said: "I never realised Russia and Japan were so close together!" He gave her rather a look.

'Churchill was so keen on maps that his secretaries used to say: "We can't get him to read his boxes."'

Although no WAAF ever (officially) flew an aeroplane, another kind of airwoman did. These were members of the Air Transport Auxiliary (ATA), the female ones known colloquially as the Attagirls.

The ATA was the idea of Gerard d'Erlanger, of the banking family, who was a director of British Airways (later, with

---

* The Map Room was part of a deep underground complex known as the Cabinet War Rooms. The building above them, facing St James's Park and only a few steps from Downing Street, was built on the sites of earlier stately homes – hence the deep wine cellars that served as the starting point for this network of chambers, tunnels, offices and dormitories that Churchill and his staff referred to as 'The Annexe'. Outside the Map Room a signpost had slots describing the weather overhead: COLD, SUNNY, WINDY, FINE. Either optimism or wishful thinking dictated that there be no sign for RAIN. A notice near the Prime Minister's bedroom – the Churchills lived there for much of the war – warns, 'There is to be no whistling or unnecessary noise in this passage.'

Imperial Airways, to become the British Overseas Airways Corporation). Allied to his belief that war was inevitable was the conviction that in such a war Britain could use the help of her many amateur aviators.

For by the late 1930s, flying had been opened up from an exclusive sport for the wealthy to a recreation for the many with the formation of the Civil Air Guard. This was started by Lord Balfour of Inchrye, a fighter pilot in the 1914–18 war and Minister of Aviation and Under-Secretary for Air in Neville Chamberlain's Government, who realised the need to train more pilots as quickly as possible. In the Civil Air Guard, young people could learn to fly for as little as 7s 6d an hour, and many did so.

At the same time, as war became more and more inevitable, aircraft were being produced as fast as possible. But little thought had been given to how they would be moved, first from the factory where they were produced to a maintenance airfield where radios and guns would be fitted and testing undergone, and then on to their destination airfield where they would enter service and become operational.

In both cases the aircraft would have to be flown there. With trained pilots in short supply, d'Erlanger's scheme was launched at the beginning of the war. To get it off the ground, a thousand-odd holders of 'A' flying licences were written to, of whom around a hundred responded.* After tests, thirty of these were selected. Within three months, eight women had joined them – the first time women had flown in the service of their country.

---

* To achieve an 'A' or private pilot's licence, candidates had to be over the age of seventeen, pass a medical examination, produce evidence of having completed at least three hours' solo flying time within the past year, and pass two flying tests. The first was to climb to 2,000 feet above the aerodrome, close the throttle and glide down to land within 150 yards of a point chosen by the examiner; the second was to fly five horizontal figures-of-eight, at no more than 600 feet above the ground, between two posts 500 yards apart, followed by shutting off the engine and landing within 50 yards of a previously chosen point.

Although all of the Attagirls had clocked up far more than the minimum of 250 logbook-recorded flying hours required even to secure an interview – all had over six hundred flying hours to their credit and one had two thousand – at first they were only allowed to fly training planes, notably the two-seater biplane Tiger Moths from the de Havilland factory at Hatfield.

For these early women ferry pilots, life was tough. They had to fly their open-cockpit Moths to Scotland (considered a safer place for pilots to train than English airfields) during the first, freezing winter of the war, then travel home through the night in a dark, icy train, usually full of troops, with only their parachute bags as a seat. Later a 'taxi service' was introduced, whereby one ATA pilot would make a round trip, picking up a number of others from different airfields round the country.

As the months passed, the need for more ATA pilots to fly different types of aircraft became obvious. The Attagirls, still confined to Tiger Moths, were gradually allowed to fly other types of aeroplane and the ATA Conversion School was set up to teach them. From July 1941 they moved on first to twin-engined trainers, then to single-engined fighters, then to light bombers, until they were flying every type of plane produced, from Spitfires to heavy bombers. With a four-engined plane they were accompanied by a flight engineer; otherwise all these flights were solo.

One of the Attagirls was Diana Barnato, the daughter of a famous racing driver, who had taken up flying before the war and had flown solo after only six hours' training at Brooklands Flying Club. Owing to a riding accident she had to postpone joining the ATA for six months, by which time their excellent training programme had been set up. This included dual and solo flights, classroom lessons and thirty cross-country flights. Cross-countries were essential as, without a radio, pilots had to fly below cloud-level and find their way simply by roads, railways, canals and rivers.

'They taught you wonderfully,' said Diana Barnato. 'All the

aircraft were put into six different categories and you learned to fly on one aircraft in each category and then were let loose on all the rest. Then you went back to school and learned the next category in the class above.

'Sometimes we flew two or three different types in a day and one might be of a kind you hadn't flown before. So you couldn't always remember the variations of stalling speed and so forth – you couldn't just kick the tyres and spit in the petrol tank and just go.

'We had a little book of words, six inches by four, with every aircraft you might have flown on loose leaf. So even if you'd flown the aircraft before, you'd turn to this page before you took off as the Marks were different and so sometimes you had to take off or land at a different speed. We couldn't have done the job without that little book. It was called Pilot's Notes and the Yorkshire Air Museum has now made it a game.'

The prejudice not only against women doing what were seen as men's jobs but against women wearing trousers that had been rife in the 1914–18 war still lingered on. The uniform of the female ATA pilots was extremely smart, in navy-blue serge, with black buttons with ATA on them, gold badges on the shoulder, gold wings and rank stripes, a belt with brass buckle – and a tight, knee-length navy-blue skirt.

'Finally we rebelled against this,' said Diana Barnato. 'When you flew, you had to put your parachute harness over your shoulders and the other straps came up between your legs, which was fearfully awkward in a tight skirt.

'Also, we said we couldn't climb up the side of a Barracuda or other aircraft in a tight skirt, with wartime stockings that ended just above the knee showing our suspenders and parachute-silk panties – you made eyes at the parachute packer and when he had a torn parachute he would give you a piece of silk – as it would expose a great gap of thigh. We were incredibly modest in those days.'

Modesty nearly cost Diana her life on one occasion. 'We'd been told by the ATA that trained ferry pilots were worth more to the war effort than an aircraft, so that in a bad situation we were to save ourselves if we could and forget the aeroplane.

'One bright January day in 1943 I was skimming happily along in a Spitfire – the twenty-second I'd flown – over the Cotswolds to the airfield where its instruments would be installed. I was wearing my best uniform jacket and tight skirt, as I'd just come back from leave and hadn't had time to change into dungarees.

'Suddenly, in literally just a few seconds, I was in thick cloud. First I climbed but I was still in thick cloud. Then I went down in a shallow dive to my break-off height [the lowest ATA pilots were allowed to go] in the hope I would be in clear air. But I was still in cloud.

'I was faced with two alternatives – to try, probably vainly, to find lower ground where the sun was shining, or to do the sensible thing and bale out.

'But I *couldn't* bale out! My skirt would have ridden up with the parachute straps and anyone who happened to be below *would have seen my knickers*! No, it simply couldn't be done.'

By sheer luck Diana managed to land her aircraft at a tiny nearby airfield, spotted through a gap in the thick cloud cover, to the astonishment of those on the ground, who assumed incredible skill and bravery instead of the real reason. Later she learned that the cloud that had unexpectedly condensed over central England (owing to an unusually high moisture content in the air) had caused the deaths of two ATA pilots and damage to a number of aircraft.

As D-Day approached, preparations became frenzied, with near-impossible weather conditions threatening the Allied invasion of Europe. Pamela Joyce, working in the Admiralty Meteorological Department, had first-hand experience of the constant changes of plan. 'It was off, the tides were wrong, the moon was wrong, there were storms coming up – it was a nightmare. People like Churchill and Monty and Alexander kept popping in and out and doing their nut over the conditions before it finally happened.'

Diana Lyttelton and her Map Room colleagues were kept virtually prisoner. 'The whole week before, we were locked in while we worked so that no one could come in by accident and see the maps. The night before D-Day the PM came in, with Mrs Churchill, and she reminded him of a lovely little restaurant they'd often gone to in France.

'That same night there was almost a disaster. There was a particular German reconnaissance plane that used to take off every evening from northern France and fly straight across the Channel to have a look at what was happening here – you could always tell these planes that took reconnaissance photographs because they always flew absolutely straight.

'The night before D-Day it set off as usual but must have developed engine trouble halfway as it turned back. If it had gone a bit farther it would have seen all the boats coming out and all the troops massing and, of course, been able to report this well in advance of the landings.

'After work I went home and quickly washed my hair because I didn't think I'd have time later. It was a very odd feeling, to be in my little flat washing and drying my hair and knowing the boats were on their way.'

~

A week later, on Tuesday 13 June, 1944, a new weapon hit London as dawn was breaking. This was the V-1, a small pilot-less plane with a one-ton high-explosive warhead. 'It made a noise,' said one near-victim, 'like an old motor-bike or a huge clockwork toy.' These new weapons were quickly christened 'Doodlebugs'. They travelled so fast that air-raid warnings were useless; those in their path learned that when the engine cut out this would be followed in about twelve seconds by an explosion. London was the principal target, and the damage they caused was such that within weeks there was a fresh wave of evacuation.

Lady Cynthia Keppel was working for the Ministry of Aircraft Production at Thames House, Millbank. 'When the engines stopped we got under the table and hoped for the best.' Anyone inside a house within 50 yards of a doodlebug explosion was likely to be buried alive as it crashed on to them.

The RAF, Allied guns, and bombing of V-1 launching sites drastically reduced the number of these missiles, but in September 1944 a new weapon appeared: rockets, or V-2s. These arrived with no warning and were so powerful that their one-ton warheads could raze to the ground a whole street of thirty terraced houses and scatter bodies on to roofs in the surrounding area. The V-2 was terrifying in its sudden, arbitrary devastation: such was the force of its blast that the windows of houses a mile away could be blown out – even some of the windows of Buckingham Palace remained covered with Cellophane for months. Broken glass was everywhere and the streets were often strewn with the contents of shop windows.

'What I mostly remember after a bad blitz was the smell,' said Cynthia Keppel. 'It was terrible – a smell of burning, an awful, awful smell of destruction.' The rocket attacks ended on 29 March 1945 when their units were withdrawn from Holland into Germany.

～

By 1944 the ATA had 458 male pilots and 108 female pilots, with a backup of three thousand secretaries, mechanics and parachute packers as well as flight engineers and ground engineers on attachment. As many as 174 pilots had by then been lost, as well as one cadet.

ATA pilots always flew solo, but in four-engined aircraft,

where certain of the controls could not be reached from the pilot's seat, the pilot was accompanied by a cadet, who had been taught how to change the petrol intake or work the emergency controls. ATC cadets, aged between twelve and fourteen, were attached to each of the twenty-two different 'ferry pools' around the British Isles.

Diana Barnato, in the women's ferry pool at Hamble, near Southampton, was one of those who had graduated to piloting Spitfires. 'We flew them as fast as they were made from the Spitfire factory at Eastleigh and also the Sea Otters and Walruses from Cowes in the Isle of Wight. I loathed the Walruses and they loathed me – my least favourite aircraft. There were 143 different types of aircraft we might have flown, of which I flew eighty-two during the course of the war.'

The main problems were the weather, and barrage balloons – the flyers were not permitted to mark these on their maps. 'They went up to at least 5,000 feet and they were all round the various important cities, towns and factories,' said Diana Barnato. 'They were on steel hawsers as thick as your wrist that could slice through a wing like butter. They were painted silver, therefore difficult to see anyway and in fog impossible. I think they probably brought down as many of us as the enemy.

'One of our ATA chaps had an amazing escape from a balloon accident. There was a ring of balloons round Langley, in Berkshire, where they made Hawker Hurricanes. They always took one balloon down for you so that you could take off, and another at your arrival airfield. As this man took off the plane swung round and he got the balloon cable in his wing. It didn't bring him down but it broke the cable. He went all round the outside, round the ring of balloons, and managed to land with this great bit of cable in his wing root.

'I was nearly brought down once myself, on one of my training flights. It was a cross-country one and I wasn't exactly sure where I was within a mile or so, so I circled – we had to fly contact, within sight of the ground. This was for two reasons:

first, so that we didn't somehow fly out over the sea in thick weather and secondly so that we could be protected by ground defences and the enemy kept off our tail. So we weren't taught how to fly on instruments and we didn't have radio – anyway, there were only about four channels and they were all in use for the RAF. Nor did we want the enemy to know where our short trips were going to, in case it gave anything away.

'As I circled, at about 1,000 feet – I was near Gloucester – I looked down and there I saw a large octagonal concrete slab, and a lot of RAF chaps jumping about and waving and pointing. I thought: Oh, they've seen my little aeroplane and they're pointing at me. Suddenly I saw an enormous barrage balloon being wound down – I'd been flying round and round its cable without seeing either.'

'Friendly fire' was another hazard. Diana was among many who experienced it. 'We did the milk run, flying Hurricanes every morning from the factory in Langley to the maintenance unit in Cardiff. When we flew from England to Wales, across the Bristol Channel, we frequently saw little puffs of black smoke around us, like raspberries in the air, but black, and one's aircraft shook. It happened to me when I was flying along towards Cardiff, away from the English coast, and I suddenly realised I was being shot at. Aircraft recognition was very difficult – I don't know how anybody did it, especially in a fog. So I didn't say anything about it.

'But one day when I went back to my unit at Walsham, by Maidenhead, there was a notice on the CO's board which said: "Will all pilots who think they've been shot at over the Bristol Channel please report to the CO." There was one hell of a queue because it had happened to everybody.'

Enemy aircraft were an occasional hazard. When ATA pilots were not ferrying, they had to be collected from destination points, often waiting for a day or two until there were several of them, and taken back to their units. This 'taxi' service used Anson and Fairchild aircraft. Diana was once in an Anson 'taxi' being flown by the famous pilot Jim Mollison,* the husband of Amy Johnson – both of whom were in the ATA – with a full load of ATA pilots, their parachutes and flying gear.

'As we came over Reading I saw a great plume of smoke rising up. I thought it was a train letting off steam – Reading was a big railway junction. We were flying towards the sun, with a dark cloud in front of us, when suddenly a little aircraft popped out of the cloud. At first I thought it was a Mosquito, because they were just coming out of the factory at Hatfield.

'Then I saw the tracer lights. Jim said: "Jesus! A Jerry," and put the Anson back into the overcast above us and the German aircraft, with the swastika on its back and the gunner firing upwards at us, passed underneath.

'It was a hit-and-run raid. The enemy came over in a line of cloud, popped out, dropped his bombs, and then flew back into the cloud and home. This one had dropped one lot of bombs on the goods yard, turned round for another sweep and found us in his way so he had a go at us as he went by. When we landed, sirens were blaring and everyone was running around in tin hats. "Did you see that Jerry?" everyone asked us. "Yes, of course we did," said Jim. "Let's go and have a cup of tea."'

Amy Johnson herself was one of the ATA casualties. She had taken a plane up to Prestwick and was going to come back in an Airspeed Oxford which she was ferrying to Kidlington, Oxfordshire. She stayed the night of 4 January 1941 with her sister in Blackpool (ATA pilots were only allowed to fly in daylight) and in the morning the weather was terrible. She should not really have taken off but she must have balanced her immense experience as a pilot against the risk and, thought Diana, might also have been anxious to get back for a party at Hatfield that night. Visibility was so bad that she did what was

---

* A leading British flyer who made the first solo flight across the Atlantic from Europe to America. When he married Amy Johnson they were dubbed the 'flying sweethearts'.

strictly forbidden: instead of flying under the cloud, so that she could recognise where she was, she flew above it.

While flying over the Channel searching for landmarks she ran out of fuel near Gravesend. A convoy coming in, led by HMS *Haslemere*, heard an aeroplane in the mist, saw a parachute coming down and shortly afterwards heard an aeroplane plop into the water; it floated for about twenty minutes before going down. A high sea was running but a boat was launched and had almost reached the parachutist when it was caught by the wind and swung against the reeds.

As the driver of the boat opened up the throttle to counter the wind the boat swung and hit the parachutist, who disappeared. The brave officer in the boat saw what he thought was a body, dived into the icy sea and recovered it – but it was Amy's overnight bag, not her body, and a long search failed to find her. When they returned to HMS *Haslemere*, her would-be rescuer was taken to hospital but subsequently became delirious and died of exposure.

~

Sometimes aircraft suffered strange mishaps. Diana Lyttelton was the embarrassed victim of one at the end of a wonderful visit to Italy in the spring of 1945. 'Field Marshal Alexander, who knew my friend Joan Bright, asked her if she would like to come and stay at his headquarters in Italy and bring a friend, and she asked me.

'We went on the *Franconia* to Malta – with all the priests gazing from the cliffs – stayed the night with the Governor and then flew to Naples in a Hudson, accompanied by crates of beer. There we were put up in an hotel, and officers were sent along to show us round, including taking us to the famous opera, and then we went on to Rome.

'On our last night we had dinner with Alexander and various generals in the Mess. Alex asked Joan to take back a handbag he had bought for his wife and General Morgan asked me to take back something to another woman with whom he was having an affair – little did he realise that she was a cousin of my mother's so we knew all about it!

'Anyway, next day we set off in the aeroplane. Joan and I were the only girls – the other passengers were thirty or forty officers. When we were safely airborne the captain came back and squatted down between us.

'"We have no lavatory on this plane," he said. "But if you need one we will land somewhere."

'The journey lasted eight hours. It was all right for the men, they just went up to the pilot and were presented with a sort of bottle. But the honour of the WAAF was at stake and we survived – just – until we landed at St Mawgan, Cornwall. There we spent the night in the Mess and told them about it. They made enquiries and later told us: "That particular plane flew a little too close to Brest and a very well-placed shell shot the Elsan* out of it.'"

The favourite aircraft among most ferry pilots, as with fighter pilots, was the Spitfire. 'I delivered two hundred and sixty,' said Diana Barnato, 'and not one had anything wrong with it, except perhaps a slightly faulty airspeed indicator. Whereas with some of the other aircraft, things were really wrong.

'Once, in a Typhoon, when I was just south of the Reading railway, there was a loud bang and I thought: Oh, goodness, the engine's blowing up. I throttled back and put the nose down so it didn't stall and began to look for a place to force-land – luckily it was a lovely day.

'Then I realised the engine was all right. I couldn't think what was the matter until I looked down and there was no floor – I could see the ground through my feet. The whole of the underside of this new Typhoon, from nose to tail, had ripped off and all I was looking at were the control wires.

* A portable lavatory.

'It was very windy. I tucked away my parachute flaps that were banging round and hitting me in the face and climbed up. Because it was so jagged with the wind, the airflow would have been spoiled and the plane would have stalled at a much faster speed. Even at 5,000 feet I found that it stalled at a tremendously high speed which meant I would have to come in at that speed if I was to land.

'I flew on to my destination, which was Kemble [Gloucestershire]. I flew across Kemble very fast, thinking: No doubt the Crash Wagon will come out, ready to catch me when I land.

'But nobody came out. They hadn't noticed the floor had disappeared – they just thought it was a beat-up. I did a circuit, very fast, thinking that I couldn't put the flaps down as they'd blow up at this extreme speed, and all the rules said it was too fast for the undercarriage to be lowered.

'But I had to do it if I wanted to land. At first it wouldn't go down, then I pressed the emergency – fruitlessly – then I rocked the aircraft and finally the legs came down, locked, and I went in. Luckily it was quite a long runway. The legs didn't come off so I taxied to the shed where we got the chits signed and left the aircraft. The chap in charge, whom I knew, peered out of his hut and said: "Hm, Miss Barnato, why are you bringing us only half an aeroplane?"'

Chapter 17

Afterwards

'The war made us feel capable of doing something'

On everyone who went through it, the war had an indelible effect: like a deep ravine across their lives. 'Everybody had their lives changed. You couldn't go back to what life was before,' said Fortune Smith (later Duchess of Grafton). 'Personally, I was just completely immersed in it.'

'I suppose it was the most important thing in my life apart from my first husband,' said Val Canning. 'I'm still reading books about it.'

When it ended came the realisation, sometimes quickly, sometimes gradually, that the kaleidoscope had been shaken and had settled in a different pattern, an enormous social change at first masked by the continuing shortages and grey monotony of the immediate post-war era.

'I can't *believe* the life that we led before the war,' was a remark made to me over and over again. 'Looking back, it seems extraordinary – it's so *over*,' said Elizabeth Lowry-Corry. 'It makes you feel a hundred when you think you were involved in that' – 'that' being not only the Season but a whole way of life with its customs, shibboleths, sports, wealth, power and privilege unknown to the rest of the population.

A few of the debs' parents refused to believe that the life they had known before would never return. Virginia Forbes Adam, who had disliked the idea of coming out before the war and set her face firmly against it, found that her mother was still determined that she should have a Season. 'She took a little flat in Dorset Street and gave another ball for me, at 23 Knightsbridge [a well-known venue], to which Princess Elizabeth came.

'After this I got asked to a lot of balls and dances but I found them incredibly boring because they were for eighteen-year-old girls and their contemporaries, and I was twenty-four and had been through the war. So I was often a wallflower and hated that.'

She met her husband Hugo, whose sister was married to Esmond Rothermere and who worked on the *Daily Mail*, in 1947, married him in 1948 and a few years later went with him to 'the remotest part of Sutherland. There Hugo wrote and I had babies.'

Often the physical response to memories of the war was hard to shake off. 'I still get a feeling now if I hear a siren,' said Fortune Smith.

'When the war ended I went to Spain as the Foreign Editress of the *Daily Sketch*,' said Renée Merandon du Plessis, who had married Lord Iliffe's son Edward just before the war. 'It was really to see my aunt but you couldn't leave England without a reason. When I arrived in Spain the first thing I saw was a plane with a swastika on it and with pure reflex action I bolted back into our plane, up the gangway, before I pulled myself up.'

'It went on so long that in a way you became very numbed by it,' said Elizabeth Lowry-Corry. 'One really got bored with longing for it to end.'

The huge social post-war metamorphosis that took place was, of course, hastened by political change and, no less powerful, a groundswell alteration in attitude. Soon after VE Day, the Labour Party held its annual conference. Churchill would like to have kept the Coalition Government going until after the Japanese war was over. A number of senior Labour politicians – including Clement Attlee, the leader of the Labour Party – agreed with him, but the party as a whole, scenting the possibility of the first Labour Government since 1931, wanted a return to party politics and an election. When Attlee told him this, Churchill realised that the days of the Coalition were over.

Polling Day took place on 4 July 1945, after which there was a three-week gap to allow for votes to be sent in from members of the Armed Forces still overseas or unable to reach a polling station.

In the interim the Potsdam Conference was held. Diana Lyttelton, now a conference veteran, went out to Germany with Churchill's beloved maps and on 15 July 1945, the Prime Minister met both Truman (who became US President after Roosevelt's death on 12 April) and, again, Stalin.

'We put up our maps in HQ and were billeted in houses along the main street. All went on fairly normally until Churchill had to fly back to hear the result of the election – Stalin, who thought he would have rigged the election, gave him a terrific nudge of complicity.

'We returned to England with Churchill, who said he wanted to see the results of the election in the Map Room. So we transformed it into constituencies. He came in in his siren suit and sat there all day. We came rushing in, calling out: "Labour gain! Labour gain!" and marking these on the constituencies. From time to time he said: "Dick [Captain Pim], ring up Central Office – how many did we expect to lose?"

'I happened to tear off the result of his own constituency, Woodford, so I took it in. Lord Beaverbrook was with him then. I said: "I have the results from your constituency, sir." "Am I in?" he asked me. The main parties did not oppose him in his own constituency but an independent stood against him on the platform of a one-hour day in a one-day week – and got 10,000 votes. I gave this result to the PM, who said: "The country's gone mad! A madman stands against me and gets 10,000 votes!"

'As the afternoon wore on Anthony Eden came in, looking as though he had been hit on the head. Then Oliver Lyttelton,*

---

* In 1954 Oliver Lyttelton became the first Viscount Chandos. Diana Lyttelton's family was a collateral branch.

saying: "It'll do the Tories good, a little time out of power," followed by Mary Churchill, who had left much of her luggage in Potsdam, to tell me where to find her clothes, and Jock Colville.

'Eventually Winston went off to change into his morning coat to resign. We waved him away from the top of the steps with tears in our eyes. After this, the Map Room rather died away.'

The final results were 213 Conservative MPs elected, compared to 393 Labour (in the National Government of 1935, 432 Conservatives had been elected and 154 Labour). No one expected quite such a landslide Labour victory, with its immediate jettisoning of the leader who had so triumphantly brought Britain through the war; but the people, who had given everything they had to the war effort, who had absorbed the idea of 'fair shares for all' through rationing, wanted reform and a new, fairer, post-war social order.

'A lot of my friends were deeply shocked after the war at this total Labour victory and couldn't understand it,' said Frances Grenfell, veteran of both the Wrens and factory work. 'But I could, absolutely. And if I'd been on the electoral register – which I wasn't because of being too young last time and having moved house – although I wouldn't have wanted to vote against dear old Winston I would probably have voted Labour.

'The Welfare State and the National Health, you knew it had to happen. You were told stories by the people in the factories of how they had to deal with health in their families. Sometimes they had a good nice doctor on the panel, sometimes not. Something absolutely had to be done about it.'

For the upper classes, the change was seismic. The elaborate infrastructure that had made their pre-war lives possible – other people to look after them – had crumbled fairly rapidly in the months after war broke out, as their servants left to fight or were called up. In contradiction to the aftermath of the 1914–18 war, when the dearth of jobs forced women and some men back into domestic labour, the men and women who had fought, often side by side, through almost six long years did not want to go back to taking orders from others thanks to an arbitrary accident of birth.

Underscoring this was the huge drop in the incomes of the rich. To pay for the new social reforms and the various nationalisations, taxes shot up, dramatically affecting those at the top end of the financial scale. Although the top rate of income tax (raised from 5s 6d in pre-war days to ten shillings out of every pound during the war) had been reduced by one shilling, surtax on a sliding scale was imposed in the October 1945 Budget of the new Government. Beginning at an (extra) two shillings in the pound for those with incomes of £2,000, it rose to a top rate of ten shillings and sixpence in the pound for anyone (husbands and wives were assessed together) with an income of £20,000 or over. Effectively, this meant that these people were paying the Chancellor 19s 6d (95p in today's money) in the pound. With death duties (as inheritance tax was known) now at a scale that rose to 65 per cent, the easy living of pre-war days had begun to seem a distant dream.

The young and adaptable took such changes in their stride. For most of the pre-war debutantes, the war gave not only a sense of purpose but of self-belief, in a way that would not have been possible before, when the majority would have passed smoothly from the parental home to that of a husband. 'The big thing the war gave me was self-confidence. That was the enormous plus – the feeling that you can cope,' said Fanny Gore Browne, who went straight back to work after her demobilisation and continued working during her marriage.

'You had to stand entirely on your own feet – you grew up,' said nurse Penny Woosnam, whose mother had died during the first winter of the war and whose father had sold their home and remarried. 'Really I had no home to go to during the war so I was always on duty on Christmas Day – but you worked so hard you didn't have time to feel lonely.'

For her older sister, Denise, war brought a sense of liberation. 'Living in the country in the way we did one would never have been thrown into a wider, more purposeful world. The way we lived before wasn't purposeful.'

'The war made me much more self-reliant and independent,' echoed Ursie Barclay. 'It gave me a sense of purpose.'

For some, it gave a boost to their self-esteem. Lady Elizabeth Montagu Douglas Scott, granddaughter of the Duke of Buccleuch, found that 'working in the hospital and being a Wren allowed me to live as myself, without my family background – without being somebody's daughter or somebody's sister. One had been defined by the men in one's life. I was completely under the thumb of everyone in my family – I hardly dared say boo to a goose. I was quite frightened by my mother, as she had very high standards and I felt I wasn't really clever enough or bright enough or anything like that.

'The war helped me hugely with my self-confidence and feeling of independence – in fact, it was the making of me. Otherwise I'd have probably gone on being a dull, shy country girl. Getting away like that and being one's own person made a terrific difference – finding that people liked one for oneself, that one could actually go to places by oneself, do things on one's own. I grew up with a dreadful inferiority complex – never really lost it! – but I got much better through my wartime work. It was wonderful to feel I was liked for myself, not for anything I happened to be.'

For many, there was a sense of liberation, freedom and possibility. 'I would consider my life started with the war,' said Diana Quilter.

'Before, I wasn't exactly stopped from doing things but I was administered to, and allowed to be – it was very passive. But one didn't ask and one didn't expect anything,' said Jean Falkner. 'The war gave me a great feeling of independence, that I loved. I felt I was in a different country.'

Still others confessed, rather guiltily, to enjoying it. 'It's an awful thing to say, I know,' said Fiona Colquhoun (by then Lady Arran), 'but one enjoyed the war. Women in the old days were kept as a useful bargain, to wash and to cook. The war made us feel capable of doing something more.

'My sisters, who were very much under my parents' thumb, joined the Wrens, which they loved – they said it was the happiest time of their lives. It gave them both a lot of confidence and one of them, who had been very shy, really running away from everything, absolutely blossomed.

'The war made one stronger in the direction one was already going – one was much stronger then than before or after. The war brought out the best in one, there's no getting away from that.'

'I adored my war,' said Lady Moyra Ponsonby. 'I got a rather priggish kick out of finding that I was good at nursing. One would go with one's name into a hospital situation, everyone thinking that Lady Moyra Ponsonby would be no good, and then finding that I was.' Moyra, who married the surgeon Sir Denis Browne in 1945, became a State-Enrolled Nurse in 1946 and went on to become, first, the Deputy Superintendent-in-Chief and then Superintendent-in-Chief of the St John Ambulance Brigade, and Vice-President of the Royal College of Nursing.

'I wouldn't have missed my army life for anything,' said Sheila Parish who, after first caring for her brother's children, went on to work for the Commissioner for South-East Asia, spend ten years in the Hospitality Department of the Victoria League for Commonwealth Friendship, and then become one of the most popular Dames at Eton. 'The war gave me a sense of purpose and independence.'

Diana Barnato, who had the war to thank for her thousands of hours of flying time, was also able to pursue an extraordinary career. A year before the war ended she had married Wing Commander Derek Walker, a bomber pilot, who was killed in an air crash in November 1945.

'I took out a "B" licence after the war and I was Corps pilot for the Women's Junior Air Corps, now the Girls' Venture Corps. It was the first time most of these children had been airborne. The Corps had bought its own aircraft, initially a Fairchild, and we went all round the British Isles, giving these girls air experience. I did three flights an hour. I went off on Fridays, flew myself silly on Saturdays and Sundays and came home on Mondays.'

In 1963 Diana gained the women's unofficial speed record with 1,262 m.p.h. in a Lightning – the first woman to fly one. Following three (successful) cancer operations, she became Master of the Old Surrey and Burstow Foxhounds for thirteen seasons while continuing to fly as Corps Pilot for the Women's Junior Air Corps.

After her demobilisation Diana Lyttelton went to the Foreign Office Conference Department, working on the first United Nations Conference of 1945. Then, one day in 1947, she was telephoned by Michael Adeane (the King's Assistant Private Secretary) and offered the job of Assistant Press Secretary to George VI. 'I happened to have an abscess on my face and I remember walking down the Mall thinking, Shall I say that I don't usually look like this? Then I thought: Well, I'm not being taken on for my beauty, so I'll say nothing.

'When I got there Lewis Ritchie – Bartimeus – was there.* When Princess Elizabeth's engagement was announced I was on my own – Tommy Lascelles was probably having a lie-in, but luckily all the Private Secretaries were my cousins and helped. Then Richard Colville arrived,† and we galloped on together towards the royal wedding. I worked there for ten years – I met my future husband [Alexander Hood] in 1955.'

* Sir Lewis Ritchie wrote short stories, often sea-based, under the pseudonym Bartimeus.
† Commander (later Sir) Richard Colville was a former naval officer who became the royal press secretary in 1947, remaining as the Queen's Press Secretary from her accession in 1952 until his retirement in 1967.

A lot of girls who had seen the plight of others, from evacuees to slum dwellers, felt that they wanted to help people less fortunate than themselves.

Lady Anne Spencer, who had married early in the war and left the Wrens in 1944 when expecting her first child ('Pregnancy was the only reason you could leave'), did a lot of charity work afterwards. 'What the war had mostly given me was the feeling that one was doing something worth while, and what it taught me was how to get on with other people in all walks of life – and how nice they were.'

Fortune Smith, who had nursed professionally during the war, married the Duke of Grafton's heir Lord Euston in 1946 but continued with her work as an SRCN at Great Ormond Street Hospital, joining their Board of Governors in 1952. She combined this role with serving as a Lady of the Bedchamber to the Queen. In 1957, three years before becoming Duchess of Grafton, she was appointed Mistress of the Robes.

'I feel passionately about the state of nursing. I think there ought to be one lot of nurses caring for the patients – feeding them, washing them, seeing that they are all right – and another lot who manage the very difficult equipment, both of equal merit. I don't like a degree in nursing – some of the girls coming out with a degree in nursing today can't get a job and often haven't had very long in the wards. Equally, people who couldn't do the exams might be excellent at caring. I've been in hospitals where the food was just put down and a person with arthritis was unable to reach it. You can't over-stress the need to care for patients.'

Jean Falkner found that the war had left her wanting to do something for less privileged children. 'I wanted to have a village school but I was too frivolous. My father had once said to me angrily when I was looking for a job: "When I think of all the money I spent on your education and at the end of it all you can do is dance and talk French." So I did a few months' training in the Montessori method and worked in a private day school in a London flat. I got asked to parties and met my husband Richard, who had been a prisoner of war and was a very severe asthmatic. We married in 1948 and he died in 1958.'

Most of the pre-war debutantes married either late in the war, or soon afterwards, some with much of the grandness of pre-war days. Lady Margaret Egerton, a lady-in-waiting to Princess Elizabeth, became the wife of Jock Colville in 1948 at St Margaret's Westminster, in a dress of white, silver and orchid pink. One of her bridesmaids was Princess Margaret and Meg set off on honeymoon with her lady's maid and twenty-six suitcases.

While most of them married exactly the sort of man they would have chosen if there been no war, a few stepped outside the confines of class, kind and even country.

'I always say that I have lived three totally different lives,' said Lady Barbara Legge, who married her Polish officer husband, Adam Kwiatkowski, just before the war ended. 'Before the war – which I can hardly believe was true now – during the war, and now.' After the war, Adam went to Birmingham University, studied engineering – coming out top in each of his years and ending up with a scholarship – and, after various jobs in industry, became a lecturer at Birmingham University for twenty-five years.

Cynthia Keppel admitted: 'My life was totally changed by the war, in that I would never have married someone like my husband without it. For one thing, I would never have met him. The war in that sense was a great mixer.'

They had met when she went to work for him – Michael Poston was a Cambridge professor seconded to London for a job in the Cabinet offices as munitions historian. 'He was eighteen years older than me and previously married, but his wife had died tragically in 1940. I met him in 1942 and I knew from the word go that this was it. I'd had lots of boyfriends before but this was the first time that I'd never had one moment's doubt.

'My family were against him because they thought I was marrying absolutely out of my background and that I would lead a completely different kind of life – as indeed I did. Especially as my husband was Jewish and non-practising, a totally non-religious person, which again was against my family tradition. My father didn't like that at all, as he was a child of his time – in my childhood we went to church every Sunday and either my father or my grandfather [Lord Albemarle] would read the lessons. It was a totally conventional country background.

'We moved back into my husband's Cambridge house, where I lived for the rest of my married life. I was always interested in learning and I've never stopped learning from the day I met him. I've had a wonderful time and a lovely life.'

One or two found themselves worse off emotionally. Val Canning, whose husband, her childhood sweetheart, had been killed in the war, leaving her with two small children, remarried. 'I knew I had to be sensible and not go to pieces. I didn't really want to get married again – I had rather a tiresome time when a whole lot of soldiers came back, particularly the ones who came back from POW camps or the Far East, as they naturally wanted marriage and especially children.

'I had known Peter Sutcliffe during the war. He was in the Royal Air Force and five years younger than me. He'd always had his eye on me. Though I'm afraid that in a sense I married for money – or really, for the security that money could give me for my children. I was hard up.

'Because I'd been married to such a wonderful person for only a short time, I naïvely thought all husbands were like that. But he was the old-fashioned kind, couldn't be bothered with girls – my children were both daughters – wouldn't let me work and refused to discuss money with me. By the time he died we weren't getting on. He wouldn't speak to me. I wouldn't have left him, though – that wasn't my code.'

After the war, ex-FANY Lavinia Holland-Hibbert was able to take up a career. 'If there hadn't been a war I'm sure I would have led a very full but rather purposeless life.

'After it, I began working for the Foreign Office, re-educating young German soldier prisoners of war, to show them what Germany was like before they went back. I worked there for two years, with a salary of £400 a year, but as I hadn't got a degree I couldn't progress in the Foreign Office.

'So I went on a teacher training course and got into the Outward Bound movement. I was rather a good teacher and thought it would be my career. But the first time I was there, in Germany, the local regiment was 15/19th Hussars and friends in it asked me to dinner. "We've got a chap coming who's just joined," they said. "Don't talk to him about children because he's been divorced and is very upset about his child." I arrived in my mauve cotton dress made by our Oxfordshire dressmaker and there was this lovely young man with red hair, a major, which was quite a low rank for me. He had a dog with him, a labrador with no tail. Afterwards, I forgot all about him but the following week I rode in a horse show, and when I didn't get past the second fence he came over and commiserated with me.

'We were engaged by the end of my first term. I had to go back for another term to fulfil my contract. We married in 1953 and went straight back to Germany as he was stationed in Schleswig-Holstein. Then the regiment was sent to Malaya. Going over, a five-week journey by ship, I ran the ship's school, then I taught at schools in Malaya with children of twenty different nationalities.' At home in Northumberland, Lavinia taught special needs children on a voluntary basis for twenty-one years.

'The war taught me that you have to be engaged in something worth while materially and spiritually – and that you must both be tolerant of people's endeavours but not want them to waste either their lives or their potential.

'We felt such a sense of purpose in the war. Denis Healey [a boyfriend of Lavinia's in 1944] said later: "You can tell the people who've been in the war because they feel the nation is one. We had the same purpose and we trusted our leaders. We were doing interesting jobs, which we were good at because we had been properly trained, we were given lots of responsibility – and we had lots of people to admire.'

Several women talked of those they venerated. 'Admiral Ramsay* was my hero,' said Fanny Gore Browne who spent the happiest two years of the war in Dover. 'Without him, none of us would be here now.'

Overwhelmingly, the women I spoke to talked not only of the sense of purpose that the war had brought to their lives but the sense of community with others. 'It gave such a tremendous sense of people pulling together,' said Lady Barbara Legge.

'The war bound people together in a way nothing else ever could – or has,' said Denise Woosnam. It turned strangers into friends; it linked those who had worked or fought side by side in a bond that has lasted to this day; and it gave a revalidation to ordinary life and communication that few had experienced before or since. 'In the war, when you met somebody you knew and you said: "Goodbye and good luck," you really meant it,' said Rosemary Hodson. 'Because you didn't know if he or she would get home – or if you would.'

---

* In command of all the naval forces in the Channel during the D-Day landings.

Bibliography

Argyll, Margaret, Duchess of, *Forget Not: The Autobiography of Margaret, Duchess of Argyll* (W. H. Allen, 1975)

Baring, Sarah, *The Road to Station X* (privately printed by Wilton 65, 2000)

Barnato Walker, Diana, *Spreading My Wings: Wartime ATA Flying Adventures by One of Britain's Top Women Pilots* (Patrick Stephens, 1994)

Bidwell, Shelford, *The Women's Royal Army Corps* (Leo Cooper, 1977)

Blacker, General Sir Cecil, *Monkey Business: The Memoirs of General Sir Cecil Blacker* (Quiller Press, 1993)

Clark, Sir Kenneth, *The Other Half: A Self-Portrait* (John Murray, 1977)

Clive, Mary, *Brought Up and Brought Out* (Cobden-Sanderson, 1938)

Colville, John, *The Fringes of Power: Downing Street Diaries, 1939–1955* (Hodder & Stoughton, 1985)

Croall, Jonathan, *Don't You Know There's a War On?: The People's Voice, 1939–1945* (Hutchinson, 1988)

Enever, Ted, *Britain's Best Kept Secret: Ultra's Base at Bletchley Park* (Sutton Publishing, 1994)

Flanner, Janet, *London was Yesterday: 1934–1939* (Michael Joseph, 1975)

Gardiner, Juliet, *Wartime: Britain 1939–1945* (Headline, 2004)

Gathorne-Hardy, Jonathan, *The Rise and Fall of the British Nanny* (Hodder & Stoughton, 1972)

Gavron, Kate (ed.), *Peter's War* (privately printed, 2004)

Gilbert, Martin, *Churchill: A Life* (Heinemann, 1991)

Healey, Denis, *The Time of My Life* (Michael Joseph, 1989)

Laver, James, *Between the Wars* (Vista Books, 1961)

Lees-Milne, James, *Prophesying Peace* (Chatto & Windus, 1977)

Mack, Joanna and Steve Humphries, *London at War* (Sidgwick & Jackson, 1985)

Margetson, Stella, *The Long Party: High Society in the Twenties and Thirties* (D.C. Heath, 1974)

Bibliography

McKibbin, Ross, *Classes and Cultures: England, 1918–1951* (Oxford University Press, 1998)

Meade-Fetherstonhaugh, Jean, *A Handful of Beads* (Serendipity, 2002)

Miller, Christian, *A Childhood in Scotland* (John Murray, 1981)

Montgomery-Massingberd, Hugh and David Watkin, *The London Ritz: A Social and Architectural History* (Aurum Press, 1980)

Morrah, Dermot, *The British Red Cross* (Collins, 1944)

Page, Tim (ed.), *Diaries of Dawn Powell, 1931–1965* (Steerforth Press, 1995)

Price, Alfred, *Blitz on Britain* (Sutton Publishing, 1977)

Pringle, Margaret, *Dance Little Ladies: Days of the Debutante* (Orbis Publishing, 1977)

Rhodes James, Robert (ed.), *Chips: The Diaries of Sir Henry Channon* (Weidenfeld & Nicolson, 1967)

Ross, Josephine (ed.), *Society in Vogue: The International Set Between the Wars* (Condé Nast Publications, 1992)

Shaughnessy, Alfred (ed.), *Sarah: The Letters and Diaries of a Courtier's Wife, 1906–1936* (Peter Owen, 1989)

Smith, Michael, *Station X: The Codebreakers of Bletchley Park* (Channel 4 Books, 1998)

Stuart Mason, Ursula, *The Wrens 1917–1977: A History of the Women's Royal Naval Service* (Educational Explorers, 1977)

Taylor, Eric, *Women Who Went to War* (Robert Hale, 1998)

The Proudest Badge: The Story of the Red Cross (British Red Cross Society, 1953)

Wilson, A. N., *London: A Short History* (Weidenfeld & Nicolson, 2004)

Wood, Emily, *The Red Cross Story: A Pictorial History of 125 Years of the British Red Cross* (Dorling Kindersley, 1995)

Index

Index

Index

Index